D1095418

BLASTS AND BENEDICTIONS

BLASTS AND BENEDICTIONS

Articles and Stories

by
SEAN O'CASEY

Selected and Introduced
by
RONALD AYLING

MACMILLAN
London · Melbourne · Toronto
ST MARTIN'S PRESS
New York
1967

MACMILLAN AND COMPANY LIMITED
Little Essex Street London WC 2
also Bombay Calcutta Madras Melbourne

THE MACMILLAN COMPANY OF CANADA LIMITED
70 Bond Street Toronto 2

ST MARTIN'S PRESS INC
175 Fifth Avenue New York NY 10010

Library of Congress catalog card no. 66–16761

Printed in Great Britain by Richard Clay (The Chaucer Press), Ltd.,
Bungay, Suffolk

CONTENTS

v

O'CASEY ON O'CASEY

Part Two: On Books and Writers

Part Three: People and Places

Part Four: Stories

Contents

PREFACE

REVIEWING a volume of G.B.S.'s letters, Sean O'Casey exclaimed: 'What a man Bernard Shaw was for sending his blasts and benedictions everywhere, falling over the land like the thistledown from a blown-out dandelion.' As it was with Shaw, so was it with O'Casey. Both were prolific writers whose articles and reviews were published in periodicals and newspapers all over the world and who wrote copiously to unknown as well as famous people everywhere. Indeed, when O'Casey's correspondence is published, a further significant dimension to his personality as well as his writing will be revealed. Like D. H. Lawrence, it was virtually impossible for him to write a dull letter, whatever the subject; even his letters to the Inland Revenue, though containing more blasts than blessings, are no exception. O'Casey's concern for all sorts and conditions of men, his receptivity to all aspects of human experience, and his inexhaustible comic spirit make even his journalistic writings of absorbing interest.

The playwright admired the essays of many writers, but although he himself wrote occasional prose pieces on a great variety of subjects, he was always scrupulous to avoid the words 'essay' and 'essayist' in a personal context, for to him they suggested a formal art form and a polished style which he emphatically disclaimed:

> *I am not an essayist.* Hazlitt, Lamb and Emerson were, and fine ones, but not O'Casey — neither an Emerson nor an Addison. Not even a Steele. . . . Essay writing is a high art, and I have never practised it.[1]

[1] Letter to George Braziller, Nov. 9, 1955.

In prefatory comments to three earlier volumes of reprinted articles O'Casey emphasised in particular the personal quality of the writings, their spontaneity and occasional nature: *The Flying Wasp* was described as a 'laughing look-over' of contemporary dramatic criticism; *The Green Crow* was a 'nest of Ids and Trends'; while *Under a Colored Cap* comprised 'articles, merry and mournful, with comments and a song'. These titles were chosen despite the advice of various publishers, one of whom wanted *Towards a Living Theatre* as a title instead of *The Flying Wasp*, while another would have preferred *The Collected Prose of Sean O'Casey* rather than the writer's choice, *The Green Crow*. The dramatist thought the alternative titles 'too academic and professorial' for him to use, and regarded his own as 'more lyrical, and to the point'. (Similarly, he declined to accept honorary degrees from one Irish and two English universities[1] and membership of the American Academy and Institute of Arts and of Letters and the German Academy of Art, because he thought that academic honours should be accorded only to writers whose work was scholarly.) He knew his own strengths as well as his limitations and ignored academic language in order to stress the personal character of his prose writings: he is himself both the stinging wasp and the hoarse croaking bird. Each of these books is largely autobiographical in content, and *Blasts and Benedictions* is in itself mainly of interest as a composite self-portrait.

Here, then, is a posthumous collection of articles and reviews, most of which originally appeared in periodicals with small circulations, but none in book form before. Here we have the playwright greeting Russian and Hungarian readers as well as English, Irish, and American ones; doffing his cap to the East as well as nodding his head to the West. Here is O'Casey discussing a great variety of topics, from his beloved theatre to peoples and places, politics and religion. As often as not, perhaps, readers will disagree with the writer's views; but however deep the dissent, it is impossible not to admire the imaginative energy of the

---

[1] Trinity College, Dublin (*c.* 1961), and the Universities of Durham and Exeter (1960).

prose, the original quirks of style and expression, and the sheer
delight of his sometimes outrageous as well as outraged pug-
nacity in defence of his own writings.

In this collection there are several important articles in which
he discusses his own work at length and with candour and in-
sight. There are also many shrewd comments on literature in
general, as well as on plays and players, and, in particular, a long
article entitled 'Literature in Ireland' which is, for O'Casey,
unusually comprehensive and systematic in its evaluation. Here
we really see O'Casey as a literary critic. Usually, in writing of
books, he deliberately limited himself to generalities, expressing
his often generous appreciation and his dislikes with a minimum
of illustration or analysis. A good example is shown in his choice
of plays for a repertory season in 'Melpomene an' Thalia Beggin'
for Bread'. In such an article we may admire his catholicity of
taste and the charming descriptions of works that he would
choose as an ideal repertoire, but there is no serious attempt to
dissect the plays. Quite apart from the occasional nature of many
of the pieces — 'Melpomene an' Thalia' was commissioned as
a short contribution to a symposium on the repertory theatre, for
instance — O'Casey deliberately eschewed detailed examination.
His attitude is perhaps best expressed in the following remarks
which, though on Russian writing, are equally applicable to his
approach to literature in general: 'I am not a literary critic. I
am not competent to pass a judgement, but [am] ready to give
an opinion or two, be they right or wrong. . . . I tend to remember the spirit of what I read rather than the letter; and it
is the spirit of Soviet Literature that moves me rather than the
letter.'[1] He did not pretend to be a critic and was consistent in
refusing to be described as one. His reading was wide and per-
ceptive, however, and 'Literature in Ireland' is a good illustration; written shortly after the publication of *Finnegans Wake*, it
pays a humble tribute to that work and to its creator.

Blasts and Benedictions, chronologically, continues Robert
Hogan's excellent miscellany, *Feathers from the Green Crow:
Sean O'Casey, 1905–1925*, but different principles necessarily

[1] Untitled article written for *Komsomolskaya Pravda*, May 1959.

guided the selection. Dr Hogan rightly included the majority of
O'Casey's early writings up to 1925. It is impossible to do the
same for his later work, as two volumes containing reprinted
pieces are still in print; moreover, even excluding these writings,
the number of articles which remain unpublished in book form is
sufficient to demand a more selective choice. There are therefore articles and reviews which are of interest in themselves that
have had to be excluded. I have attempted to include as many as
possible of the pieces in which the playwright discusses his own
work, though I have omitted his fine reply to James Agate's
attack on *Within the Gates*, 'The Cutting of an Agate',[1] because there are several other articles on the play in this collection,
none of which have appeared in book form before. I have also
tried to give as much elbow-room as possible to O'Casey the
book reviewer, for in this field his generous appreciation of
many of his contemporaries, as varied as Joyce, Shaw, D. H.
Lawrence, Yeats, Gorki, and Lady Gregory, gives his writing
a lilt and sparkle that is particularly attractive.

The latest in date of the essays — 'The Bald Primaqueera',
which was completed only a few weeks before his death —
continued his long running battle with recent trends in the
drama, notably those of the Theatre of the Absurd and the
Theatre of Cruelty. His essay brings together several of his main
criticisms. As we know from *Under a Colored Cap*, O'Casey
disliked what he regarded as the pessimism in theme and the
negative portrayal of much of the violence on the present-day
stage. He was also fundamentally opposed to the current distrust
of language as the basis of drama. In 'Behind the Curtained
World' (1942) we see his long-standing antagonism to the
'silence is golden' school of playwriting. Many contemporary
authors have deliberately sought for ways by which to restrict
the rôle of language in the dramatic experience, portraying in-
articulate characters and relying primarily on visual effects and
mime to realise the play's meaning. O'Casey's attitude, expressed in *The Flying Wasp* in 1937, was quite clear: 'A good
acting play that is not also good enough to be enjoyed in the

[1] Originally printed in *The Flying Wasp* (1937), pp. 39-50.

study is not worth a dying tinker's damn.'[1] At the same time he put forward a positive view on the importance of language in the theatre:

> The critics have said *ipso factum* that all on the stage must be an exact imitation of life, and so nothing spoken there must dare to be above a whisper. (As if there were no shouting in real life.) And most of the dialogue used isn't worth even a whisper; but when every word shall be heard, and passion raises her voice again on the stage, when a shout in its proper place shall have the importance of a silence in its proper place, then the dramatist will have to think more about the words he gives his characters to say, and more still about the way in which the actors say them.[2]

It is thus not difficult to see why the Irish author prefers the work of John Arden before that of his young contemporaries, for Arden is not afraid of challenging themes and he is always highly articulate.

It may seem strange that a socialist like O'Casey should oppose the aims and objects of Centre 42, an organisation designed to bring art to the working people. The title, Centre 42, was derived from the number of a Resolution passed at the Trades Union Congress in September 1960. Resolution number 42 on the agenda for that year pledged Congress to recognise 'the importance of the arts in the life of the community' and requested the General Council of the T.U.C. to 'conduct a special examination and to make proposals to a future Congress to ensure a greater participation by the trade union movement in all cultural activities'. In fact, more than forty years ago, O'Casey had urged Irish trade unions to encourage cultural activities among their members, believing that:

> this is the silent need of the workers: loss of ignorance and acquirement of culture. However the worker may shout for an increase in his wage, or protest against a reduction, be he at work, or waiting wearily in the Unemployment Exchange, his greatest need and most urgent claim is a share in the culture of the society of men.[3]

[1] Ibid., p. 94.
[2] Ibid., pp. 189–90.
[3] *The Irish Statesman*, Dec. 22, 1923.

It is easy to say this when one is not a manual worker oneself. Yet O'Casey was in fact still wholly dependent for his living on his wage as a manual worker when he wrote these words. Even in the midst of strike action and in the most militant of national and labour disputes, he always tried to remind his fellow-workers that material betterment, necessary and important as it is for its own sake, is, ultimately, merely a gateway to a spiritual enrichment. In 1941 he wrote:

> There is a Persian proverb which says: 'If you have two pennies, with one buy bread, and with the other a lily.' But if we have but one penny, we can buy only bread. It has been my fight for a long span of years now to try to bring about a condition in which the worker spending his penny on bread, will have one left to buy a lily.[1]

In 'Behind the Curtained World' the playwright urged the Labour Party and 'the mass members of the Trade Unions' to recognise the importance of the drama in the life of the people and to encourage it.

His opposition to Centre 42 — demonstrated in the essay, 'Mr Wesker's March Past' — is, in fact, not to the aims of Arnold Wesker's group but to the way in which they were to be realised.[2] O'Casey thought that rather than getting professional companies of actors and singers to visit factories and clubs, the unions would be better occupied in encouraging their members to participate in cultural activities themselves, including writing and acting plays. He believed that only in this way, and by a school education where every child should experience drama and the arts as a living and meaningful experience, could culture in any enduring form be fully accepted by the working people. Thus O'Casey returned once again to the importance of education, a theme which has pervaded his work from his first published article, 'Sound the Loud Trumpet' (1907), until his last. From this point of view, whether or not we accept his

[1] Letter in *The New Statesman and Nation*, Aug. 2, 1941.
[2] Recent statements by Mr Wesker suggest that there is, probably, less disagreement than O'Casey thought in the views of the two playwrights on this point.

strictures on Centre 42, there is a consistency in his outlook underlying the seeming incongruities.

Several articles in the present anthology were written for readers in communist countries. Indeed, O'Casey published many articles in the U.S.S.R., particularly in the last ten years of his life; and a number of these contributions were specially commissioned by Soviet journals. Distorted views of the playwright's attitude to communism and to Soviet Russia have been published in recent years. These impressions have been given by his friends and admirers as well as by detractors. Several American critics who were friendly with him were obviously embarrassed by his avowed political standpoint and seemed unwilling to believe that a man of such humane and compassionate vision could *really* be a socialist of any kind, or an agnostic either. Certain of their criticisms, therefore, have tended to portray him as a half-hearted communist, or a naïve idealist fallen among Marxists. Another erroneous picture, of O'Casey as a conceited and schizophrenic personality, has been presented in a recently published book; in this work we find the following statement:

> I note that he [O'Casey] has told his latest biographer that he was always a Communist. If he was he managed to conceal the fact from many of his early friends. So far as I was concerned his Communism began to thrust itself forward only toward the end of World War II *when it was obvious that the Allies were likely to win and the Russian tanks were now pointing westwards.*[1]

From the gratuitous aside that I have italicised it is to be assumed that O'Casey only backed winning horses and that his political ideas were dictated by expediency. Nothing is farther from the truth. O'Casey joined the editorial board of the *Daily Worker* in 1940 when the Nazi advance in Europe was proceeding without check, and his most obviously communist play, *The Star Turns Red*, was published and produced at the same time. His wholehearted support of international communism and his admiration for the achievements of the Soviet Union never wavered before, during, or after the Second World War.

[1] Gabriel Fallon, *Sean O'Casey : The Man I Knew* (Routledge, 1965), p. 152.

Occasionally, like all men carried away by excessive enthusiasm, O'Casey said and wrote silly things, and at times, in his praise of the Soviet system, he seemed to ignore, or pass over too lightly, mistakes and weaknesses that were apparent in it, and which, whether one supported it or not, one might reasonably expect to find in any fallible human society in process of evolution. The present collection of essays is not free from such blemishes: in the essay on 'Censorship', for instance, we find the assertion: 'I have never yet heard a whisper of the banning of play, poem, or novel by the officials of the U.S.S.R., good, bad, or indifferent.' This may have been his experience in 1945; it was to be altered in 1958 when Pasternak's novel, *Dr. Zhivago*, was banned in the U.S.S.R. and the poet expelled from the Soviet Writers' Union.

Yet though O'Casey sometimes over-simplified political matters in his writings, he did not underestimate the difficulties ahead for the socialist countries. He did not believe that communism had yet been attained in any state, though countries like the U.S.S.R. were, he thought, on the right road. He was no dogmatic party-liner, as we know from his writings, and despite his strong admiration for the Soviet Union he was opposed to any slavish pursuit of Kremlin policies. He urged English socialists to quote less from foreign Marxist theoreticians and, instead, to draw inspiration from the rich radical 'tradition' in English literature — quoting examples from the work of Ruskin, Carlyle, Shelley, Keats, Burns, and Morris. Horrified to discover, in talks with workers and party intellectuals, that writers like Dickens were distrusted because they were regarded as bourgeois in outlook, the dramatist wrote 'Empty Vessels' (1942) in order to defend such writers.

O'Casey's consistent repudiation of the theory of Socialist Realism realises a more fundamental disagreement with 'official' communist attitudes to art. For a period of time after the end of the Second World War this doctrine was firmly entrenched as an ideal to which imaginative writing should conform; and Soviet critics and politicians like Zhdanov used it as a yardstick of literary value. Even today, though Zhdanov has long been discredited, the theory has still many adherents in the literary establishments of communist countries. O'Casey opposed rules and regimentation in art — whether capitalist, theological, or socialist — and he firmly rejected Socialist Realism as a meaningless and impracticable dogma. In an article entitled 'The Flaming Sunflower' (1960), written for readers in the U.S.S.R., O'Casey declared:

> Communists everywhere seem to be afraid of any writing or painting that isn't packed with what they consider to be 'socialist realism', which is nonsense. As we have no fear of experiments in science, so we must abandon fear of experiments in art and in literature; and, above all, communists should be more tolerant of the natural gaiety of youth.

Two of the central tenets of Socialist Realism are the necessity for optimistic social themes and subject matter, and the creation of a positive hero or heroes to further this aim. While these values are in fact embodied in much of his own later work, the playwright defended the work of Eugene O'Neill when it was denounced as pessimistic and negative, and he urged Russian writers and critics to be unafraid of portraying heartbreak, frustration, and tragic experience. To a Congress of Russian writers he sent the following criticisms, in the course of a friendly article entitled 'Trumpeters in the March of Man':

> I should venture the opinion that the [Soviet] Novel and story doesn't go deep enough into the personalities of the characters; that there isn't enough of sadness and laughter within the stories. There seems to be a hint of hesitation in a lot of them. There seems to be a fear of grief, though grief can be just as beautiful as joy. A great writer once said that 'Life is a comedy to those who see it, a tragedy to those who feel it.' Let us not be afraid of those souls who see life as a tragedy. To me, the best writer is he or she who both sees and hears the laughter of life's comedy, and deeply feels life's tragedy too.

And in an article written for *Komsomolskaya Pravda* in 1959, he added:

> It seems to me that Soviet writers don't bring enough of lyricism into their more realistic writings, or enough of humour. There seems to be some fear of laughter. Your writers should let themselves go more.

They should bring more of the clown Popov into what they see and hear around them, for Popov takes his fun out of what he has seen and heard. There should be seen more of the spirit of the Russian dance, too, such wild goings on as I have seen in the performances of your Red Army Assembly; and of your wonderful joys of satire in your Puppet Displays.

The Soviet dismissal of James Joyce's work was, of course, anathema to the dramatist; and, in the face of strong criticisms, he persistently upheld the poetic value of T. S. Eliot's writings, while disliking the poet's philosophy. He also found it necessary to defend Bernard Shaw against attacks from English communists who saw him, in Lenin's words, as 'a good man fallen among Fabians'. O'Casey sternly rebuked such sneers, revering as he did not only Shaw's dramatic work but his contribution to political thought as well. O'Casey himself denounced certain tendencies in modern writing that may be attributed to the influence of Freud — 'The Bald Primaqueera' gives examples — but he never agreed with the wholesale rejection of Freud's writings by the Soviet authorities.

In many respects, therefore, the dramatist was aware of mistakes and excesses in Soviet art and criticism, and he did not hesitate to point them out to his friends in England as well as in Russia. Mostly, however, he was content to express his opinions in private letters, rather than published articles because, I think, he was afraid that the capitalist Press would distort for its own purposes his criticisms of the Soviet system. He did not pull punches in his correspondence with his many friends in the Soviet Writers' Union, and his disagreement with Pasternak's expulsion from the Union — though the playwright did not particularly like *Dr. Zhivago*, and though he thought the Nobel Prize had been awarded to the novel for political and not artistic reasons — was expressed firmly and unequivocally.

Sean O'Casey believed that, whatever its errors, the Soviet political system was the one which, with national modifications, promised the most creative future for mankind. Whether he was right or wrong in this faith, it is a fact that he used his considerable influence within the world socialist movement to help liberalise attitudes to life and art in that portion of the world controlled by it, as he consistently fought for the same principles in that portion which is more familiar to the present readers. We should bear in mind these considerations when reading his writings on communism and the Soviet system.

In an amusing aside written shortly before his death, in a passage later deleted from 'The Bald Primaqueera', the playwright 'apologised' for his life's work:

> I have said far too many things in my life, vocally and by way of writing, in book, in play, in magazine, and in papers. I have often thought that, if there be an after life, I may come up against a tough experience. The experience of those shown in Sartre's *Huis Clos* would be but a pleasant interlude, however long, in comparison with mine.

He thinks himself in hell, tongue-tied and lost, able only to listen:

> I imagine myself alone in a tight place, beleaguered by great hosts of my own words, from the time go to the time of my separation from this mortal coil; words forever sounding, pounding, expounding, and astounding my poor afflicted ears, now widened like the ears of Bottom when Puck anointed him with a magic juice.

There is no need for me, selecting words from the loquacious limbo of O'Casey's fable, to justify a collection whose eloquence and worth speak for themselves; instead, my concern in this preface has been to clarify some of the views held by the playwright, and often misinterpreted, and to show the consistency and honesty with which he maintained them.

RONALD AYLING

Bristol
1966

ACKNOWLEDGEMENTS

ALL those who admire Sean O'Casey's work are deeply in his wife's debt. Her loving care and devotion gave him several precious years of life that he might not otherwise have had; and she was, in his last years, the eyes through which he saw the world, as well as the voice which linked him to it in the reading of letters, newspapers, and books.

I am especially grateful to Mrs O'Casey for her friendly encouragement and her assistance in allowing me to examine the papers in her possession. Wherever possible I have collated typescript copies of articles with their published versions, restoring the few passages omitted by various editors, and also the playwright's titles when these have been changed.

Dr Robert Hogan and Dr David Krause have generously given me of their expert knowledge and advice, and have regaled me with their genial humour. I also wish to acknowledge information kindly supplied by Mr Wright Miller and Miss Lindis Beaulah; the co-operation of Dr R. J. Hayes, Director of the National Library of Ireland, and his staff, especially Mr Alf MacLochlainn; the services of the British Museum; and the facilities provided by Mr J. Shum Cox and the library of the University of Bristol.

Finally, I am pleased to record my appreciation of the good humour, patience, and understanding shown by my wife on nearly all occasions, and my gratitude for the many sacrifices that she has made on my behalf.

R. F. A.

Publisher's note. 'A Word Before Curtain-Rise' is reprinted from *Selected Plays of Sean O'Casey* by permission of George Braziller, Inc. We regret that we have not been able to trace the estate of the late Mr Maurice Browne, who took part in the B.B.C. discussion on 'Playwright and Box Office' reprinted in this book, but we should be pleased to make the necessary arrangements at the first opportunity.

PART ONE

THE CURTAINED WORLD

O'CASEY ON THE THEATRE

PLAYWRIGHT AND BOX OFFICE (1938)*

Discussion between Maurice Browne and Sean O'Casey

BROWNE: I know, Sean, that anyhow you are going to bruise my English head with your Irish heel, so, just to annoy you, I'll start by suggesting that the theatre, the playwright, and the box office are, as a matter of fact, whatever they should be in theory, the only possible ruling trinity in the theatrical world today with economic conditions as they are — I don't say as they should be or as you and I would have them in our pet private Utopia.

O'CASEY: Believe you me, I don't want to go dreaming in any Utopian land: but I do want to walk in the region of common-sense. We can't have perfection yet, but we can become a little better than we are. It is an unholy trinity, with the box office controlling the theatre and modelling the playwright. The trinity of the theatre used to be the author, the actors, and the audience; but now it is the box office, the manager, and last, of course, the playwright, so that the theatre and drama not only do not come into the sun, but do not even come into the limelight. This devotion to the box office is not only making it more difficult for the English drama as a whole, it is also making it more difficult for the box office itself. Managers are now so eager to get a success that to win one they will rook the box office of every penny it possesses. The more eager they are for a success, the more difficult a success becomes because of the cost. When a play is written, the first thought is: What is it going to cost? The question of money, money is at the head and tail of it

* B.B.C. broadcast published in *The Listener*, July 7, 1938.

and in the very heart of all things connected with the putting on of a bad play or a good play. When a play's doing well, the box office is a haven of light and hilarity; when a play's doing badly, the box office is a place of desolation. So we see what a mill-stone round the neck of a manager the box office really is, for so much money is lavished even on a trivial play to make it into what is called a wow, that the very success desired becomes the next thing to impossibility. And once a manager is unfortunate enough to make a pile out of some play, he immediately loses all he has gained by his frantic efforts to make a second pile.

BROWNE: Of course, you've got me when you talk about managers unfortunate enough to make a pile out of one play and idiots enough to lose it over others. I'm a bad case in point, as you know, you old rascal! But, joking apart, if you are going to buy a motor-car, or a wireless set, or a teething ring for the baby, isn't one of the very first questions you ask yourself: 'How much will it cost?' and the next question: 'Can I afford it?' I absolutely agree with you that the question of money is at the head and the tail of play production, but isn't the question of money also at the head and the tail of birth and death of every single and solitary thing in between? And do you really think that this fact has such a bad influence on the playwright?

O'CASEY: A very bad influence indeed. Everything is against the playwright who thinks of his play, and everything in favour of the playwright who thinks of the box office; and woe unto him who does, for the playwright who thinks of the box office can never write a fine play.

BROWNE: Half-a-minute: what about Shakespeare, for example, or Euripides, or Chekhov, or Eugene O'Neill, or even one or two Irishmen I could mention — George Bernard Shaw for example, to say nothing of the author of *Juno and the Paycock*? Now, Sean, you just said 'The playwright who thinks of the box office can never write a fine play'. Can you give any real reason for saying that?

O'CASEY: Of course I can. When a playwright thinks of the box office while he's writing a play, he's bound to try to model his play on the traditions with which the managers and actors are familiar. So, from the very start, he dare not write anything new. Anything new makes a play more difficult for the manager, more difficult for the actors, more difficult for the producer, and, most of all, more difficult for the poor box office. As for Shakespeare, his best works prove that while he was writing them, he couldn't have been dreaming of the box office. The length and power of the principal characters stand in the way of a long run, and without a long run there can be no success within the calculation of the box office. The parts of Hamlet, Othello, and Lear, are so huge and call for such tremendous effort that an actor playing any one of them for a year would kill the parts, and so kill the plays, or he would kill himself. The box office never dominated Shaw. He swept away the box office as he swept away the stupidities that littered the stage: but there are few playwrights with the fighting abilities of Shaw. We may have his courage, but courage may slay ourselves. Shaw's courage, so well directed, slew all who tried to slay him. O'Neill, if he ever thought of the box office, would never have written *Strange Interlude*, *The Great God Brown*, or *Mourning Becomes Electra*.

No: managers and actors are still terrified of anything new. Tell us the old, old story, say the managers, so that the theatre may be made a place fit for box offices to live in! In a programme of a play running recently in the West End, the most important things mentioned are, not the play, not the actors, but a dress designed and made by Messrs. Tweedledeedum, and gloves, bags, and silverware designed and made by Messrs. Tweedledumdee. The one thing forgotten on the programme was to mention that the author, the actors, and the audience were designed and made by God Almighty. Long ago, we used to go to see the play; later on we went to see the actors; now we go to see dresses, negligées, nightgowns, hats, gloves, and silverware. That's the kind of dramatic art we get since the box office has become the guardian angel of the English theatre.

Another sign of the evil effect of the box office: some time ago, in a kind of competition, a London management asked for plays. Before the sun could move from one solstice to another, the management was struggling with one thousand six hundred plays. Just think of it — not one thousand six hundred manage-ments fighting over one play, but one management fighting with one thousand six hundred of them! What was the result? One thousand five hundred and ninety-nine good plays and one bad one? Hardly. Out of this mass of plays there were but two having a possible chance of production. Now this management wasn't one bossing a theatre like the Art Theatre of Moscow, or the Guild Theatre of New York, or the Abbey Theatre of Dublin, all ready to put on second-rate plays, at a pinch, but eager to get plays that would make a name for themselves, at home and abroad. No: the management that dealt with the one thousand six hundred plays wasn't so eager for world-wide fame as it was eager to secure a commercial success. And out of these one thousand and six hundred plays this management got two that were possibly fit for production. We may safely assume that the writers of these plays had their eyes fixed fast on the box office. So we see that the box office has a bad effect even on those who concentrate on giving it honour and power. In fact, there are far more failures when the thoughts are of the box office, the whole box office, and nothing but the box office, than when it is completely banished from the mind of him who writes for the theatre.

BROWNE: Look here, Sean, I'm not defending the box office, but are you quite sure that you are thinking clearly? A moment ago you were talking of one thousand six hundred playwrights (yes, it's an awful thought, isn't it!) and you said that only two of them wrote plays that were possibly fit for pro-duction — good enough to sell to that management which had organised the competition. But how do you know that the management selected the two best plays? If it was half as bad a management as you suggest, it probably selected the two worst. And how do you know either that all those one thousand six hundred playwrights had their eyes fixed on the box office?

O'CASEY: Well, mainly because the theatre is so constituted today that it is next to impossible for anyone writing for it to have his thoughts anywhere else. What is the art of the theatre of today but a hang-dog attachment to the law of supply and

demand? Give the public what the playwrights and the managers think the public want — that is the law and the prophets
in the theatre of today. The slogan of a great agency is, not
'You want the best plays — we have them', but 'You want the
best seats — we have them'! And the law of giving what it is
thought the public want is based on the box office. Only the other
day a playwright who has had a box office success, is reported in
a Sunday paper as saying: 'I think the public taste is for romantic
plays with incidental music, a touch of probability, and characters taken from life.' So, I suppose, we should all strive to write
romantic plays with incidental music till the taste of the public
changes. 'The poets,' says Shelley, 'are the trumpets that call
to battle; they are the unacknowledged legislators of the world.'
Poor Shelley was wrong. Actually, it appears, the poets and
playwrights are but the miserable camp-followers of what is
thought to be the public taste. On the other hand, it may be he
who searches out the public taste who is wrong! He tells us 'he
thinks the public taste is such and such'. He thinks — he
doesn't know. That's the thing that keeps them all hanging by
the neck — the box office is never sure. Well, thank God, it's
just as easy to have a sickening failure with a romantic play
tricked out with incidental music as it is to have a financial
failure with a play by Shakespeare, Shaw, Strindberg, or O'Neill,
or any other dramatist who thinks life is something more than a
romantic glide, helped along by incidental music.

BROWNE: Bravo! I agree with every word you are saying
now. Go on, rub it in.

O'CASEY: Another sinister attraction of the box office is
that when a playwright secures a financial success with any
particular play (*The Barretts of Wimpole Street*, for instance),
many attempts are made by other playwrights to go and do like-
wise, and this imitation is encouraged and applauded by the
managers on the strength of the idea that what is once done well
can be done a dozen times badly. The managers have made
imitation the curse of the theatre, as it is, to a greater degree,
the curse of the films. How are we to bring about a change?
Private energy and enterprise have sprinkled a little theatre here

and there in England, occasionally offering a chance of production to a new play by a new dramatist. But even these little theatres are continually struggling with financial difficulties. To do anything they must be nationally and municipally supported. The theatre in Shaftesbury Avenue must become the theatre of Islington, of Fulham, of Stepney, and so on, with the new National Theatre[1] leading the way in greater things for the glory of God and the honour of the English theatre.

BROWNE: I'm not going to let you draw me off your trail with a controversial red herring like the National Theatre. But I *am* going to suggest that for those ills of our profession today which you denounce so rightly, the ultimate fault doesn't lie in the managers, nor even in the box office. Surely both fault and remedy lie in ourselves. You've admitted the law of supply and demand. In Elizabethan days England demanded the best from its theatre and got it. Today we — the audience, the people — have grown lax in our demands; we let ourselves be fed with fifth-rate stuff at extravagant prices. But we can still get the best if we want it enough. And, if we want it enough, we'll demand it — and go on demanding it until we get it.

[1] The National Theatre, constantly demanded by O'Casey throughout the 1930s, was not to materialise until 1963.

BEHIND THE CURTAINED WORLD (1942)*

WHAT is the theatre, where is it, and what does it do? Some few years ago, sitting at a round table of a big film association, while he was engaged on a production of *Call it a Day*, Mr Basil Dean, according to a famous Sunday journal, told us that 'going back into the theatre horrifies him. It was like watching little black ants crawling about the grass. The theatre will soon be as specialised and old-fashioned as chamber-music is today. It isn't in touch with the audience any longer, it's not a medium that can say anything to the mass of the people. The film medium is so much finer and more precise. You can get so much nearer your actors with the camera, and tell your story more intimately.' Then Mr Dean talked of film versions of Shakespeare, and said his next production would be Eleanor Smith's *Ballerina*. That's the first lesson from the filmic gospel, and here followeth the second lesson from the theatric gospel taken from a famous Sunday journal, and appearing, strangely enough, in the same year as the first one: 'The Soviet Union has, probably, the only theatre of its kind in theatrical history. It is called The Polar Theatre, and in 1935 has just rung down the curtain on a successful session of seventy performances given in the Arctic fishing villages, on ice-breakers and barges, and in the dining-room of the many scientific outposts and industrial settlements of the far north. The fourteen men and women, comprising the group, carried with them complete stage sets, costumes, and a collapsible stage. After long uncomfortable trips in open boats, often through stormy seas, and under a deluge of cold rain, they had to unload their equipment, often wading knee-deep in the icy

---

* Published in *Saturday Book 3*, edited by Leonard Russell (Hutchinson, 1943), under the title 'The Curtained World'.

9

waters. They played, it might be, on the shifty deck of an ice-breaker anchored off Wrangel Island, or in the small meeting-hall of a village, near the mouth of the Obi River in Siberia. The hall was crammed with the strangest audience the Polar Group had ever played before, and with rapt attention they followed a performance of Molière's *Tartuffe*. When it was over, not a hand-clap came, and the players were puzzled and a little frightened till they learned that hand-clapping was unknown there as a sign of approbation, and the dead silence was their sign of profound respect and appreciation.'

If the drama dies in one place, it springs to life in another, for drama was the first child given to the first man and woman born to the world. Wherever two or three of them are gathered to-gether, there is the theatre. Wherever we sit down, stand up, lie stretched; wherever we sing, dance, work, weep, curse and swear, or play games; wherever a child be born, or a man or woman die, there the theatre is, and ever will be. And now, wherever a soldier's camp is fixed, a gun goes off, or a bonny young airman flies upwards or crashes down to death; wher-ever a field is tilled, or machines rush round in a factory there is the stuff that drama and dreams are made on. As high as we can reach to heaven, as low down as we may get to hell, and all between, is the theatre proper and the theatre grand. It is gun-peal and slogan-cry, woe and wantonness and laughter in the midst of the grace of God. It is more than a mirror, for if what be conceived there be conceived with fierceness, joy, grace, and exul-tation it will split the mirror from top to bottom as reality cracked the glass and scattered the threads by which the Lady of Shallot wove her pretty patterns from the coloured shadows that passed her window by. It is a big, wide, wonderful world of treasures for the young dramatist from which to pull beads of glittering glass or gems of the first water from its drab or colourful and intense tapestry of life, if only they can banish fear of new things from their minds and the minds of their audience, and keep their anxious heads from being held in tight chancery inside a box-office window. Today young dramatists have a chance that few have had before for the winds of war are blowing open the gates of a newer and a

stranger day. Today all dramatists, he who has already blown a
tune on the trumpet, and he who holds an unblown trumpet in
a hand, find themselves in the midst of turbulent life and death,
for everywhere is the centre of the storm of war that has swept us
into its indifferent clutches. The last war carried the dramatist
about, more or less at his ease, round and round the edge of it;
this one has sucked him into its centre. The stone-walled castle,
no less than the gracious ivory tower, has been split to its foun-
dations, and left both naked to the blast of anxiety, and much and
grievous tribulation; so that life which was select and gracious,
full of refined security, is, today, abroad on the wind-swept heath,
without a cloak, abiding the pelting lightning-rent storm.
Tinker, tailor, soldier, sailor, richman, poorman, beggarman,
thief; silk, satin, cotton, and rags, are all there, unhooded in
the horrid hurly burly. Today the King's major audience
sport no plumes, carry no gold lace on shoulder or sleeve, but
are smoke-begrimed or asweat with labour, and he is ori-
flammed in the ruins of his people's buildings and his people's
homes.

Here we all are actors in a fight more frenzied than a world
ever saw before, touching only, if it touches anything, the fight
between Michael and his angels with the hosts of evil. The mirror of nature has become a huge magnifying-glass, showing us
ourselves as we never saw ourselves before. We have stood up to
all that has happened with brave hearts and steady hands, so it
can't be too much to hope that we shall stand up to welcome a
widening, deepening, and intensifying of our theatre. Life can
never be what it has been before; changes have come, and many
more are heralded. As it will be with us, so shall it be with our
theatre; and it will no longer be a decked-out place in which
trivial objects glide in before the eye, and glide out again to
disappear forever; but it will be an honoured place where fine
things are spoken, and where great names move and live and have
their being.

The English theatre today is nothing to be proud about;
indeed, by and large, it is a thing of poor shreds and patches, with
an odd one having a tint of colour. It is no more a part of the life

of England than are the penguins in the Zoo. Indeed, the penguins, especially the King Penguin, are more interesting to the people than are the vital treasures of English dramatic art. Down where I am now [in Devon], among a good-natured, intelligent, hard-working people, many have never seen the inside of a theatre, much less the performance of a Shakespeare play. Reckoning her wealth and vigour, concerning the theatre, England is a Cain among the nations — wearing the mark of God's condemnation on her brow through thinking she parades her dramatic glory in a suit of sackcloth. It is wonderful, too, how many among these are anxious to keep the theatre closed on Sunday though they never stir a finger to keep it open any other day of the week. Where I lived for four years in Buckinghamshire, the theatre to many of the people was still the house of Satan, and to many everywhere it is still a thing that makes God close His eyes and shudder. In this county of Buckingham with a population of a quarter of a million, and three big towns, there is, as far as I know, but one theatre holding 238 persons; a theatre but a few years old, and still in childish bib and tucker. And this theatre has to work night and day to keep going, putting on a new play weekly, mauling the unfortunate members with ceaseless work to give this little corner of England a glimpse of what the British drama is like. The one concession given to this activity by the mass of wealth and vigour that is England is that the theatre isn't required to pay the Entertainment Tax: for this relief, much thanks. Here are a few words, spoken without malice, by the present producer of the theatre in Amersham: 'The conditions under which Repertory Theatres work in England (England, mind you — wealthy, arrogant England) are, from a theatre point of view, almost unspeakable. Rehearsals all day as well as playing far into the night.' This little theatre holds less than half those fitting into the Abbey, Dublin, and, to give a spare living to its members, has to give a twicenightly performance.

And, I daresay, the tale told here is the tale to be told of all, or almost all, the other man-forsaken repertories in England. There isn't a repertory in England whose greatest thrill isn't the agonising uncertainty of what is going to happen to it tomorrow; and that is a mean aggravation against which no little theatre (or big one either) can struggle towards a fine, fierce, or graceful expression of its art. Brave and all as these tiny theatres are, they aren't many enough to give any importance to their connection with the outer and inner life of the English people.

It is a parlous thing, this, to associate contempt and indifference with our grand achievement in dramatic literature; and we are all to blame for it, particularly our leaders, political and religious and labour; right, left, and centre. The Church ever active in her own sacred theatre, drenched in her own dramatic liturgy, never now bothers her head about the theatre profane, unless on an occasion when this theatre does something which some impulsive ecclesiastic thinks is bound to be a means of stirring up the souls of her people, like a Bishop of Willesden strutting on to the stage after the first performance of *The Tents of Israel* to tell an astonished audience that 'this was a great play because it showed a whole people kneeling on their knees'. That was the Bishop of Willesden for you! Perhaps it would have been a greater play still if it had shown a whole people standing on their heads! To help to promote an interest in the theatre, we may rule the Bishops out, though they sit in the House of Lords, influencing a mass of people, and rule in an effective way over many fair demesnes in this fair land. It is a pity they don't take an odd hour off to learn a little about a play. Surely this potent and widespread organisation could form a permanent dramatic group, say in each cathedral city, from among the members of her Young Men's and Young Women's Christian Associations, the Church Army, Church Lads' Brigade, and Bible Classes so that their dioceses might, at least, hear an echo of Shakespeare's voice speak brave and gay for England still.

In the old time before us, the Church took a keener interest in the drama, and even touched drama into some of her most reverential rites. In the more dewy days of Christianity, we find a record of a dramatically performed rite celebrating the coming of the three women to the tomb of the buried Saviour, called *Quem Quaeritis in Sepulchro, Christicolae?* It is set out in

B

an MS attributed to St Gall (an Irish Saint, by the way), and this is how it goes: 'While the third lesson is being said, let four brethren vest themselves. Let one of them, vested in an alb, enter as though to take part in the service, and let him approach the sepulchre without attracting attention, and sit there quietly with a palm in his hand. While the third response is chanted, let the other three follow, and let them all, vested in copes, stepping delicately as those who seek something, approach the sepulchre. These things are done in imitation of the angel sitting in the monument, and the women bearing spices coming to anoint the body of their Lord. When he who sits there beholds the three approach him, like folks lost and seeking something, let him begin in a dulcet voice of medium pitch to sing, *Whom seek ye in the sepulchre, O Christians?* Then let the three reply in unison, *We seek Jesus of Nazareth who was crucified, O Heavenly One.* Then he who imitates the angel chants, *He is not here; He is risen even as He said before. Go; proclaim He has risen from the grave!* At this, let the three turn to the choir, and say, *Alleluia! The Lord is risen!* Then let the one sitting there, and as if recalling them, say the anthem, *Come, and see the place where He lay.* And saying this, let him rise and lift the veil, showing the place bare of the Cross, and only the clothes there in which the Cross was wrapped. And when they have seen this, let them lay down the thuribles, and take the cloth, and hold it up in the face of the clergy, as if to demonstrate that the Lord has risen, and is no longer wrapped therein; then shall they sing the anthem, *Christ has risen from the grave,* laying the cloth on the altar as they sing. When the anthem is done, let the Prior, sharing in their gladness at the triumph of our King, in that, having vanquished death, He rose again, begin the hymn, *Te Deum Laudamus.* And this begun, all the bells chime out together.'

Well played, boys! As neat as any, and much more graceful and exultant, as has ever appeared on the present-day stage. We need more of this grace and exultation, more dulcet voices of a medium pitch, of delicate movement without attracting attention, of sitting quietly with, or without, a palm in the hand, in

our play-acting on the stage today. The above little ecclesiasti-
cally-made drama was bound to set up a quietly-clamorous
emotion in the breasts of those who saw and heard it, convincing
them forever that God was in His heaven, and all was well with
the world. The world lost a dramatist in St Gall, disciple of St
Columba, or in whichever monk who wrote it. So we see —
there are many other instances — the Church not only gave the
kiss of peace to the drama without her walls, but added it to give
added effect and beauty to some of her own particular rites.
Perhaps the Church may stir herself again, some day, though I
think the chance has passed forever now. Canterbury has, I
believe, given some pageants, and has done T. S. Eliot's *The
Rock*; but these have but touched the stone walls, and have never
got within sight of the altar. It seemed to me there was a touch,
more, an embrace of make-believe about these things showing
the Church good-naturedly tolerant, rather than affording a welcome to the alleluias, amens, and glorias of the theatre which
were and are and are to come, *in saecula saeculorum*. The plays
given over the wireless were, to me, an effort to dance the story
of the Gospels into the minds of the young to the sound of
castanets. Recently, a civic luncheon was given to Mr J. B.
Priestley because of a new play of his to get production in
Bradford, and the Bishop spoke kind words over the tables;
but I'm afraid that the honour was meant, not for the play, but
for Mr Priestley because he was a son of the city. No, it won't
do: the Church must be ruled out of it.

Then there are the two premier Universities that lift, it may
be, once a year, a play by Shakespeare or Jonson, or Euripides
in original Greek, out on to the lawn for an airing, then putting
them back into a warm cupboard for a rest for the rest of the
year. There, too, is the plump and self-satisfied Conservative
Party, anxious now about putting on a little too much weight, and
sensitive now of shoulders stooping, to the right today, to the left
tomorrow; speaking, governing, and acting as if the theatre
didn't exist; never allowing vote, censure, division, or standing
orders to have any connection with the recreation of the brief
chronicles of time, moving in light and shade in quiet and tumult,

within the curtained stage; their conservative, gilded nonchalance above and beyond it all.

Following very close behind now is the brawny Labour Party, many of its officials pressing forward to the heaven of bowler hats, respectable suits, and neatly-folded umbrellas, regarding the theatre as a place for ninnies of leisure and levity, forgetful that without a vision the people perish, and that a facet of this vision should be aglow in a theatre that they and the mass members of the Trade Unions have set firmly upon its feet. It was left to a few Communists and fewer sympathisers to set about bringing the theatre back to the people, building with much labour and hard going a little theatre[1] to bring colour and a laugh and an occasional tightening of the spine to the common people in the form of play and pantomime. But to England as England the drama is as if it never had been, and never will hang out on her battlements the masks of tragedy and comedy again.

Why has the colourful, vivacious, tragic life of the theatre faded from the ken of the English people? It had a big life and a gorgeous time when the Trade Guilds went about in their wagons doing the Mystery and the Morality Plays, showing the goodness of God and the evil of Satan to the gaping crowds, clapping their hands and shouting for more, so that one couldn't get stir or breath. Again in Elizabethan times the gayest of colours swam before the eyes of the people, and the loveliest of language fell musically into outstretched ears, to become scented and clever, but a gift for the few only in the golden days of good King Charles; to burst melodramatically out into paper bloom again, and then, finally, to be shepherded with golden whips into the toy-lighted corner of London's West End, along which faintly blows Mr Priestley's whispered appeal of 'don't desert a man because a graver note creeps into his work; don't stay out of the theatre because the realities of life have crept into it'.

Some will blame the cinema, but it goes down deeper than that. The decay of the theatre, I think, began when the nationality of England began to grow pale in the rush and roar of the

[1] The Unity Theatre, London.

Industrial Revolution. Then all flocked to the towns, and the country's lore was lost, buried in the fields like the man hiding his talent in a napkin, though this was the talent of a nation. When all the spring and harvest festivals, the customs, the dances, the natural songs, the blossoms of folklore and folk music faded into forgetfulness and disrepute, a lot of theatrical inspiration went out of England's soul. They still flourish in Scotland, Wales, and Eire, and even in some of the more remote English counties; but among the masses of the people they have been swallowed up in their Daisy Bell give me your answer do's and It's a long way to Tipperaries. One has only to listen to Workers' Playtime and Works Wonders, this let the people sing business, to see what tremendous advances England has made in her own national loss. A few folk societies have tried to give these things life again, but have never got anyway near the people, and seem to preserve these treasures as national ikons, rather than to hand them out to the people as gorgeous and inspiring playthings.

We are far too ignorant of, and careless about, this great national wealth lying well outside of our national banks. Some time ago, our great Prime Minister [Winston Churchill], speaking in Edinburgh, referred to Mr Harry Lauder as Scotland's national bard, thereby giving, unintentionally, a knock on Scotland's nose. Rabbie Burns, Dunbar, MacDiarmid, yes; but not Mr Lauder. In my opinion, England's older customs, her songs and dances, her folklore must be, and should be, familiar to us before a sprightly and serious native drama can spring into vigorous being. I don't of course, mean the there'll always be an England stunt — that's as bad as the Irish wrap the green flag round me, boys, tomfoolery. I mean the deeper things that spring from the experience and credulity of life; for simple as these may be, each has the glint of colour, touch of poetry, sigh of pathos, and the ray of imagination that give a glow to song, to story, and to drama.

Only in the Children's Hour do we sometimes hear a few of these lovely things — recently, I listened to a stirring Cumberland march that I never heard before, and, maybe, will never hear again. England must sing more about herself; not of her

Empire, but of herself. That will shake her shyness off, and make
her more audible on the stage. And get the young dramatists
away, too, from the curious heresy that nowhere is silence more
golden than when it appears on the stage. For now there is a
monastic awe for silence on the stage so that actors and actresses
are losing the power of speech, and mutter and mumble their way
about behind the footlights and the curtain, keeping all their
secrets to themselves. Mr John Palmer, in one of his critical
books, claims as bold and adventurous the dramatist who said
that 'above all, the theatre is the art of the unexpressed, and has
no worse enemy than literature'. And Mr Palmer, applauding
this, says 'this "theory of silence" should be sure of welcome and
sympathy among ourselves, for it is a sacred postulate that the
more poignant emotions are too deep for words. English lovers
are expected to be incoherent; English heroes are expected to be
silent. In English drama the strong silent man will never die.
Kill him in the plays of Alfred Sutro, and he will appear, strong
and silent as ever, in the plays of John Galsworthy.' Mr Palmer
makes haste to excuse Shakespeare's *Romeo and Juliet*, saying,
'We must scrupulously beware of using the theory of silence as a
cover for mere literary incompetence or neglect, and some of us
may suspect that men are silent because they have nothing to
say.' Quite so. A lot of these dramatists hide a personality
within a mumble because they haven't a personality that can be
lifted into a shout. Shakespeare's *O what a rogue and peasant
slave am I!* would silence every strong silent man of the stage
into silent pillars of salt.

But the first apparent change to come, has already begun to
come, will be the physical method and manner of the theatre.
As the war has set our buildings tumbling, so it has set our needs
tumbling into new ways of living, and our minds tumbling into
new ways of thought. The big professional theatres of the West
End have had their day, on the whole, a dog's day, and that
day is now in its twilight, for the half-gods are getting ready
to go; and when the half-gods go, the gods arrive. Plays are
being performed where they have never been performed before,
and, by and by, the provincial cities and towns will not rest quiet

without theatrical activities of their own. This has started quicker in the United States than it has here, and a Congress of the National Theatre Conference has begun to set things moving. They have asked playwrights to give them an equal chance with the professional part of the theatre. Saroyan gave them *Jim Dandy*, and last year this play was done in forty-four centres, and is still being performed. Maxwell Anderson's *Eve of St Mark* was performed in seventy cities before it came to Broadway; and now a musical comedy has been written for production by the numerous centres of this National Theatre Conference. This outspread of interest and self-determination in the theatre will come to us, and will form new and fine endeavours, inflicting new trials on older actors and actresses staggering out of the art of acting under the burden of a huge weekly salary. It will give us a new theatre. Imagination will supersede the dressmaker's shop, and show us that man doth not live by bread alone, but by every word out of the mouth of God; by every word, mind you, and not only the word repeated by Nonconformist, Anglican, Roman Catholic, or Mohammedan; but also the glowing word spoken by every fine building, statue, poem, picture, and play. This theatre will cordially send out to show its achievement to India, to Australia, over the sea to Skye, to St Helena, or whatever may be the *ultima thule* of the British Commonwealth. It will be a theatre preserving all the delicate grace, beauty, and majesty of line that have been born before us, adding the sturdiness and lusty life of the present-day descendants of coopers, fullers, armourers, bowmakers, and all of a bygone generation, so that the theatre may become a passionate, graceful, and colourful part of English life, giving us a vision of the whole earth, not as a mourning man in the fork of a dying tree gazing over a waste land, but like unto Pushkin's beautiful princess with the moon in her hair and a star on her forehead.

THE THEATRE AND THE POLITICIAN (1945)*

STRANGERS, nearly, though they should be friends, and find each other good company. But to most of the politicians Melpomene is but a second-rate whore. And man in the mass is as much to blame as the single aspiring politician. Most of us have as odd an idea of politics as we have of the theatre and of the Church; simply because we think, mostly, that all our concerns are born and reared within the confines of our own little circle of thought and action. Politicians keep away from the theatre, and the theatre is advised to keep away from politics, while the Church has strained its heart by trying to keep away from both. They think all they say as politicians to be so important; it is important, or should be so, but not eternally so. I understand, there are stored safe under London, a hundred million copies of *Hansard*, a magazine recording all that has ever been said by the politicians of the parties. In these volumes you will find references to most things, even to religion from the refusal to admit an atheist who declined to take an oath to a debate on a reformed prayerbook that was to contain a petition to God to maintain the then present rate of interest on share and bond. But is there e'er a word in any of them about the theatre? Do we ever hear of the House moving an adjournment so that its members may go in a body to a play, led by the Speaker, with the Black Rod smiling approval by his side? If I remember right, I have heard of ministers present at a football final; and some time ago, what was called body-line bowling nearly caused a cabinet crisis; but no cabinet ever, as far as I know, took a special train to Stratford to see a play by Shakespeare, or one to Malvern to see a play by Shaw. Do any of them ever even go

* Published in *Common Wealth Review*, Jan. 1946.

to a pantomime? The politicians' indifference to such things has helped to give them a bad name, enticing Webster to say of them, 'A politician imitates the devil, as the devil imitates a cannon; wheresoever he comes to do mischief, he comes with his backside towards us.'

Not only British politicians are indifferent: it is recorded that de Valera was once only in the Abbey Theatre; and then he went, not to see a play, but to hear how a play sounded in Gaelic. Little or no notice of literature, science, art, or the theatre, though these things are as important in the lives of the people as coal, gas, bread, meat, and the houses they call home; for even primitive man chanted his guttural song, and chiselled fine forms on the walls of his hole of a house. More so then than now, and politics are partly to blame. We are letting the loveliness ooze away from the mind of man. How often have I heard a voice, a complacent voice, shouting over the wireless, 'This is so-and-so saying goodbye, and let the people sing!' Sing what, sing how? They don't know how to sing, and the poverty of song in the theatre, Archer's pride, is partly responsible for this; and the indifference of the politicians largely responsible for the poverty of the theatre. Oh, for some member of parliament that would have the courage to jump up and give the rest of them a song and a dance on the floor of the House!

It is strange the indifference to drama with drama everywhere around us — in the solemn, muttering gossip of old men and women, in the gestures we make, in what we say and how we say it, in our prayers, curses, regrets for the past, hopes for the future, our birth, our growth, our decline, and our death; all of them, day by day, tinctured deep with politics; for politics are more than a clever speech, a point gained against an opposite, a passing from one division into another. It is a searching out, a finding out of the best way of ordering life to bring out the brightest and fullest development of the mind, body, and soul of man. And no bigger influence exists for this end than the influence of the theatre. And so, then, to me, the nationalization of the theatre is as important as the nationalization of coal or transport. Every town that has a church should have a theatre,

*

not subject to the charity of wealthy persons, or to the whim of visiting companies; but with its own living staff and active workshop. Nationalization of Art! politicians will say, with their hearts beating; but such an idea means no more than the provision of means for the young to practise the art of the theatre, without having to suffer the indifference that paralyses all effort. No fear may be felt for the artists in acting, in design, or in the writing of a play. Any one of them, with the instinct and urge of the artist in him or her will just ignore the pressure of opinion, and go on his own creative way, without rejoicing, possibly, but determined to be himself. The salute so often given to bad art — apart from the views of venal critics — comes, not from this or that party opinion, but mainly from ignorance of art, the fear of what is new and unique, because, for the time, it cannot be understood; and for the easy love of the familiar and the commonplace. And this ignorance is found among the highest and the lowest in the land. The lowest can be educated; the highest must be shoved aside. In times of great crisis, like the one we have passed through, all efforts combine for the discomfiture and defeat of the enemy; but even then artists are constrained to remain themselves, as with Mayakovsky; for, in the stress of the bitterest fight for Soviet life, he was not the mouth-piece of this or that committee; in everything he did, he was always Mayakovsky. Einstein's mathematics could never evolve a universe satisfying to the Nazis. I think we may rest assured that a people's theatre will in no way interfere with the playwright's independence. No committee can create an artist's vision. No committee could have written the plays of the Shakespeare of the past, nor will any committee ever be able to create the Shakespeare of the future. But it can make things easier for him, and straighten out the path before him, in a way, too, which no commercially bound theatre could attempt.

Then there is the question of what is called propaganda in a play. There are very few plays in which the artist doesn't give an opinion about life as he sees it; or gives forth a sigh for what he would like it to be; or laughs at its follies, applauds its courage, or lashes out at its hypocrisies. There is, of course, at times, the play that is nothing but a wearisome string of political party platitudes, containing no element, in character or lyricism, of a play at all. The writers of this sort of thing have in them no spark of the love of humanity, but are merely hangers-out of opinions, voiced by puppets dressed up for the occasion in the garments of men and women. Unless what is said by a character in a play be part of the play's texture, and part of the nature of the character speaking, then the dialogue is just severely boring, and tends to injure the very cause the writer is trying to advocate.

Gorki knew this, and spoke plainly about it to the younger writers who were hurrying to write a play of all the political platitudes they had heard since their ears had opened to the many messages around them. Indeed, it would seem that since the ending of the war, the Soviet playwrights and theatre-men are taking up again the writing and production of what is called 'pure theatre'. In the *Moscow News* for October the sixth, of this year [1945], we are told of the production of John Fletcher's *The Tamer Tamed*, which, the journal says, 'is a sign of the reaction to the psychology and realism that has been the dominent feature of the Soviet stage'. There isn't any doubt in my mind that the concrete shelter is as bad as the ivory tower; worse, in fact, for the ivory tower keeps in faint touch with present life, but the walls of a concrete shelter are too thick to hear even a whisper of it.

THE PLAY OF IDEAS (1950)*

ONE cannot write about people without writing about things; for the food we eat, the clothes we wear, and the roofs that shelter us are all very near to us, and without them we perish. Even the atom bomb, so far away from us, is very close to us all. So we cannot keep ideas about things out of plays. We'd have to get ideas out of life before we could remove them from the drama. Indeed the very first glimmer of the conception for a play is an idea. There's hardly a thing written as a play, a novel, or a poem, that hasn't an idea under it, hovering over it, or in its very core. Life is constantly pummelling itself with ideas from morn till midnight.

No one can write about ideas without creating persons to express them; but it is one thing to have an idea in a head and quite another to place it in a play. It takes a master-mind to do that so that it will appeal to the imagination of an audience. Shaw and Ibsen are masters of this fancy. Shaw's plays are packed with punches for all kinds of reforms, yet there's hardly one of them that isn't glittering with the fanciful guile of a dramatist. Shaw and Ibsen are Israelites in whom there's a lot of guile, and grand guile too. And *Othello* (among other plays) is a melodrama; the acting editions showed us what they actually were, when all the poetry in them had been gutted out of them. Shaw's own play, *The Devil's Disciple*, is a melodrama, but one in which an intelligent being can sigh with safety. It is full of intelligent emotion — emotion lacking in such things as *Abie's Irish Rose*, *The Song of Bernadette*, and many plays dealing with a son's

* *New Statesman and Nation*, Apr. 8, 1950. This article was one of several contributed by leading playwrights to a symposium on modern drama: Bernard Shaw and Terence Rattigan were others.

relationship with his mother or a husband's jealousy of his wife.

Mr Rattigan seems to cherish the thought that such plays can create characters out of themselves; that relationship of mother with son, or the jealousy of a husband used as play themes will bring forth ready-born and fully matured characters into existence and into action without any tiring interference or help on the part of the dramatist; and, that, if the dramatist only chooses a suitable theme, the characters will flock, fully fruited on to the stage. They won't. It is just as hard to create a play with the theme of a mother and son relationship, or the theme of a jealous husband as it is to create one about the theme of a honeymoon or a holy well. And, anyway, what would these themes be but psychological discussions around the relationship of mother with son and a husband's jealousy of a wife? Again, Falstaff, probably the greatest character ever thrust upon a stage, had no relationship with a mother as far as I know, nor had he a wife to be jealous of.

It is exhilarating, in a perverse way, to hear it said that Ibsen's stealthy entry into the English theatre and Shaw's determined rush on to its stage killed the drama dead, though the dead drama refused to lie down. The fact is that these two dramatists brought a dead drama back to a serious and singing life again. The zeal for the theatre that had eaten them up gave them the courage and strength to drive, helterskelter, the foolish, fustian plays that had cluttered the stage for so long, as can be seen from a glance or two at the plays mentioned in Shaw's two volumes of *Dramatic Opinions* — plays so prodigiously trivial that their names even are unknown to the younger souls of today. The previous playwrights had made a simpering whore of the drama, and it took Shaw and Ibsen — though they didn't make her a lady, thank God — to change her into a vigorous, dignified, and intelligent woman, able and ready to give an answer for the hope that was in her.

There is a lot to be said for the opinion that all, or most, of the older, greater works, if not loaded, are strongly tinted with social significance; that they comment on, and often condemn, the activity and manner of their time. In England alone, from

Chaucer and Langland up to Auden and T. S. Eliot the life we lived, religious, civil, and political, and the life we live, have been examined and commented upon according to the period in which the life was lived and the works were written. The thinker, the playwright, and the poet have shared in the struggle for the rights of man; and, if they didn't wield a sword, at least they carried a banner. They have helped to immortalise man's fight against intolerance, cod custom, ignorance, and fear.

Things change life as well as thought — the railway, the motor-car, the tractor, the harvest-combine, and even the proletarian bicycle. A new kind of life is with us, whether we like it or not. And a good deal of this life will flood into the theatre. The stalls that give rest to the bums hidden in satin and silk will soon be ghosts of the past; and the new life will demand new plays that deal with and interpret the life it lives. And here comes a pause. The plays written around the new life must be currents in the mainstream of drama, must be an offspring of the great tradition. When we decide, instead of playing at being kings or queens or cavaliers, to play at being proletarians, then let us play at being them, and not send them forth as lecturers in an academy hall, preachers in a pulpit, or speakers from a political platform, important as these activities can be. The dramatist must see poetry in the smoky hub-bub of a tavern, just as he may see it in the stately ceremonial of a cathedral, though he may realise that, while the life in a tavern is always real, that of the cathedral is often a sham.

Just now, the English proletarian is immersed up to his nose in the making out of football-coupons, a minor way of getting rich quick, a method condoned by the Government and applauded by the Roman Catholic hierarchy. But this won't last: already many millions of workers and peasants in other lands are pressing towards a fuller share of the necessaries of life, and are stretching out to grasp the higher things abounding above them. I look forward to the day with confidence when British workers will carry in their hip pockets a volume of Keats's poems or a Shakespeare play beside the packets of lunch attached to their belts.

MELPOMENE AN' THALIA BEGGIN' FOR
BREAD (1958)*

I'M not in love with repertory theatres, for I have never liked
poverty, and these theatres are always asking or sighing for help,
lazarian lads and lasses who live, mostly, on the crumbs falling
from a rich man's table. Of course, the repertory theatres
have done fine work, often splendid work, and have done much
to enliven communities half-starved for drama — for instance,
the Abbey Theatre, giving Synge and Lady Gregory to the
world; the Rep. in Liverpool that enriched English acting; the
Gaiety in Manchester which gave England some fine playwrights; the Court Theatre in London which furnished the
world with such tremendous talents as Shaw, Galsworthy,
Granville-Barker, and others; and the great O'Neill who found
a first nest in small theatres near Washington Square: very fine
records, and worthy of commemoration in sculptured memorials.
But they never lasted, unless propped up by some generous rich
man, like Barry Jackson, who delved deep in a pocket to keep
the Birmingham Repertory going; but time and the commercial
Conways did down most of the others; and, always, they were
wondering where the money would come from to pay for
another week's life. Poverty was always the repertory theatre's
best robe. Here today and gone tomorrow their daily slogan.
Jesu help us their daily prayer. A cry for help was always
hovering on the lips of those who ran them. At times, they
showed infinite riches in a little room, and an hour later the
room was empty.

Thirty-five years ago, even, the repertory theatres were

* O'Casey's contribution to a symposium on Repertory Theatre, published in the *New York Times Magazine*, Nov. 9, 1958.

crawling about on all fours, hoping one day to be fit to stand up, and though some of them managed it, the stature of maturity lasted but for a week or two, and then the repertory sank down on its knees again. Then, too, in these theatres, the actors received tiny salaries, sharing the anxieties of the manager on and off the stage; the scenery and designing was a matter of rags and tatters; but, even so, it all cost at least two hundred pounds a week, so when they couldn't take the cash, they had to let the credit go. Now it is much worse, for expenses have gone up swift as a new-made rocket, and the hope of the repertory theatre now is a hope that lies still in a coffin. The amount of food a dramatist gets from a repertory production wouldn't feed a dozen of his chickens for a month; so playwrights aim at productions, not in reps, but in London's West End or Broadway's broad and jewelled bosom.

Only in the creation of municipal theatres will we find some dramatic satisfaction and some security, for the theatre should be part of the common and uncommon life of the people. If not bone of the people's bone, flesh of their flesh, then one of the pulses of the people's heart. In any of these theatres, plays would get fair rehearsals joined to settled and competent actors, with no reason to bother about where the money was to come from; all thought would be given to the play; any play of worth, home-made or one from a foreign mind, would be welcome; but for a season, maybe the first one, I should select the following plays as works that give me enjoyment and thought. *Heartbreak House*, which Shaw thought to be his best play, for its small but piercing voice of prophecy in the rooms and life of Horseback Hall and Heartbreak House; *The Cherry Orchard* for its lovely muted melody and the unnoticed coming of another age, shown in the cutting down of the trees, presaging the future time when the axe would be laid to the root of the tree; O'Neill's *Mourning Becomes Electra*, for its haunting power and its dread vision of envy, hatred, and uncharitableness driving a soul from life into a secluded ruin; Strindberg's *Dream Play*, with its sad longing and its infinite compassion for humanity; Saroyan's *My Heart's in the Highlands*, for its heart of an old man beating hope and its bugle-calls turning life's disappointments into a fair, sweet tune; Gorki's *Yegor Bulychov*, for the play's joust with humbug and cant, Yegor's rebellion against God as the people rebel against the Tsar, and the revolutionary reincarnation in young Yashmak of the dreaming student in *The Cherry Orchard*; Wedekind's *Spring's Awakening* for its tender and tragic poem on the pain of adolescent sex impulses in a technique far and away in advance of those who wrote plays beside him; Shakespeare's *Midsummer Night's Dream*, for its wonderful words, its magical songs, and its glorious comic interludes; Thornton Wilder's *Our Town*, for the simplicity of its adventure upon the stage, its gentle pathos and humour in its brief passage from life's youth to the heart-breaking silence of the dead; Pirandello's *Six Characters in Search of an Author*, for its symphony of psychological logic showing that he knew almost too much about us; and Giraudoux's *Enchanted*, for its poetic simplicity, and the play's charming blending of realism with poetic fantasy, enabling the actors to become familiar with, and to practise, the new form that seems to be gradually changing the form and the style of drama.

These for a beginning; all beautiful, and all worthy of the best efforts of any theatre, worthy, too, of the best actors who at present tread the stage.

SHAKESPEARE AMONG THE FLAGS (1964)*

AT last all the flags are out, all the pipes of the great organ play, and the commemorative postage stamps are out. The four-hundred-year-old grudge against the acknowledgement of Shakespeare has given way to a national acclamation. The dramatist has made a wonderful fight of it. He began within the torment of an inferior education, separating him from the more fortunate writers of his time. His father had failed in business, so he was poor, possessing nothing but the urge of the genius within him. The university wits more or less despised him, though they couldn't altogether shake his confidence out of him. One of these wits, even when he was dying, cursed Shakespeare as an upstart, and warned his fellow-wits against this impudent, ignorant interferer. So, alone and warming his five wits, the young grammar-school lad sat down to begin the work that was to sweep the others aside, and make the lonely one the greatest poet and dramatist of them all. Fortunately he was helped by the Earl of Southampton, about whom Shakespeare wrote many of his sonnets; and by the time that patronage began to be transferred to a dangerous rival, Marlowe, Shakespeare was independent, and able to whistle 'Merrily, merrily, shall I live now, under the blossom that hangs on the bough'. He was a freelance, able to probe and prod anyone, anywhere he liked.

What a different tale today to the tale of thirty years ago! Then Shakespeare was as quiet as a mouse, for the theatre then

* An article written to commemorate Shakespeare's anniversary, published in *The New York Times Magazine* on Apr. 19, 1964, under the title 'Ode to an "Impudent Upstart".' The conclusion to the manuscript, published here, is slightly different from that of the version printed in the *N.Y.T.*

30

was the theatre of Pinero, Lonsdale, Barrie and Coward. One playwright of that time whose play[1] employed six or more companies surging through the English cities and towns was a lad who was then regarded as England's herald and hope in drama. He had neither seen, nor heard, nor read a Shakespeare play, an experience then suffered or enjoyed by millions of English people. A sin of omission, a grave sin of omission! So he was hurried off to see *Hamlet*, and as he and his friends homeward plodded their weary way, he was asked what he thought of it! The play would be better without the Ghost, he murmured. Was he moved? Well not half as much as he had been moved by a performance of *Young Woodley*. That was just the temper of the times.

An Irishman in England at the time came seeking out Shakespeare; he had received from the then President of the Soviet Union of Writers a gorgeous golden book, with a frontispiece of the poet, and a host of illustrations showing the designs and characters of the plays that were being performed in Moscow, Leningrad, Kiev, and other towns in honour of England's genius. Pinned to the cover was a letter asking him to write an account of the many productions reeling through the English theatres, giving their bow and obeisance to the Elizabethan literary giant.

The Irishman sought in vain. Shakespeare was in the land of Erewhon — the Stratford Theatre was shut and no play was on from Penzance to John O'Groats. He had become a mere neglected English antiquity. Some day, maybe a literary archaeologist would ferret him out, and critics would lazily wonder if the find was a genuine one. The Bright Young Things of the period found him heavy going, and kept him at a safe distance; while the sombre group, the Angry Young Men, blew themselves up into a tappertit revolt against capital and convention, and so had no time to pick a leaf from Shakespeare's laurels for a badge, or pluck a rose from his great bush of blossoms for a-wearing in their coats.

There is wonder in it that one said to have been dead for so

[1] R. C. Sherriff's *Journey's End*.

long can still prance and pirouette about as if in the virile and idyllic year of his youth. Why is it that the great Marlowe and the equally great Ben Jonson are so relatively stiff in their stride to-day compared with the gay and supple agility of Shakespeare? Chiefly, I think, because the two loved so little and loved so few, and the third loved so much and loved so many.

Yet Shakespeare could be terrible in his bitterness about the things of life: of man's ingratitude, of friends remembered not, that most love was mere folly, most friendship mere feigning. But in all, and through all, ran the pulsing vein of compassion and love for all things. He loved all things; he missed nothing, for nothing was too lowly for him to touch with a beautiful phrase. He looked up at a lofty tree and looked down at the speckled cowslip; rosemary, rue, wild thyme, and the pansy grew by his doorway, or scented the ways he walked in, and he often saw the morning dew shine for a moment before it slid off like a blessing from God. There was nothing of the literary popinjay in Shakespeare as there was in Marlowe, or of the literary swashbuckler as there was in the rare Ben Jonson. Bottom, Falstaff, Dogberry, Feste, and even the humour-obsessed Nym, were his companions as well as King Richard, Hamlet, Anthony, and Cleopatra. He seemed to know Bible and prayerbook like the palm of his hand, and used both to add point and flavour to the dialogue in his plays. Marlowe, Jonson, and the other University men wove most of what they wrote out of themselves as spiders weave silk threads from their own bellies; but Shakespeare gathered a lot of material for his miracles from the talk, the mannerisms, and eccentricities of those with whom he mixed and had his being. They stood still in the centre of learning; he walked, talked, and ran around in the centre of life.

The world of life was Shakespeare's oyster, and, unlike Auden who found it empty, Shakespeare found it packed tight with good and grand things. He saw all, heard all, tasted many things, felt all the emotions, and he scented the sweet perfumes coming from the hearts of flowers and shrank from the rotten smell that came from war. The great Marlowe, too, had his five wits that clubbed together in a mind keener, possibly, than Shakespeare's, but they never seemed to warm towards anyone outside of himself and confined him to a reckless importance alone among his university companions. He was cold and had little sense of humour. Whenever he tried to raise a laugh, it was clumsy, and dull, falling on the ear like clay falling on a coffin's lid. Shakespeare's sense of humour was heart-felt and full-bosomed, for he loved liveliness and his feet tapped out many a dance, for he would foot it featly here and there on yellow sands or in a candle-lighted room. For these reasons, Shakespeare has lived on, forever young, forever the supreme playwright of his time, of yesterday, today, and will be supreme tomorrow too. This is why when Marlowe, or even Jonson enters our home, we meet him with a deferential bow; but when Shakespeare comes, we cry welcome, and shake his hand, and set him down in the cosiest seat by the fire.

But Shakespeare isn't all smiles by any means. In his plays, he can be a man of sorrow and acquainted with grief. He has no delusions about life; he knows that man, born of woman, has but a short time to live; that he cometh up, and is cut down like a flower; he fleeth as it were a shadow, and never continueth in one stay. He was able to see change and decay all around him, as he showed in a sonnet to the young and handsome Earl of Southampton. He counted the clock that struck the time, saw the brave day lost in the night, noticed the fading violet past its prime, lofty trees barren of leaves, summer's green gathered into sheaves and borne on a bier with white and grizzly beard, saw sable curls turned white with age; then questioned the beauty of the Earl that in the waste of time must go:

> *Since sweets and beauty do themselves forsake,*
> *And die as fast as they see others grow.*

He saw change and decay as keenly, and felt it far more deeply than we present-day dramatists do, but he saw new growth as well. He knew that man cometh up and dieth as a flower in the field; but beside every fading flower, he saw a fresh blossom rising. A brief candle blown out gave place to another: *lux mundi* never goes out, never grows less. There is always someone in the house with Dinah playing on the oul' banjo.

I usually listen to the B.B.C. Schools Broadcasts, junior school as well as sixth form. I enjoy all the programmes, especially the one called 'Time and Tune', for it teaches me something about music, of which I know very little. One item recently was a gay, simple song, most enjoyable, which went like this:

> *We are dancing as we sing,*
> *Gaily, gaily are we singing,*
> *We are dancing in a ring,*
> *Come and join us dancing.*

Were he here to listen to this simple song and see the fun, the great poet who knew well that man's life fleeth as it were a shadow, would have been within this ring, this round O of hilarity, in the twinkling of an eye.

As long as Shakespearean flags fly, bugles blow, drums beat; as long as his glorious and graceful words sound in our ears, we need care little about the wolf-howl of the Avaunt Garde, or, in any way, be afraid of *Who's Afraid of Virginia Woolf?* The dance and the song no less than the requiem and the funeral march is Shakespeare's way with life.

JOHN MILLINGTON SYNGE (1946)*

AN odd, 'silent, drifting man', afflicted with cancer, who, almost in the twinkling of eye, became a great playwright, combining, in the fineness of his dramas, the lusty vigour and exuberant gaiety of Breughel with the grace and charming sensitiveness of a Botticelli. For twenty-eight years he remained an insignificant man, his name unknown in Ireland, or anywhere else, except for a few acquaintances who casually met him, casually talked with him, and, an hour after, as casually forgot him. Then the last eight years of his life flamed into prominence from the charm and power in the plays he wrote, and because of the tumult they roused in Ireland and many parts of America. For eight years this once dim star burned brilliantly, then, weary with the terror and torment of cancer, Synge murmured he could fight for life no longer, and calmly placed himself in the arms of gentle, but disturbing, death, and the shining star of drama became but a bright reflection in the sky.

Synge was born in Dublin in 1871, graduated from Trinity College, a university founded by Queen Elizabeth I; a university antagonistic to everything Irish, though, paradoxically, giving to Ireland some of the first and fairest patriots who ever fought and died for the natural and national freedom of the Irish people. It would seem he made no friends in the College, or any outside of it; so, unconscious, apparently, of any ties with his native land, and equipped with the modest income of two pounds a week, he left Ireland to wander over the continent of Europe, settling down eventually in a cheap and rather drab lodging in Paris. Here he whiled away time writing faintly-scented articles on French

* This article, commissioned for foreign distribution by the British Ministry of Information, was published in *Britansky Soyuznik* (Moscow) in June 1946. This is its first appearance in English.

literature, losing himself, and lost to Ireland. So for some years, hidden away in his meagre flat, known to a few, honoured by none, unaware of the music of words in his nature, sat and slept the strange man who was soon to cause uproar all over Ireland, and send thousands of the people in the United States into a tempest of argument, the sides dividing into hatred and repudiation on the one hand, and affection and profound appreciation on the other. Here Yeats, the poet, found him, persuading him to leave his unprofitable toil, and come back to Ireland, where the touch of the people would give him a life he had never known before. Synge found companions among the common people, and he was at home equally beside the sea in the West, aglitter with the shine of the sun, or in the deep, dark, lonely valleys of the county of Wicklow. In Wicklow he placed his first play, and the title — *The Shadow of the Glen* — and its description of scene, 'The last cottage at the head of a long glen in County Wicklow,' show how Synge could satisfy himself in the deep recesses of a gloomy glen, as *Riders to the Sea* shows how easy he was facing the fierceness of the stormy sea beating riotously on the rocky coast of Aran, where life was hard, and all lived dangerously.

When his first play was produced, Ireland felt a decided tremor of resentment and dislike. It wasn't what was wanted. The play was thought to be an insult to Irish women. It is an old theme — that of a fine, lusty woman tied to an old wheezy man, who, to find her out, pretends to be dead. She engages herself to a timid, callow young farmer, who thinks he owns the woman. To them a tramp enters the cottage for shelter from a stormy night. She is a courageous woman, for when the tramp suggests that she should be afraid of him, she says, 'I'm thinking many would be afeard, but I never knew what way to be afeard of beggar or bishop, or any one of you at all.' The tramp, a natural poet, after her old husband had jumped up from where he lay, supposedly dead, to denounce her, and order her out of the house, persuades the woman to come out of her loneliness and go the roads with him, saying, 'It's not my blather you'll be hearing only, but you'll be hearing the herons crying out over the black lakes, and you'll be hearing the grouse and the owls with them, and the larks and the big thrushes when the days are warm; and it's not from the like of them you'll be hearing a tale of getting old, . . . losing the hair off you, and the light of your eyes, but its fine songs you'll be hearing when the sun goes up, and there'll be no old fellow wheezing, the like of a sick sheep, close to your ear.'

In a short preface to this play Synge says that his plays hold no message; but here, in this one, is the call of a brave heart for the fullness of life; a character ready, at last, to go through life with a steady step, and add its vigour to the energetic and everlasting song of nature. The play is alive with realism (as all of them are); but the realism is coloured gaily with imagination, and a gay, or a lovely sad song sings a merry and delightful way through each of them.

Synge's next play, *Riders to the Sea*, restored the harmony. The work is a lovely melody of pain. In it is the past, the present, and the future sorrow of all those who live along the harshly-beautiful coasts of western Ireland, and who depend largely for their livelihood on the temper and generosity of the sea. In the Isles of Aran it is worse: hardly a family there who hasn't had one relative, at least, flung motionless and dripping on to the rocky shores; or, maybe, one who never returned, but stayed to tumble about forever in the deeper waves of the Atlantic Ocean. In this play, we see an old woman who has lost her husband, four sons, and now loses the last one; she sees the last male stay of the house, one stormy day, carried in by the neighbours, 'a thing on a plank, with water dripping out of it and leaving a track by the big stones'. A calm-eyed sister asks, 'What way was he drownded?', to be told that the grey pony he was taking to the hooker to be sold in the market, 'knocked him over into the sea, and he was washed out where there was a great surf on the white rocks'. And death by drowning is so usual, so common in these islands, that the old mother, stony-hearted with grief, rejoices that she has no more sons that the sea can take: 'They're all gone now, and there isn't anything more the sea can do to me. I'll have no reason now to be up crying when the wind breaks from the south, and you can hear the surf is in the east, and the surf is in the west, making a great stir with the two noises, and they hitting one on the other. I won't care what way the sea is when the other women are crying.'

Aran, the scene of the play, is a group of islands in Galway Bay, very bleak and very beautiful. The hardy people live by fishing, and by selling an odd cow or an odd pony. They range the ocean in long frail boats, called currachs, made of wicker framework, covered with stout canvas, and thickly coated with pitch. They are so light that few waves, however high or swift, can overthrow them, they shoot so suddenly to the wave's crest. When seeking the safety of the shore, after being caught out in a sudden storm, the boat has to be guided in on a favourable wave; the crew has to sweat and toil to keep the boat back when caught on a wave that will overwhelm them on the beach; so the relatives watch on the shore, knee-deep or waist-deep in water, to shout to the crew when they see a wave that will sweep the boat so far in on the beach that, with the help of the relatives, boat and men may be hauled out of the suction of the receding waters. The islands where they live are rocky, and their little vegetable plots are built up from handfuls of soil taken from rock crevices, with the addition of piles of kelp seaweed, gathered by old men and women, which they allow to rot, or burn to ashes with which they make excellent manure. Their small ponies nibble whatever life they can find growing in the rock crevices, though, oddly enough, these ponies are among the sturdiest and most intelligent in the land. The people wear raw-hide sandals, which they call 'pampooties'. These they can whip off in a second, so allowing them to wade through the countless sea pools spread over the face of the islands; and the white 'bawnees' the men wear are woven by themselves from the wool of their own sheep.

Here, liked by all, Synge lived as often and as long as he could, travelling with them in their hookers to the mainland, among cattle, pigs, and turf, eating with them the simple meals they built up on the fish they caught and the potatoes they grew in their tiny gardens, sleeping with them in an attic reached by a ladder, or in a corner of the stone-walled kitchen. Here he listened to what they said, shared their funny stories, sympathised with their boasting, and mourned with them when an accident or a sudden squall tumbled a relative into a medley of roaring surf from which there could be no escape. In the winter Synge fled the islands, for his lungs weren't fit to stand the battering of the ocean waves or the rushing, tearing winds that sent the sharp, cold wave-spray showering over the islands from one end to the other, often carrying off the labour of months in the little patches of soil that timidly held the tiny crop of cabbage and potato.

To the political-minded and to the puritanical Irish, Synge was an atheist and a most untoward man. To them 'Nora' [in *The Shadow of the Glen*] was a woman who 'wore her lusts on her sleeve'; for then — and now, too — the Catholic Irish can see a play only in what they think to be the light of the Catholic conscience. But the surprised disgust that met *The Shadow of the Glen* was a tame thing compared with the roaring, raging resentment that hailed the performances of his *The Playboy of the Western World*. Prelate, priest, and layman, Press, pulpit, and political party rent their garments before what they shouted out was blasphemy, insult, and ruinous travesty of the Irishman's clean mind, and the Irishwoman's unchallengeable modesty and virtue. For many nights the Abbey Theatre, Dublin, was a bedlam. The roaring of the resentful audiences made the play a dumb show from beginning to end; things were thrown at the actors, and violence was threatened so vehemently that the directors had, eventually, to call in the police, so that the performances might proceed. The same violent opposition was encountered in America when the company went on tour there, and, finally, through the pressure brought on the authorities by ignorant members of religious and political organisations, the company was placed under arrest for 'performing an obscene and an indecent play'. Eventually, the Abbey Theatre won its battle, and the play travelled over America without let or hindrance. But all that is over long ago, and the play is acknowledged by almost everyone for what it is — by far the best play that Synge wrote. In Ireland, now, it is received graciously, and even warmly, by the bulk of the play-going people, and is recognised as conferring honour, rather than shame, on the great name of Ireland. The full account of the fight in Ireland and America can be found in Lady Gregory's *Our Irish Theatre* (1913).

Synge had his own ideas about drama. He says, 'The drama, like the symphony, does not prove anything. Teachers and their systems soon become old-fashioned — look at Ibsen and the Germans — but the best plays of Jonson and Molière can no more go out of fashion than the blackberries on the hedge. Of the things that nourish the imagination, humour is one of the most needful, and it is dangerous to limit or destroy it. Where a country loses its humour, there will be morbidity of mind, as Baudelaire's mind was morbid.' There is certainly no direct teaching in any of Synge's plays, such as two and two make four in morals, but in the gay loveliness of their conception, in many a laugh at human feeling, flimsiness, and frailty, there are laughing lessons for all; or, in *The Shadow of the Glen*, when Nora, counting sound money out [of] a stocking, wistfully wonders if she was a fool, when, playing for safety, she married an old man, to sit with loneliness, 'looking out from a door, and seeing nothing but the mists rolling down the bog, and the mists again and they rolling up the bog.' And in *The Well of the Saints* we sense the idea that it is not well to destroy even the illusions of loveliness, and that imagination can see Helen's beauty in a brow of Egypt.

It is a strange thought how Synge draws these humble, ill-educated people, living in sordid surroundings, their hands forever handling mean and trivial things; yet though their feet stick deep in the mire, their heads are often singing in the golden clouds. Professor A. E. Morgan says of him, 'He laughed and wept with man's joy and sorrow. He had the power to show his vision of life in a form beautiful in detail and balanced in design. Above all, believing in the greatness of mankind, though fully aware of its littleness, he created works of art which were not only clever and meritorious, but were in the real sense great.' And George Jean Nathan, the famous American drama critic, says of him, 'Of the Irish dramatists who have gone to their

Maker, Synge stands pre-eminent in after-glory. *The Playboy of the Western World* has not its match in Keltic satirical drama, and one would have to search wide and deep for an equivalent of the melodious pain in *Riders to the Sea*. Both are classics of the modern Irish — of the modern world — theatre. Synge combined in himself an ironic humour of rare and fruity power and a compassion for humanity drenched in the tears of a great pity's understanding.'

Like the opposition that harried Mayakovsky, the resentment that Synge encountered wearied him, and, undoubtedly, hastened his end. In the month when the daffodils come before the swallow dares, Synge grew too tired to finish his last play, *Deirdre of the Sorrows*, and, stretching out in his hospital bed, he murmured to the nurse, 'It is no use fighting death any longer', then he turned his face to the wall, and left the Abbey Theatre behind him. A sad year for Ireland, 1909, for then it was that Synge bid her farewell.

ONE OF THE WORLD'S DRAMATISTS (1943)*

THERE are not many when one comes to count them; but
certainly Anton Chekhov is one of them. It is hard to say what I
think of this fine dramatist and master of the art of the short
story. I am not a critic, and have never set out, either by experience or by training, minutely to describe and unerringly explain the beauty, power, and grace in great plays; or, indeed, in
any other art. In the beginning (for I had to painfully educate
myself), I followed those I liked and reverenced afar off, till I
could honestly go to them, and say, Be my friends. So it was with
Shakespeare, Milton, Shelley, Burns, Keats, Walt Whitman,
and others; and so it was with Chekhov, who has been a friend
of mine now for over thirty years. To me Chekhov is one of
God's gifts to man, a generous and a rare gift. He is one of the
unmitred bishops of men. Chekhov was kind to me, greeted me
cordially, though he spoke Russian and I spoke English. He is, in
my opinion, a writer of whom the greatest nation and sturdiest
people may be well proud; and I am very glad to know how the
Russian people cherish and honour his memory. Some time ago
(some still do it) the communists, in their stern and detonating
sincerity, rejected as against the people, and alien to the future of
the proletariat, the creative works of the race when they happened through no fault of their own, to be attached to any other
class than what they called the workers. 'These didn't belong,'
they said. In doing so they threw away many a goodly pearl —
for the time being. It was a nonsensical and ignorant attitude of
mind, and many a cool nod, and many a hard word, I got for
daring to tell them so. Indeed, only a year ago I wrote an article

* This article, written in 1943, was written for publication in the U.S.S.R.;
this is its first publication in English.

for *Irish Freedom*, called 'Empty Vessels',[1] in which I deplored their indifference to, and contempt for, the fine works of man in literature, painting, and sculpture. I maintained that I was no less, rather more, of a communist for the love and reverence I had for the riches poured out by the mind and imagination of man. I never could agree with this perverse opinion (sometimes transformed into a dogma), and argued that all lovely and sturdy things were the property, not of this or that man, but of the race which they in themselves glorified. These were treasures that no man could persuade me to cast away, and Chekhov was one of them: a fine graceful pearl of great price.

His plays have, of course, been done here, but not near often enough; and sometimes they have been done badly.

I have seen performed two fine productions of *The Three Sisters*, one of *Uncle Vanya*, and a comparatively poor production of *The Cherry Orchard*. I shall remember for a long time the performance of *Uncle Vanya*, for I went straight to it on my arrival to England from Ireland nearly eighteen years ago. Jean Forbes-Robertson gave a fine performance of Sonya (by the way Jean and her husband recently gave a performance of *Distant Point* in a town near us as a short holiday in their tour through the war factories), and the whole production was a delightful one to me. It was the first time I had seen one of Chekhov's plays on the stage, though I had been familiar with his plays and stories in book-form for a long time before; and it was the very first play that England showed me, which augured well for the English theatre, though, unfortunately, the augury proved to be an unsubstantial one. I have yet to see *The Seagull* performed, and shameful it is to have to say so, but it is a lamentable fact. But now that a thorough awakening of the English Theatre is promised, I hope to see the plays of Chekhov helping to make our stage a livelier and more lovely place than it has been for a long, long time. A Russian producer gave us the *The Three Sisters*, and a very fine production he made of it, showing us its tenderness, its longings, its sad and graceful beauty with the

[1] See pp. 158–61 in the present volume.

gentleness of a sensitive and pretty woman showing her beautiful self to her lover for the first time.

Great argument has gone about and about as to which of his works is his best play, *The Cherry Orchard* being the one generally led forward as undoubtedly the most lovely of the dramatist's children. James Agate, the drama critic of *The Sunday Times*, in a book published in 1933, says, while he is encouraging English people to become unafraid of the unfamiliar, 'I have views on most matters, and am as willing as a politician to change most of them. But there is one view which I will not change for anyone living or dead, or to be born in the next thousand years, it is that *The Cherry Orchard*, by the great Russian dramatist, Anton Tchehov, is a world-masterpiece. You are thinking,' he goes on (he is writing in a conversational manner), 'it is some gloomy, doleful piece, praised by the high-brows for the simple reason that they can't understand it and therefore think it must be wonderful. It is nothing of the sort. A great deal of it is as funny as *Charley's Aunt*, though parts of it are as pathetic as Adelina Patti singing "Home Sweet Home". This play is perfectly easy to understand, and it is written in language as simple as a child's book called *Reading Without Tears*.' Well, I agree with Mr Agate that *The Cherry Orchard* is a masterpiece, but it isn't as 'funny' as *Charley's Aunt*; it isn't as pathetic as Madame Patti singing her song of 'Home Sweet Home'; it isn't a play that is 'perfectly easy to understand'. It is full of thoughts too deep for tears; its humour is of the texture of the play, colours, some vivid, some softly pastel, threading their way through the graceful, lovely, gentle grey of the play. Then Mr Agate makes a curious statement. He says, 'It is hard to believe that this play may be no longer performed in Russia. It is forbidden because it deals with the woes of the aristocracy; and the new order, realising that there is pity here as well as condemnation, will not allow the piece to be played.' Well, there's information for you! This talk was given over the wireless by Mr Agate in 1925 and the book in which it appears in 1933, so there is no excuse for Mr Agate. Had he read Huntly Carter's *Theatre and Cinema in Soviet Russia*, he'd have seen not only that this play was produced there in those years and the years before, but also the other plays of Chekhov, in company with plays by European playwrights, including [one based on] Dickens' *Cricket on the Hearth*. He might have advantageously read the words of Lenin, too: 'If we cannot comprehend clearly that a proletarian culture can be built up only on the basis of precise knowledge of the entire culture created by humanity during the whole period of its development, and by adapting that culture to its own needs — if we cannot comprehend that, then we will not be able to solve our problems.' He could have read that in the magazine called *The International Theatre*, and have discovered that the founder of the Soviet State would certainly not show the back of his hand to Chekhov.

Well, to return — which play by Chekhov is his 'master-piece'? Personally, I don't like that word. A great play, a beautiful play, a fine play, are words much better with which to honour a work worthy of any of those tributes. When I read the plays of Chekhov, his best play is always the one first read, to be changed for the one that is read afterwards; and it is so when I see them on the stage. The truth is that his plays are all lovely, and fit to step out with the foremost. Here is the sombre pine, the graceful beech, there, the pearly-jacketed birch, with the nuances of many birds in their branches, bannered by a silvery sky overhead, tinted with a delicate mauve hue; and voices everywhere praying, sighing, calling for more life, more light, more evidence for the vindication of the nobility of man. Honour, too, to this man's grandfather who freed his family from serfdom, thereby giving the world the chance to produce this great man, Chekhov, who in his great work manifested the loveliness and strength of his own nature, and added another glory to the life of man.

c

DRAMATIS PERSONAE IBSENISENSIS (1932)*

If there had been no Ibsen, there would have been no Pinero, no Shaw, no St John Hankin, no Miles Malleson, perhaps not even a Frederick Lonsdale. France would have had no Brieux, Germany no Georg Kaiser or Ernst Toller, Italy no Pirandello, America no Eugene O'Neill. — *Hannan Swaffer.*

IBSEN stood still and thought, thought as he stood still in the snow on the highest peak of the tallest mountain in the most northern corner of northern Norway. He stood still a long, long time, and thought long and thought deeply. It was the middle of the six-month night of the northern land, and, turning his back on the green, purple, and golden plumes of the Midnight Sun, he faced forward into the darkness.

'I must have more, I must have more,' he murmured, 'I must have a crowd of kids. I must have them there, here, and everywhere. The prophet has spoken, saying I, Hannan, declare unto thee that thy seed shall be even as the sands of the desert for multitude.'

Then Ibsen turned himself round and bowed low, three times did he bow low down to the green, purple, and golden plumes of the Midnight Sun, saying as he bowed, 'Farewell, great coloured candle, companion to the northern darkness, for I go now on many far and toilsome journeys to achieve that which was, and is not, but shall be in the days to come.'

He bent down and tested the straps of his skis, tightened the belt round his middle, pulled down his fur cap over his eyes and ears, while a terrible look of determination came over his face. He plunged his alpenstock into the ice and gave himself a fierce push forward. Away he went down the slippery slope of the

* Published in *The American Spectator* (New York), July 1933.

mountain peak. Quicker and quicker he went, one thousand seven hundred and sixty yards to the mile, and three hundred and sixty-five and a quarter miles to the hour. Over crevasses, cliffs, and mighty fiords, white with the foam of the waves of the incoming tide, over one and over all with a gliding spring, such as A E, the Irish poet, when he dreams is said to give when he skips from star to star. To the edge of the land he came, and swept over the nose of Norway with a mighty bound which landed him with a gentle bump, right in the middle of the heart of Midlothian. He tramped over the bracken and the fern; wandered through the heather and the gorse, till he came to the borders of a lovely lake. He saw thousands of butterflies changing into women fairies, and back again into butterflies; and thousands of bees changing into fairymen, and back again into bees. Suddenly he felt sharp pangs of pain, and, sinking down on the bonnie, bonnie bank of Loch Lomond, he begat Barrie. He gave a look at the kid, and was silent. Suddenly the little fellow began to sing 'The Blue Bonnets are over the Border', and Ibsen hastily wrapped him up in tartan ribbon, put a lump of candy in his little fist, lifted him up, planked him in the corner of a kail-yard, and fled away down the lanes and the roads till he was down the hills and up the dales, till he was well over the border. He goose-stepped into a city of fiery furnaces and flame, and in the middle of the noise from hammers falling on red-hot steel, and the whirr of revolving bobbins, he felt the pains of labour coming on him again, so sinking down, he begat Hankin. Ibsen looked at the kid for a moment and murmured, 'It's a little better than the last, anyhow, but not good enough to persuade me to waste any time in nursing.' Then he visited a store and bought a natty lounge suit, a dress suit with tails, for he wanted to be fully prepared if special pains should come upon him. Carrying them in a box on his back, he walked and tramped and trudged for miles and miles, till he staggered at last into London. Feeling very hungry, he hurried into a corner shop and had a good meal. Then he went into the wash-and-brush-up department where he put on his dress suit with tails. Then he returned to his place, had a glass of port, and, while smoking a cigarette, without a pang of pain, he begat Pinero on his right hand, and Miles Malleson on his left hand. He went out, engaged a nurse, hired a pram, bought a little Eton suit for Pinero, a little plus-four suit for Malleson, packed the kids in the pram, and sent them off to join the Sunday morning parade in Hyde Park.

Strolling off in the opposite direction, he looked into the shop windows, and suddenly found himself in a huge building, crowded with excited men, some speaking, some sitting down, and many lying down asleep. He noticed that each speaker as he began and as he ended his speech, made over his breast the sign of the cross of St George. He saw, too, that when all had spoken, and the last man ended his speech, the first speaker began all over again. He asked an attendant boy scout if the talk ever ended, and the boy scout answered, 'Never.' Ibsen then asked what it all meant, and the boy scout answered that it meant nothing, but was simply a never-ending hymn to intellectual beauty. After many days, Ibsen crept out of the place on his hands and knees, murmuring that there was no chance of a fertilising air there, rising to his feet and running when he reached the gates, just as Big Ben by mistake boomed out the angelus.

Speeding down Whitehall, such terrible spasms came into his belly as made him throw himself flat on the ground and yell for the police. Policemen rushed over and blew their whistles for more policemen, who came running, and they all rubbed Ibsen up and rubbed him down, telephoned for an ambulance, flung him in when it came, and hustled him off to hospital, where he was put to bed and surrounded by many doctors, some saying it was a wish-fulfilment dream, some that it was syncopated bloodpressure, and one or two that it was pure imagination. The pain got worse, and they gave him chloroform. Then Ibsen heaved a mighty heave and begat Shaw, which, when the doctors saw, they made off, saying that if they had known what was coming, they wouldn't have lifted a finger to help. The kid refused to be nursed, saying that he was bloody well able to take care of himself, and asked for pen, ink, and paper to jot down a few remarks about past, present, and future tenses.

Lawyers in crowds came and whispered to Ibsen that if he took their advice, he'd slip off the first chance he got, for his latest creation'd get him into serious trouble before long. So Ibsen, frightened, slipped on his clothes, gathered his belongings together, and slunk away while the little Shaw was writing a long letter to Man and a postscript for God.

As Ibsen was hurrying along, a cardinal who had heard of him, stopped him and blessed him; lighted a holy candle before him, and rang a holy bell behind him, blessed him again, saying, 'Increase and multiply and replenish the earth with dramatists, Ibsen, that the words of Hannan, the prophet, may be fulfilled'. The blessing bucked Ibsen up tremendous, and he hurried into Italy, where he begat Pirandello; hastened out of Italy into Germany, where in the evening he begat George Kaiser, and during the fourth hour of the day after, he begat Toller.

Without a minute's rest or a second's hesitation, Ibsen then ran like hell down to the nearest seaport, journeying up and journeying down the quays till he found a trim, little schooner just hauling up its anchor with a heave and a heave yo ho yo, before it slipped out and away for the shore of America. So hitching up his trousers, he gave a great leap and went flying over the gunwale, with a heave ho and a heave ho yo, and to keep himself fit, he raced round and round the poop, turning, when he felt giddy, racing the reverse way round the prow. He jumped over the taffrail, and back, and over and back again. The sailors cheered as they stood up to the winds and up to the waves, and reefed and furled and set the sails of the trim, little schooner which ploughed on and on till at last on a windy winter's day, she crept into the harbour of New York. Without waiting for the gangway to be put down, Ibsen jumped on to the landing stage, and ran all the way to the woods of Pennsylvania, where, under a lofty elm tree, in roaring spasms of pain, he gave birth to Eugene O'Neill.

Ibsen wiped the sweat from his brow, and looked down on the lusty kid who cried with a loud cry; and Ibsen, looking at the kid again, murmured to himself, saying, 'I've done enough, be dammit, I've done enough to last me for the rest of me life.'

He went back to New York, entered a store and bought a second-hand frock coat and tall silk hat, took passage on board a great liner that brought him back to his native land. As he came down the gangway, a long thin man, covered with a long black cloak, and wearing a wide-brimmed black hat, came over to him, chucked him under the chin, slapped him on the back and said, 'Well done, well done, old sport; thou hast done all that the prophet, Hannan, an aitch an ay an en another en another ay an another en, 'annan, commanded thee to do. Henceforth all majesty, might, dominion, and power be Ibsen's, forever and forever more, amen.'

NOT WAITING FOR GODOT (1956)*

IF your magazine [*Encore*] be seen and *read* by five hundred students, then you have a very important audience, for I hope none of them is a grey-beard. What would my old raucous voice be doing among your young, shrill, eager ones? It is you who have, or ought to have, the say in the world now. My world is gone, gone in the winds of yesterday, and I don't intend to run back after it, like a man running after his hat. You will have to write for yourselves — a Magazine of the Students, by the Students, for the Students.

Beckett? I have nothing to do with Beckett. He isn't in me; nor am I in him. I am not waiting for Godot to bring me life; I am out after life myself, even at the age I've reached. What have any of you to do with Godot? There is more life than Godot can give in the life of the least of us. That Beckett is a clever writer, and that he has written a rotting and remarkable play, there is no doubt; but his philosophy isn't my philosophy, for within him there is no hazard of hope; no desire for it; nothing in it but a lust for despair, and a crying of woe, not in a wilderness, but in a garden.

The earth isn't either a grave-yard or a roaring camp — save in a war, when it is both; but today war is a *non est*, for with the new nuclear explosive power, all are within range of death; the rich and the poor, the ones who go out to fight, the ones who remain at home; the Catholic pope and the Catholic peasant share its shivers, and so aren't ready to nod the head in favour of strife. And there is life and energy even in decay (not Beckett's, but nature's), for dead leaves turn to loam, and dry bones to phosphates.

* Published in *Encore: A quarterly review for students of the theatre*, Easter 1956.

What witnesses does this Beckett call? A dowdy and a doleful few: Camus, Kafka, Orwell, Graham Greene, Huxley, with T. S. Eliot a wan follower, cross on breast and hands clenched in an obscure prayer. And what witness have we? A cloud of them: Copernicus, Newton, Beethoven, Angelo, Shelley, Whitman, Balzac, Faraday, Titian, and, yes, by God, and Shakespeare, too, with ten thousand others close up to the greatest!

As for the English theatre, it is but a ghostly memory, with the Irish theatre a runner-up. There is, of course, Joan Littlewood's Theatre Workshop in East London — a cinderella without a fairy godot-mother; a theatre that should get what is given to the Old Vic, for it is as adventurous as the other is timid and tired and lazy. There's the People's Theatre in Newcastle, a venture that is spreading into what may become a sanctuary for the drama, the film, and chamber quartet. A nest of amateurs who have kept the rose of Lancaster, rose of York, and Tudor rose in a state worthy of wearing: colour and scent are in them still. But what are these among so many? The rest is silence; or a mutter and a *moue*, hurting a silence that would be a finer honour. Today, bar the musicals, *Waiting for Godot* and *The Wild Duck*, there isn't a play worth a penny on the London stage; and these are by an Irishman and a Norwegian. No, sir, English drama is the bird in the golden cage, and it is safe in the vaults of the Bank of England.

MR WESKER'S MARCH PAST (1963)*

In the May–June issue of the little drama magazine, *Encore*, Mr Arnold Wesker gave an interview[1] outlining the aims, claims, and games of Centre 42, an organisation for the promotion of the theatre among the heathen working-classes. The movement was begun by a small number of people of the theatre, including a number of playwrights like Alun Owen, Shelagh Delaney, and, of course, Mr Wesker himself. Centre 42 has a startling list of patrons, and their well-known names sound like a roll of drums. Names are of little use, unless each comes bearing a thousand pounds on its back. The list of big names attached to Centre 42 is very imposing, but once uttered and silence comes again, they don't do a damn thing. If this drum-roll of names could march in front of the organisers, hammering away at the drum-bellies, they might give some exhilaration, but silence is theirs, and not a stick stirs. Even could they keep up the drum-beats, it wouldn't be any good, bar sounding a little picturesque for a while; but their drumming would soon become tiresome, and soon sound ridiculous. The drum-roll, however loud, could give no life. The lullaby in the 'Last Post' can't soothe into a deeper sleep any dead warrior; neither can any reveille arouse into life again

* The coda to this article was dated Nov. 1963, but the article was obviously begun in 1962. This is its first publication.

1 'Centre 42: An Interview with Arnold Wesker' in *Encore : the Voice of Vital Theatre*, No. 37, May–June 1962, pp. 39–44. The aims and intentions of Centre 42 have grown and expanded since its inception in 1961, and this evolution may be traced in the Annual Report of Centre 42 for 1961–2, in Wesker's article 'The Secret Reins', in *Encounter*, Mar. 1962, and in his pamphlet *The Allio Brief* (1964), published by Centre 42 Ltd. These accounts make it clear that Mr Wesker's ideas are closer to O'Casey's than one would gather from 'Mr Wesker's March Past.'

any soldier dead before it sounded. So no organisation can spring to life following a drum-roll of names, however imposing they may be. It must have the seeds of life within itself. Given life, and the seeds strike root, a lot, maybe all, depends on him, on her, or on those who tend it, and coax it into a strong, vigorous, and pliant plant, giving both flower and fruit. Such was the Moscow Art Theatre and the Abbey Theatre of Dublin; but, then, the one had Stanislavsky and Chekhov, and the other had William Butler Yeats and Lady Gregory. Has Centre 42 any such remarkable souls to guide and goad the movement upwards and onwards? Oh, no, John, no, John, no, John, no!

They had no star to guide them; or, at least, the few they had weren't of such a magnitude to light a way, ahead, stronger than the ineffectual fire from a glow-worm. So they set up a watch-tower; rather did they put one together, for when I last heard of Centre 42, they hadn't decided where to set it down — in London, in one of the large provincial towns, or in a completely new town, where the plaster was still wet on the walls, and only the first puffs of smoke were rising up out of the chimneys. Wherever they set it down, however, that place was to be the Centre. Mr Wesker added that they hoped to form branches all over the country. How many? Oh, say twelve. (A sacred number — twelve months of the year, twelve signs of the Zodiac, twelve apostles; I wonder will these proposed twelve Centreens form another of the sacred numbers established already?) Each centre will, it is hoped, form a pool where the best of artists will be gathered, ready to hurry off, on hearing an artistic SOS call for help to run a show in that particular district. Since the artists cannot be expected to lodge in the centre, but must live outside of it, I suppose, as in the case of fire somewhere in Torquay district, a siren will sound a long continuing wail, summoning the absent ones to assemble and hear where they have to go, and what they have to do.

All very fine and large, but how are the finest artists in the district to live while they wait for a call? Are they to get a re-taining fee; and, if so, how will they spend the lagging days that pass by while they wait for a call to get cracking? Mr Wesker in the interview seemed to be anchored to a broadline, saying that the various details would be decided according to circumstances, and the things learned by experiences as the work went ahead. Well, a helluva lot of details require a helluva lot of experiences, and failure will do far more harm than good. The calls will hardly come in quick succession, so what will Mr Wesker's Retainers do during the long vacations between the calls? Will they spend the time, arise and go to where the good Christian, Rank, has changed a cinema from a den of trivialities into a temple of scholastic, mathematical study and meditation? Bingo!

Of course, the scheme is laughingly impossible; it would have been so even in the early or late days of Queen Victoria, when there was nothing for the artist but the theatre and the music hall. Now we have the artists forever staring in at the windows or knocking at the doors of film studios, or, more numerous still, the many television studios scattered over the country, places where the artists come to dig for diamonds. The theatre now has sunken into a shameful and shameless *pied à terre*, a bridge-head, a jumping-off ground into television or into the slavering maw of a film studio. The playwrights are, of course, usually there before the artists. We are all on the runways, and Mr Wesker's rosy plan can't stop it any more than a twig can stop the rush of a swollen river. To me, at its best, it seemed to be a conceited idea to think that this really insignificant group carried the English theatre on its back, like a pedlar with his pack, who imagined he carried silks from Asia, whereas the pack held cheap cottons and cheaper jewellery.

One can't make a desert blossom like a rose with a quart-size wateringcan; or fix the attention of a community by bursting into it, then bursting out again. Nor is it the way by which a civilised and educated community is evolved out of life; nor yet the way a coming generation continues to be as civilised and educated, or more so, than the older one passing out of life.

Care has to be taken as to what is offered to the unaccustomed for the first time. It should be remembered that today the mass of the people, as far as the arts in general are concerned, are not only unaware of them, but very suspicious of them, imagining that if they try to mix with artistic things, they will be shamed by their ignorance of them, and so made to look ridiculous before those who know a little more about these odd things. We are but children when we are faced with the strange and whirling intricacies of the arts. Most of us over thirty years of age are ignorant of them, and so are afraid of them too. For myself, I was introduced to what is known as Classical music by our three children. Once on a sunny evening, I entered a lounge where the three of them were listening to a broadcast, and I was startled by a sudden, vehement, and simultaneous hiss of Hush! I sank down on a seat, and waited, holding my breath for the thing to finish. When the end of the first part came, I was asked if I wanted to listen? Giving a hesitating ye . . . es, I was told to keep quiet and to just listen. I stayed quiet, but I didn't listen; I just watched the three others, two leaning back, apparently rapt up in the stream of music, the third leaning forward, hands on knees, his head slightly turned to one side as if he turned a finer ear forward so as to catch the faintest note or volley of notes flooding from the symphony. So I learned to keep still, to listen, a great step forward. Since then I have listened to, and enjoyed, many a symphony, many a quartet, many a concerto too. I suggest that these evangelists, before they take off their coats, should listen to the Schools Programmes given over the B.B.C., by which they could learn a little about how to introduce arts and literature to those who have little interest in any of them before they start out to teach. The schools, the schools, the schools! After the home where the green blade is fed and warmed in the arms of an earthly mother, after meeting its first touch of literature from the mother's stories, its first sense of music and song from the nursery rhymes, after learning civilised habits, the child, yet a seedling, goes to school, the bedding ground that gives more vigorous growth, all tending to introduce the young life into a fuller plenitude of enjoyment and understanding. The schools, the schools! In 1963, over a thousand concerts were given by first-class orchestras or first-class chamber ensembles in the English schools — more than Centre 42 could do in a long, lingering lifetime. I myself listened to one given in the Festival

Hall to over a thousand young school-people from schools all over greater London. It was a delightful experience, and I wish I could have been among the young and enthusiastic people. Could Mr Wesker ever hope to do for drama anything better, anything equal to this concert? Oh, no, John, no, John, no!

Another programme was the musical composition of what would be called, I suppose, a 'pop piece'. It was entitled 'The Pied Piper', and the broadcast gave the children (including one 83 years old) a cheery and profitable half-hour. First we heard the drums giving the rhythm, then the melody first from two guitars, tenor and bass, then a tambourine was added, the rhythm and melody being played right through; next, the piccolos joined in, and lastly trumpets were added, and 'The Pied Piper' was played by the full band. Finally, what they called 'an echo' was given as a background, and this distilled an odd and charming tone to the music of the song, all being guided, modelled, and deployed, by the experienced mind and cunning hand of the recording engineer.

The music isn't all pop, of course; today I listened to an interesting and simple talk on Bach's 'Christmas Oratorio' and the other day a talk about Bach's younger years; of how Buxtehude offered him his own job as organist and the fine house which went with it, if only he consented to take the daughter of Buxtehude to wife as well.

There are other talks beside those on music. I have heard talks on How Things Began, Brain and Eye, on things familiar to us — water, its cycle, why some things float and others sink; on the uses of air; on the Southern Apes, now surviving only as fossils; how these apes walked upright, their heads farther back on their bodies, like man's; that they were able to think, and use their hands, having abandoned the trees; that they were hunters, could ambush animals for food, and make offensive and defensive weapons from the bigger bones of the animals they killed. It is believed that it was from these apes, or some offspring of the species, that the trumpets of Nature sounded forth the appearance of man. These were talks for juniors. I haven't enough knowledge of things yet to find myself at ease among the enthusiastic intellectuals of the sixth form; but nevertheless, find the simpler talks intensely interesting. Interesting: they are made to be interesting by lively and clever writers; and in any effort to make the genera of the working people like the theatre, it must be made interesting to them, made vivid, bright, gay, in one way or another; otherwise, they will hoot every effort off as dull and drab efforts deserve to be. They get the bird. We should remember that those had little chance to do anything or learn anything but to live as best or as worst as they could. Even today the schools have broken doors and cracked windows, more like tabernacles of darkness than of light; but they are far better than they were in their way of talking and their way of walking. We of an earlier time know little more than a use of mind and hand to give a good chance to the few to squat down their arses on cushions of gold and cushions of silver. The giant of the Industrial Revolution gave the few wealth, and to the masses, they gave a calibanic civilisation. We have come out of this into the light, but the effects of the past cling round a lot of us still. If we be ignorant of the arts, then the bosses are more ignorant still. Now, willy nilly, they are forced to call in the scientist, the designer, and the craftsman to guide and help them, for man is demanding that everything around him, everything he handles must be better and brighter than it was in the past. Thus revolution towards better taste began years and years before Mr Wesker and his bonny bunch of roses-O set out to hunt the mass of city workers into the corralled concept of the arts and drama sprouting out from the heads of Mr Wesker and his pennon-bearing troops. I remember years and years ago, a current canting way of enlivening or cheering up another, was to prod a finger into one's ribs, uttering an ejaculation of 'Pip Pip!' This is used by the great Shaw in his play *Major Barbara*. Centre 42's effort was no more than a timid finger-prod in the ribs of the masses, escorted by a feeble imitation of Shaw's enthusiastic 'Pip Pip' to Lady Britomart.

We know that for the first five years, at least, the child spends all his or her time at home; afterwards, from five to fourteen, at least, the child, developing into youth, spends far more time in the school than she or he does in a theatre; so that if there be no familiar contact with things theatrical during these years, then the young person will enter the world utterly ignorant of the theatre, and wholly indifferent to the drama. At home, the child does come into contact with the drama when it learns a nursery rhyme for the first time. It comes into contact with the theatre in the story of 'The House that Jack Built' and all that happened around it. In the ballad of 'Who Killed Cock Robin' the child can shake a fist at the savage sparrow, can admire the bull, strong enough to toll the bell, listen to the solemn rook who read the burial service from his little book, and sorrow with the dove who became the chief mourner. What further contacts the child may have at school will depend on the kind of school she or he goes to, and the teacher who controls it. Education is realising now how important the theatre is to the mind of the child, with its music and song, dancing, architecture in the building of sets, painting in the colouring of scene and costume, timing, use and balance of the body, development of voice in the right and melodious use of words; indeed each school is itself a centre 1, of far more possibilities for creating audiences than a dozen Centre 42s, working overtime, and taking no rest on Sundays.

Centre 42 seems to have held one Festival — in Wellingborough; a success, remarked Mr Wesker's interviewer; but was it? We heard few details, bar the news that the audiences which came to the show were of the middle-class and intellectuals, with the workers contemplating Bingo in other moods and postures bold. Of this show, Mr Wesker is reported as saying: 'When it was over there was a fair amount of chaos and I remember deciding that we should not stage any more festivals until the Centre was firmly established. But then invitations came in from six other Trades Councils all wanting similar festivals and we were on our way.'

On the way to Mandalay or on the golden road to Samarkand? A costly caravan, for a full-page advertisement in *Encore* tells that Centre 42 is asking for £25,000 to pay for the running of these six festivals. The call of the curlew is less plaintive than the cry for this big sum of money. I remember once that Totnes asked the people for a mile of pennies to help a cause, and a line of pennies began to stretch along Fore Street, High Street, as well as a side avenue right down to the fringe of the town. But pounds aren't strewn about streets like leaves from Vallombrosa's vale. The rich don't scatter their wealth except when they wish to evade tax, or to give their modest names renown and honour. Centre 42 won't hear a loud jingle from these boys. Mr Wesker has been disappointed by the poor response Centre 42 got from the Left. They, the socialists, the students, wouldn't accept the concept Centre 42 asked them to believe and accept: to be not faithless, but believing.[1] Small wonder, this, for those who organise and lead the venture can hardly be called inspiring, and the creations they are to carry with them are dull and lifeless as clay-made marbles jumbled together in a schoolboy's pocket. The one work of worthiness mentioned by Wesker was the play, *Serjeant Musgrave's Dance*, a play of eloquence and a good deal of power, a work that is of higher dramatic value than all the others heaped together.[2]

Of course, Mr Wesker believes in himself; he is armed with sincerity, and he has made genuine sacrifices for what he is trying to do: but sincerity is disregarded at times, self-sacrifice is often made in vain. It looks as if this has already happened, for activities have ended, and, it is said, that where Centre 42's name was brass-plated on the door of the name's local habitation has been shuttered up, and all the glory departed.

But there was method in the madness, though even the method had madness in itself. The proper prop and pillar of the efforts made are described by Mr Wesker himself at the ending of the interview. He says he was worried for two years that the

---

[1] In the interview Wesker says: 'The other and fairly upsetting thing is that the response of the Left in this country to the idea of Centre 42 has been so poor. Socialists in this country are so battered and bruised that they don't believe in themselves let alone anybody else. . . . I've found out that there is no greater sceptic than the left-wing intellectual and this is very depressing.'

[2] Apart from John Arden's play, the other plays mentioned were *A Taste of Honey*, *The Lily-white Boys*, and Wesker's own *Chicken Soup with Barley* trilogy.

drama movement he and his comrades had joined would vanish, a worry he set forth in 'articles in *Encore* and in a letter to *The New Statesman*'. He adds, 'I was conscious that if the new writers didn't watch out we would all be handled simply as a fashion and bundled out of the way as soon as the new fashion arrived. I see Centre 42 as a means of consolidating what we have gained. An exciting new movement is under way in all the arts and I don't want to see it (as so often happens) divided and annihilated.'

Looks like the core of the cause isn't sound, so watch out, new playwrights, for Time is a whoreson trickster! Looks like Centre 42 isn't out, after all, to bring drama as such; only those whose plays are favoured of themselves. A cause ceases to be one when it concerns, directly or indirectly, the personal works of those who are organising it. Although Mr Wesker, when he suggests plays that might be done, refers to his own in an apologetic and negative way, it is conceivable that if the venture had been a permanent success, his own plays, willy nilly, would have shone forth in the list of works done. So it seems to me to be rather a tall order to appeal (publicly) for £25,000 in order to push a fashion or a clique a few feet further into the future. And what a futile hope! Not all the gold in the banks of the world has the power to make a work of literature or art live a day longer than time allows; and no power can hold it up on its feet but the living power within itself. The Elizabethan outburst in literature was a fashion; the Restoration period was a fashion. Ibsenism became a fashion; hundreds of plays written in each of these active times perished, and only the few of the greater ones lived on to be an honour and a pride to all men. Mr Wesker and his comrades will save themselves worry if they realise that plays, just like everything else, are subject to the law of the survival of the fittest, receiving no favour from indifferent Time, just like bird and just like beetle.

Tempo dramateria Damnatus.

Oh Miserere mea!

CODA (November 1963)

It has been recently reported that a generous donor has presented Mr Wesker with the remaining fifteen years lease of a huge building in London, free of all rent, and a good-will wish that he should go ahead, and do what he can with it. Mr Wesker has welcomed the gift with a bang of cymbals, though fifteen years seems all too short a lease for the dream in his mind to come true. His vision is of a theatre holding a good-sized audience and a smaller one for experimental drama; a hall for music and one for lectures; a conference room, offices, a restaurant, maybe; all to form a striking and imposing Headquarters for Centre 42. What Mr Wesker needs now is a donor or donors to give him six hundred pounds to enable him to get cracking.

If he can transmute this vision into fact, he will have given to the London theatre something fresh, exciting, and challenging. I sincerely hope he may. I should advise him to give himself to this, and forget all about bringing culture to 'the masses'. This is a national problem, and hinges itself on numerous other problems — of many more schools, crowds more teachers, many more hospitals with a tremendous increase in the nursing sisterhood; and homes for the masses so that every mother may be able to cherish and lead her children in freedom and light.

THE BALD PRIMAQUEERA (1964)*

Oh, don't tarnish the memory of the marvellous play we've just seen. Let not your heart be troubled, nothing ridiculous can linger longer so. Let us steep and seep our souls in the gospel, the last gospel according to Artaud.

> *Artaud! Artaud!*
> *Pounding a play to a wordless thesis,*
> *Beating up life into bloody pieces,*
> *An' the birds of Swan Lake to a gaggle of geeses.*
> *Artaud!*
> *Cut down the ivy, hack down the holly,*
> *Life is sure gruesome, death is most jolly,*
> *Keep the axe poised over Pineapple Polly.*
> *Artaud!*
> *Rape, murder, and suicide for brave British writers,*
> *And a kicking to hell for the song-singing blighters.*
> *Artaud! Artaud!*
> *For man is a louse and woman's a folly,*
> *An' the way to the grave's the way that is jolly,*
> *So hack down the ivy and burn up the holly,*
> *Into black urns with each Mick and his Molly,*
> *An' keep the axe poised over Pineapple Polly.*
> *Artaud!*

There are mild Mabels among the axe men, those of calmer and more civilized propulsions, who rarely go farther than marauding invasions into bedroom curiosities, and spectroscope probing into the mysteries of the toilet, the lavatory, or the water closet, according to the more or less refinement of the several writers of the several plays.

* This essay on the Theatre of Cruelty, completed on Aug. 21, 1964, was the last article written by the playwright.

There was a play[1] done on B.B.C. Television in which a man and woman, visiting a couple, met in the hall, came up together and exchanged remarks when they had settled down on chairs, one making himself known to the lady, explaining that he lived in a certain road, to be surprised by the lady saying that she lived there too, adding that it was 'a remarkable coincidence' followed by the coincidence of living in the same house, the same floor of the house, the same flat on the same floor, the same bedroom in the same flat, the same bed in the same room. All just coincidence, variously called 'Marvellous, Amazing, Extraordinary, Astonishing, and Tremendous'. Seeing that though they came so close together in so many ways, even to him, presumably, mounting her while they were in bed together, yet could never become acquainted, they were persons of very poor powers of observation. Then in the midst of the coincidences came the climax — a maidservant slipped forward to tell the audience that she had bought a chamber-pot, and in the production of this play, as a suitable coat of arms for it, a chamber-pot was planted in the stage centre, plumb and ferocious, in plain view of the audience, their rosy faces trying to keep calm, and look ahead as if they had seen nothing. It was the consecration of the house.

Apart from being old-fashioned, the chamber-pot is almost non-existent now. It used to be the third piece in a set of three for a bedroom. The ewer, the basin, and the pot, in the upper-class and middle-class homes in the day of my youth, but times and new dispositions displaced them from favour, and now it would be hard to spot them, even in an old-fashioned junk shop. Apart from this, these peering, leering playwrights have no natural or supernatural licence to jeer at these essential bodily practices. None of them is the mental and physical outcome of an immaculate conception. Each has a mortal button on his belly.

These are the pacifist Freudians of the theatre who see sex in a raincloud, the way a spoon is used, and the way one holds a knife and fork. These, too, are half-brothers with the dare-devil

---

[1] *The Bald Prima Donna* by Eugène Ionesco; entitled *The Bald Soprano* in the U.S. translation.

Horrorhawks of the theatre of murder, rape, and cruelty and all are arm in arm with the Theatre of the Absurd. As Minerva is said to have sprung from the head of Jupiter, so these playwrights seem to claim they have jumped from the head of Freud, a shocking mishap to happen to anyone. They dibble and dabble in their plays with the Freudian faculties, turning them into neurotic fixatives and erotic fribbles and frabbles of their own. There must be some Freudian reason for their frequent leering, sneering among the lower depths of the human body. To them a body is a vile body, and it is nothing more. The Christian Church nourished and nursed this idea, aiming at getting out of the body to be present with the Lord. The idea didn't work and it doesn't work now — except among a lot of playwrights, busy making the mind worse than the body. The comic thing is that their plays declare that they know little or nothing about either. Psychology and psycho-analysis are sciences, life studies, and cannot be acquired by just reading a book at bedtime. Freud spent his life studying the human mind, yet, at the end, admitted he had learned little about it.

Yet a lot of these boyos sit in the minds of their characters like a spider in a web's centre, noting every vibration and agitation in their characters, as if, like the spider, they themselves had woven the mysterious and multi-multiple web of the human brain. Freud knew the first thing about it, but these know the first and last about it. Each is in his own swollen ego, the Alpha and Omega in the know-how of the whole psychological nature of man, the peak of mammals, yet scientists are now studying the psychology of captive animals, in relation to their food and habits, and they aren't finding it as easy as kiss hands.

Do they know much more about the body which they so often abuse by sneer and snarl in their plays? It is odd that the body from the waist down should be used as a gibe in the plays of so many present-day playwrights. It would seem that they resent being endowed with a belly. They seem to regard it as an unnatural and unwarranted degradation. They don't relish the idea of having to carry a basement department with them, they refuse to admit that the lower storey is just as wonderful as the upper one, that there can be no *apartheid* here, for the upper, lower, and middle body, brain, and mind, are one unified whole.

It is the middle parts of fortune which hold the golden issues of life. All our wealth of great minds through the ages, in art, science, literature, music, and great and small buildings, all have to make their first passage to life through the belly, and the clash together of complementary bellies has given the world a bewildering mass of wonderful animation in hand and head, with many more to come, all giving problems that keep hands and heads busy trying to keep things steady, shipshape, and cheerful.

It was Artaud — the latest trumpeter of the Primaqueeri — or one of his brethren, who gave us a picture of a beautiful girl, naked, with a malignant tarantula spider between her lovely thighs. An ugly guardian for the seat of life, a vision that could only be seen by a savage Primaqueera — one who is thinking he is looking through a lens which reflects back into the mind of the onlooker, showing that this tarantula spider is squatting, not between the lovely thighs of a woman, but in the searcher's skull, weaving its tendrils in and out of the web of his brain. It is an opposite vision seen by Peter Keegan [in Shaw's *John Bull's Other Island*], but is, too, the vision of a madman. All the greatness of man in wealth of science, art, literature, human healing, the fire of vision, the urge of effort, have all come in a little life from between the thighs of a woman. Such writers blaspheme against humanity, for even the tarantula spider has its place in nature, and in its own haunts is harmless to man.

These fellows rarely mention animals, and when they do they make them as horrible as they make men and women. The tarantula has been shown by Artaud ensconced secure, ready to pounce and poison, between the soft thighs of a young woman. None of these Primaqueera playwrights seem to like either beast or blossom. When they do mention any, they seem to give them a sinister or savage symbolism. A travesty on the old and charming tale of *Androcles and the Lion* told us that when the lion and his master had gone through their romance in the arena of Rome, and they were returning home at night in the dark, with the busy streets empty and still, the lion turned on Androcles, rent him to pieces, and ate the poor bugger up, leaving not a wrack behind. Another story tells us of a fellow absorbing the nature of a dog; not a gay dog, but one apparently on the way to madness. Now a mad one is no more a true dog than a poor demented person is a true human being. Soon there will be no necessity for a da to buy his daughter a bow-wow, bow-wow, for with little effort, apparently, he can become one, and a fierce one, too. Ionesco, the playwright, tries to show us men and women turning into rhinoceroses, with but one man left opposing the Muttamorphosis. Funny, this, for while there is no fear of the rhinoceros exterminating man, man has to engage in a feverish fight to keep a few of these strange and remarkable animals alive. There is no fear of us turning into rhinoceroses, but there is a possible chance, if these playwrights get their way, of us all turning into Ionescos, a more terrible fate still.

Hitchcock is the latest champion in the fray, but he, in a film, gives the venom and the violence to the birds. Our feathered friends become our spear-beaked enemies, according to the talk I've heard around me. The birds (very different from those imagined by Aristophanes) set themselves to overthrow the dominance of the human family; to pierce and rend them as the frenzied women of Thebes tore their king, Pentheus, to pieces for ignoring and mocking the power and divinity of the god Bacchus. Euripides was bad enough, but he rent but one man, and him for blasphemy against a god. The present literary group, in their work in drama, novel, poem, and film, seem to revel in the sending of all men, mentally and physically, to act like Shakespeare's wanton boys with flies. They get sport out of it all. They want to be the *avant-garde* gods. They are a kinda requiem get-together group, and there dare not be any sing-along Saturday in their poem or play.

The most recent addition to the dark stars that have swum into the sky of English dramatic literature is the play *Afore Night Come*.[1]

[1] *Afore Night Come* by David Rudkin, produced by the Royal Shakespeare Company at the New Arts in June 1962 and revived at the Aldwych in June 1964.

The scene is a pear orchard on the outskirts of the Black Country. A group of casual labourers gather the fruit under the direction of a bluff, harassed foreman deficient in power of command. Into their midst wanders an outsider — a scrofulous, defeated, defiant, cringing, elderly Irishman, Roche, a lazy visionary who offends and frightens the rest. They kill him, decapitate him, bury him, and go their ways in the dusk.

As among the denizens of these dark stars, this latest one, too, has a psychopath and a homo. The other *personae gratae* are ignorant and stupid country labourers. They are busy gathering a pear harvest, and they are backed by three pear-trees placed so as to be a symbol (it is said) of the Crucifixion, and the murder of the Irish tramp is said to be encased in or enthroned on a Ritual.

We read that after the scrounger had been polished off, the rhapsodic labourers beheaded him with a hayfork. A playful little group, certes! Clever, too, to be able to behead any mother's son with a hayfork. What is a hayfork doing at the gathering of fruit anyway? Fruit is gathered from the trees with the prongs on a hand, not by those on a hayfork. It is said that the play is partly naturalistic, partly documentary. I have watched the gathering of plum and cherry, but never saw a hayfork used in the work. The trees were lofty, fifteen to twenty-five feet high and they were clustered with fruit. Indeed, the men and I were already treading on fallen plums, and among these sappy ruins lay several blackbirds and some smaller birds I couldn't identify. Against two of the trees were odd-looking ladders, splaying out at the base, narrowing as they mounted, till they tapered almost to a point at the top, so that they could easily be thrust through the higher branches, and placed so that the picker would have the widest possible radius for the reach of his arms, and gather all the fruit within touch of them. It was a job of skill, needing quick and flexible hands and delicate fingers, so that the fruit in its plucking and its deposit in the basket might never be bruised. No clumsy, stupid worker could do it, for it required an intelligence far above that embodied in the nature of the primitive men who selected one to be a god for a season and then slew him so that the pieces of the body could be scattered over the fields in honour of the Corn God and so ensure a plenteous harvest for the coming year. Ritual of any kind isn't a haphazard thing! it always has a custom, a reason in the background — a ritual in the churches, on Remembrance Day, the ritual of Freemasonry, the ritual of the old music hall! but here we have neither rhyme nor reason for it. This 'sacrifice of a victim' seems to me to have nothing to do with any pagan rite described in *The Golden Bough*, but to have been the act of a group of psychopathic maniacs.

The strangest thing of all is the foolish and hateful way in which playwrights and critics regard the farmworkers as ignorant, stupid, and given to ferocity. It is an odd contemplation of the country worker, and could be very questionable if it were not ridiculous. Even in my early days, although the field-worker was often ignorant in the ways of formal education, he was never stupid, was highly intelligent as far as the farming knowledge of his time went and had a great deal of natural knowledge. They had none of the gaudy or gorgeous knowledge of the higher airs within them, but they were well versed in the knowledge of the good earth they husbanded, of the earth that gave us life, and provides the wherewithal to maintain it. They knew the odd ways of the sky, the clouds, the wind, and the rain, the ways of the Farmer's Boy, and all the ways of the things around them, the fields, the animals, wild and domestic, the trees, the silent turmoil that went on in hedge and pond, and all this made them one with the most remarkable mysteries of life. Under conditions which would be dreadful to the farmworker today, these harassed folk reared up sturdy children, thousands of them following the drum to widen Britain's empire, dotting foreign fields with their dead from Crécy to Tel el Kebîr. To say that these were stupid and brutal, if said seriously, is a bare and malignant lie. These fellows with their women have given us over the centuries a rich heritage of folk music, lore, and song, which could never have been composed by the brutal, ignorant, and the stupid.

Yet today, when the farmworker is more alert, well up in general education, firmly organized in a sturdy union, is something of a mechanic dealing with complicated machines, in this play they are presented as a group of savage and senseless thugs. Even in Chaucer's day there were good reasons for the peasants' anger, defiance, and rough usage of a few nobles during their great revolt against intolerable conditions and the deprivations made on their scant possessions by landlord and parson whenever the head of a family died! but even here there was no ritualistic nonsense when a pike speared a body or a billhook slashed at a head! Nor are there accounts of these goings-on by the rude 'mechanicals' during the time Spenser wrote his *The Shepheardes Calender* and Shakespeare set down the rough-and-ready manners of the country folk, ignorant but vivid beings whom he knew so well and loved so much. Nor can it be safely alleged that the persecution of what were called 'witches', mostly women, was ritualistic. It was the nobility and the learned of the land who used to condemn these poor beings to the stake. Yet on the possible happenings of this play a critic has said: 'The play is unbelievable, yet somehow, unbelievably, makes the unbelievable real. In the end it is inevitable that the menacing outsider must be killed by the group.' We need time to tease all this out. In such circumstances as fruit-gathering, no time would be wasted in killing an intruder, however menacing he might be. So they bury their victim under the pear-trees, the victim that died for the peace of the group. How did they dig this grave? They had no spade, and a hayfork could but scratch the grass. The group should have left him where he fell, lying on top of the world, should have gone home in the darkness, having called upon the robin redbreast and the wren.

Mr Harold Pinter is more of a gentleman; you could never see him going about with a hayfork. Yet all critics admit, nay, agree, that he is a sinister fellow as far as his work is concerned. Not only every sentence, but almost every word, is sinister in its menace; hidden, but none the less visible in emotional penetration. Rudkin works barehanded; Pinter wears gloves so that not even a finger-print is deposited in the writing. Rudkin roars like any sucking dove. Prim Pinter is genteel, he rarely shouts, but uses the voice like the sibilant purr of a Siamese cat, ready to change to the dangerous hiss of a snake at any minute. His quicker dialogue, as in that of the mother in *A Night Out*, is like the hammering of a woodpecker's beak against the trunk of a tree! His slower tense is like the tap tap tap of the stick of Tiresias. Pinter doesn't behead his *personae non gratae* with a hayfork! He pulls them to pieces in his pauses; the one kills with a shout, the other in a silence. His silence is like that of a cemetery, menacing and creepy, making each individual hair upon one's head stand up like quills upon the fretful perkypine. In these plays we know not the why or the wherefore. No one knows whence the persons come or whither they goeth. Hecuba doesn't know where she stands. Pinter and Rudkin keep their mouths shut. To any questions they answer not. No names, no packdrill.

They must be meant for NO plays. Neither Pinter nor Rudkin likes people. Indeed, Mr Rudkin declares with a flourish that he despises audiences. Perhaps he means only that he despises them as audiences but really loves them for themselves alone. He dislikes them only when they get in his way. They certainly are a nuisance to all playwrights when they don't come. Mr Pinter's play *The Birthday Party* is a tour de farce of the menace in the common word, the cliché, and the menace in the pause. It seems to frighten the critics. One of the radiant members of the Sunday School of radio critics referred to a pause as a 'bumbinating vacuum'. I imagine that the characters as well as the pauses are other kinds of bumbinating vacuums. These are the woman of the house, her husband, a chair attendant, and a lodger named Stanley. There is a young girl, too, and, later on, two visitors who turn out to be megatonic, bumbinating vacuums, who, towards the play's end, take away poor Stanley. The play opens with an overture on the theme of cornflakes and fried bread for breakfast! A brilliant line of chatter which is apparently meant to make a heart stand still. It is Stanley's birthday, so a boy's drum is bought and presented to him, apparently for his amusement, or to encourage his musical tastes, for he was once a pianist in some kinda show or pub. He fixes the drum round his neck, beats a simple stepping tap tap, and parades around the

table to the delight of the woman of the house — left — right
— left. He increases the beat quicker and quicker, he walks
faster, then beats a frantic roll on the toy drum, facing the
woman! His whole aspect changes; he looks terrible so that the
lady collapses away from him in abject terror. The dolldrum!
The dolldrum! The Congo is strongo, the Congo will how do
hoo doo voodo you! Coming events cast their shudders before,
the gods arrive in the shape of the two visitors, Goldberg, an
effusive Jew, and a surly brutish Irishman, members of the two
races which have given a lot of trouble to a too-complacent
world. They have no trouble here. Goldberg, when he hears it is
Stanley's birthday, calls for a party, the woman of the house says
she'll wear her party dress, and hopes she'll look well, Goldberg
replying that 'she'll look like a tulip'. In the end Stan is taken
away by the visitors for God knows what to God knows where.

As far as the mind can go, this is the one instance in the plays
of the *avant-garde* where a flower is mentioned. The tulip
suddenly flowers, but only in mockery, and is swiftly sheared
from the mind of any who noticed it. A flowering plant would
be an obnoxious intruder into any *avant-garde* play. If one was
brought in it would be a festering lily, for we are told 'Lilies
that fester smell far worse than weeds'. I wonder if any of the
avant-garde playwrights has a garden, and if he has, do flowers
grow in them, and if flowers grow there, does he notice them in
his goings out and his comings in? If he doesn't, then he is contemptuous of a large part of the loveliness around him, and so is
contemptuous of life, for plants are living things as he is a partly
living thing; they spring from seed as he does, and germinate in
the earth's womb as he does in the womb of a woman. They eat
and drink as he does, they are attacked by enemies under the
earth and above it, as man is by bacilli and virus, but in spite of
these distresses they express themselves in beauty of colour and
scent. They are useful, too, for man could not go on living on this
earth without them.

One play belonging to what we are told is 'Theatre of the
Absurd', *A Resounding Tinkle*,[1] mentions a garden, but no

---

[1] By N. F. Simpson.

herb or shrub grows there, but an elephant romps around in it. Small chance for a plant or shrub where an elephant is, for an elephant in a garden is as damaging as a bull in a china shop. In the mind's eye one might see a lovely woman in a garden, like Maud among the musk roses, or see the beautiful lady Handel saw walking in a garden shady, bathed with the evening air, with a glory of golden hair. Or a simple farmworker on seeing a daisy might say:

> *Wee, modest, crimson-tippèd flow'r,*
> *Thou's met me in an evil hour;*
> *For I maun crush amang the stoure*
> *Thy slender stem.*
> *To spare thee now is past my pow'r,*
> *Thou bonie gem.*

But not they. Tree, shrub, or herb grow nowhere near them. They may have glimpsed a tree as they raced past, but their eyes never seem to have rested on the graceful beech, the sturdy oak, the immemorial elm, or the tender ash. They live in a silent spring. Of course we know that this elephant was put into the garden as an item of assurance that this play belonged to the Theatre of the Absurd. For the life of me I can't find anything humanly absurd in any of them. These playwrights seem to be vying with each other as to which can be more absurd than the other. A kinda 'what you can do well, I can do better' slogan. Shouldn't be surprised if one day we had a hippopotamus, not in a garden, but in the cage of a canary, and he singing away like any nightingale. They see none of the wonder of animals. They don't even take a passing interest in them. All kinship is lost between animals and them. If they be mentioned, they are but mentioned in mockery, like the rhinoceros trotting through the town and the elephant in the garden. A Pinter play mentions a slug, and that is all, as far as I have read or can remember.

Arden, of course, writes about a workhouse donkey, but he isn't one of the *avant-garde* and doesn't deal only with nonsense and savagery. Indeed, it seems to me that Arden's *Serjeant Musgrave's Dance* is far and away the finest play of the present day, full of power, protest, and frantic compassion, notwithstanding that, on its first presentation, it was scowled and scooted from the theatre by most of our intelligent and unintelligent drama critics. I wonder why! What dazzling Freudian id or idiom swept this rejection into them, making them reject the denunciation of war's horrors, and led them to embrace the plays which despise and hate life. They take all they can get out of life, like the most of us, enjoy its sweets and recreations, pilfer its pleasures, and dial 999 as soon as they feel a chill in body or in bone.

There was one lone but grand exception — Mr Harold Hobson, drama critic of the *Sunday Times*. He told his many readers, without any qualification, how much he regretted the cold reception he gave to such a fine play. He had been greatly mistaken in his first opinion of the work and went on to give the play the fullest and most eloquent praise any intelligent critic could give to any fine and powerful work. It is naturally hard for a critic to proclaim a mistake in the first estimation of a play, and so Mr Hobson's handsome admission of one was a very courageous thing to do, and it shall be counted unto him as righteousness.

PESTSCRIPT

The newest example of the theatre's condition of mind is a play now appearing in London, called *Entertaining Mr Sloane*.[1] The author gave an interview on the B.B.C. network recently. The interviewer asked him to explain the plot, the meaning of the play, or to say something about it. The author responded as readily as any of Chaucer's storytellers wending their way to Canterbury. No, he wasn't influenced by either Oedipus Rex, or Oedipus Rix. It was a gathering together of many phases and psychologically disturbed characters, woven in and out into a simple dramatic pattern. Shakespeare did the same kind of thing. The play told of a house where dwelt a father with his two adult children, a man and a woman. The woman met a man in a

[1] *Entertaining Mr Sloane* by Joe Orton, published in *New English Dramatists 8*, 1965.

public library who happened to be looking for a lodging. She invited him home to see if a room would please him. He went with her, was very pleased, and decided to dwell in the tent of the scarabs. Within the space of eight pages of typescript — say five minutes — she succeeds in getting his trousers off — the outer barbican stormed. Then the brother of the woman enters, and he too, immediately desires to take the young man's trousers off. Yet no homosexual he. The author gives us a plump assurance that he is bisexual, so, while remaining a man, he can, at a drop of the trousers, become a perfect woman-impersonator. Another trivial point — the newcomer, before he arrived, had murdered an old man, and the other old man upstairs knew of it. Someway, the brother and sister become aware of it too, and she blackmails the lodger into her bed with a hey nonny o. Afterwards, the brother succeeds in blackmailing him into his bed in rare counterpoint style, and to brighten the borders, the newcomer kills the old fella upstairs.

Here we have a theatrical gallimaufry of murder, odd sexual surges, a kinda incestuous indulgence on the part of brother and sister, with a man lodger in between, and a variegated assortment of psychiatric phases. A play to make a man pull his trousers up. The future is to have the inheritance of the theatre of the ridiculous, of the absurd, of rape, of murder and sudden death, of incest, of futility, of violence, and of a basilisk pot of sexual distortions; the land of Hope and Glory will disappear beneath the mud of a dull inferno.

Alfred Hitchcock has added an addendum crescendo to all these by his many films of mystery and horror. In a recent interview over the wireless he recounted with opulent satisfaction all he had done, and all he might yet do. Without seeming to see any difference between fear and fright, he told us that people like to be frightened, that they came to the cinema to be absolved from some kind of psychic fear. They joined their emotions with those shown in the picture, leaving the cinema chastened, and easier in mind and stronger in body — the film director adding with a beaming and patronizing air that all this fear and need to be frightened, sprang from the nursery tale of Little Red

Riding Hood. Does the child really carry this tale in his or her mind from the cradle to the grave? There was a wise man who said, long, long ago that 'When I was a child I thought as a child, but now, having become a man, I put childish things from me', but maybe he didn't know what he was talking about. There are many more nursery rhymes than one, and any one of them might become a psychic influence as the one quoted by Hitchcock. I would shove aside his for this:

> *Ride a cock-horse to Banbury Cross,*
> *To see a fine lady upon a white horse;*
> *Rings on her fingers and bells on her toes,*
> *And she shall have music wherever she goes.*

Today I heard on the wireless of a fifteen-year-old lass diving into the sea to save a boy of ten. The boy was saved, she was lost. And of a policewoman who risked her life on a roof-ridge to save a baby which a half-mad father had in his arms, ready to jump off the roof, baby and all, had the brave woman not snatched it from the frantic father. Brave woman, brave teen-ager lass. Ah, to hell with the loutish lust of Primaqueera. There are still many red threads of courage, many golden threads of nobility woven into the tingling fibres of our common humanity. No one passes through life scatheless. The world has many sour noises, the body is an open target for many invisible enemies, all hurtful, some venomous, like the accursed virus which can bite deeply into flesh and mind. It is full of disappointments, and too many of us have to suffer the loss of a beloved child, a wound that aches bitterly till our time here ends. Yet, even so, each of us, one time or another, can ride a white horse, can have rings on our fingers and bells on our toes, and, if we keep our senses open to the scents, sounds, and sights all around us, we shall have music wherever we go.

ART IS THE SONG OF LIFE (1960)*

And the theatre has, of course, an honoured niche in life, but it is only a part of many arts which together make a grand and merry chorus when life sings in harmony. What is called Culture isn't just the theatre here, the other arts there, music yonder: Culture is the life we live; and unless the theatre, music, and the arts be within us, around us, essential to us, not cultivated, but naturally part of ourselves, always with us in field, factory, and workshop as well as on a stage, in a concert hall, hanging on the walls of a picture gallery, then it is outside of us, and we have little or no part with the arts. They should be with us in some form or another from our childhood to the time when old age tells us we must soon go. Culture is expressed, shown, in the schools where we are taught, the homes where we live, the factories and fields where we work, the streets we walk through, the simple things we use when we eat and drink, and the packages that carry them safely into our homes, the very bindings on the books we read, the clothes we wear, the way we live and move and have our being. It is far more than books on our shelves and pictures in our galleries. It is all that is within us, all without, colouring all our activities.

The theatre is part of all this, an important part, and a very popular part too, next perhaps in familiarity to the papers and magazines we all read, and so it has a tremendous variety of scene, meanings, colour, and locality; mirroring the life of the people, it shows differing pictures, says different things in different countries. The great dramatist, like Shakespeare's poet, 'gives to airy nothing a local habitation and a name'. Every play,

* An article written for readers in the U.S.S.R.; it was published in the Moscow *Literary Gazette* in April 1960.

in whatever form, however written, must deal in one way or another with the life of the people meeting the dramatist who writes it, of those whom he has worked with, lived with, and of those whom he has watched in every conceivable way within the locality where he has lived himself. He weaves all these things through his mind, his imagination, using the technique of the stage to place there what is called a play — a pattern in words and movement either in poetry or prose, which must, if it is to be a fine work, bring to all who see and hear a new and an exciting experience.

Technique is useful and important, the marshalling of a play within a limited allowance of space and time; but imagination is all: it is the focus of all achievements by man, it sparked off the American Revolution, it began the discovery of Evolution in the mind of Darwin, it flamed forth from the mind of Lenin, inspired Shakespeare's plays and all his songs; and is the burning core of form and eloquence which is present in a fine play, novel, painting, or musical creation. Imagination can be born and developed from what we see and hear, mingling with the experience we get from life.

Present-day drama is beset by the worship of realism, by 'illusion', by the proscenium or 'picture-frame' stage. Said an English critic, 'All stage plays are pictures of a world removed from the spectator, cut off and presented to the spectator's consciousness by the gilt and moulding of the proscenium'. Presented by gilt and moulding! What if there be no gilt or moulding? Is the play then lost to view, unseen, unheard, and less than a vapour? But Shakespeare's plays in their first productions had neither gilt nor moulding, no scenery; and whatever illusion there was present was gotten from the magical poetry and rhetoric that flowed from the imagination of the dramatist. But the picture-framed stage is precisely the stage of the time of the sedan chair, the candle, the linkman, the silk- and satin-clad ladies and gents who had become wholly separate from the people. In patrician Greece the theatre was the theatre of the people, high-minded and low-minded; in Shakespeare's day, the theatre was the theatre of the people, high-minded and low-minded; but when the picture-frame was lifted on to the stage, the theatre and play crept away from the people and became the theatre of the dandies — very clever dandies to be sure, but dandies that made it impossible for any play to serve any entertainment interest but their own.

Here in England and yonder in America, we have something similar, though dramatists and actors have changed the bawdy gaiety of the dandies into the despairs, the futilities, the hopelessness of what they evidently conceive life to be; and the audience who go to these plays are one in mind with the dramatists, so that the theatre here has again become the theatre of the few. Says an American drama critic, Brooks Atkinson of *The New York Times*, the other day, writing about the 1959–60 season: 'Shabby Season! Anyone who has looked at fifty-four productions since the season started in August last has sufficient reason to feel depressed. Last year was on the whole banal. This season so far is worse. Although the theatre keeps going through the motions with technical skill, it is not headed in any direction. There is nothing creative at the centre of things, pushing the theatre into significant areas of thought and feeling'.[1] A sad picture of American theatre. Even the musicals are no better, for the same critic says: 'Although the musical stage has been spending stupendous sums of money and huffing and puffing desperately as usual, *Fiorello* is the only musical that has a fresh spirit.'

This New York story is identical with that of London. The plays shown here are as shabby, without significant thought or feeling; indeed without a flicker of life and often without meaning. The other day an excerpt from a play called *One Way Pendulum*[2] was shown over the London Television, and the one in charge, introducing the play, told the viewers that the play was, such as it was, not possible of understanding by any human being. So it is with most of the later plays — not only miserable, but as incomprehensible as the Christian dogma of the Trinity. The London theatres are kept going by the stalls and these can be filled only with those who have money to spare. These people support the trivial play on the one hand and the incomprehensible one on the other; and all are pleased, if none is enlightened. These are the barriers impossible to cross by the serious and creative dramatist who takes a comic or a critical view of the life around him.

That's how it is here: the old proscenium with all its gilt and clumsy ornament and its silly or un-understandable plays. You [in Russia] are much farther ahead. I have already heard of your Institute of Social Building, of Briantsev and of Zavadsky; and in this morning's (January 11, 1960) London *Times*, there is an article on Soviet theatre building, with a picture of the model of Leningrad's Theatre of the Young Spectator. It seems to be a very fine building, precise and supple, ready for the days to come. I wish we had something like it. You are on the way; we are among the decayed and dilapidated in building and in drama.

Brooks Atkinson says in another paragraph: 'The dramatists are citizens of a world that cannot cope with its troubles, and accordingly become increasingly morbid, ingrown and trivial. The little Freudian maladies that preoccupy the dramatist represent the common state of mind. When a civilization lacks the vigour to deal with big problems, it becomes fascinated with the small. Life becomes small and petty and the psychoanalyst's couch becomes the theatre's most popular forum'. Well, not a hopeful-looking future for the English-speaking theatre, though we should remember that a drama full of hero and heroine may, too, be small and petty.

What the future of the theatre may be I cannot tell — it depends on so many things. I do not agree with those who would banish emotion from the theatre (Brecht seems to imply this), for, to me, emotion burns within the veins of life. We all feel it in sorrow, in joy, in fear, in hate, at births, weddings, burials, and when we achieve things. Even calmly-minded scientists feel its thrill; and your own scientists must have felt the emotional surge of elation when they sent the first sputnik careering round the earth. I believe that all the arts should meet in the drama — architecture in the framework of the design, painting in the scenery, music in an occasional song and dance, and literature in a play's dialogue. One more important thought: the dramatist must make his imagination serve him; he must control it; if he doesn't, it will make all the difference between an interesting but disorderly play and a fine work of dramatic art.

AN IRISHMAN'S PLAYS (1957)*

IN a recent number of *The Times Literary Supplement*, a reviewer writing about the expected new departure in drama, heralded by Mr Eliot and Mr Fry, and disappointed that the hope had, apparently, faded away, said: 'This irresolute leadership has been the fading of a dream, the dream that poetry was about to return to the stage, and a flurry of eagerness, as the night's tents are struck for a further march, to be off in some other direction.' The fact is that poetry has never left the stage, but has danced on the stage from the beginning, and will dance on it all the days of the drama's life, which will end only when man ceases to be. Within our very lifetime, Yeats, Synge, Shaw, Lady Gregory, Ibsen, Strindberg, Arthur Miller, and Giraudoux, were poets, if not of the sanctum, certainly of the stage; and a folk-poetry runs through the melodramatic plays of Dion Boucicault: indeed, as Shaw says somewhere, the drama has a far older and more consecrated apostolic succession than the Church herself.

In my opinion, no one who hasn't a quivering fibre of poetry in him can write a fine play, though one who may be afire with the spirit of poetry will often write, and has often written, a very bad play; the dramatic help to the poetic spirit was far away in other souls. Of course, there are plays destitute of poetry in colour or line or form that strut the stage for a thousand and one days, but when the last night of their performance dawns, and the curtain falls, they fall, too; fall like Lucifer, never to hope

* This article was written as an introduction to a broadcast season of O'Casey's plays which opened on the B.B.C. Third Programme in Jan. 1957; it was published in the *Radio Times*, Jan. 25, 1957, under the title 'The Drama of the Future'.

82

again. It is the plays that influence the mind and the emotions, however brief their appearance may be on the stage, that live a lasting life. And this is what every dramatist should aim at, even though he may never achieve it.

Be the effort a success or a failure, I aim, as I have always aimed, at bringing emotion and imagination on to the stage, in the shapes of song, dance, dialogue, and scene; each mingling with the other, as life does, for life is never rigid (except in political parties, respectable families, and old-fashioned schools like Eton and Harrow); nothing changes so often, so inevitably in city and country, in field, factory, workshop, and home. The best of dramatists throughout a long life can but get a glimpse of it, and this glimpse is confined to the life and chronicle of his time. And he can catch this glimpse only if his eyes are ever watching and his ears ever open to catch the merest whisper.

Some say, I believe, that the theatre of the future will be an intellectual one. I don't think so; for intellects differ, the one from the other; different intellects are superior in differing subjects, and can the future dramatist's intellect be so supernatural that it will understand all, and put an incontestable synthesis of them all, glowing, upon the stage? And intellect, even the best of them, is but a part of the life of him who owns it: the intellectual has to live through the commoner nature of man, has to move through the seasons, has to sweat in the sun, shiver in the frost, has to work while it is yet day, for the time cometh when no man can work, has to spend time with the sauciness of girls, maybe a life with one of them, has to have a family, has to grow old, and, finally, has to be gathered unto his fathers. There are great intellectuals in the world today who couldn't write a line of dramatic dialogue to save their souls, and many inferior ones whose imagination gives them the power to write many plays: imagination is a far greater power in the drama than intellect of the highest. Imagination that can look upon a thousand years as a day, and a day as a thousand years; that can spring from one mood to another a thousand miles away with a hop, step, and a jump; that can make from airy nothing a folkal habitation and a game.

Intellect can never banish emotion from the theatre, for emotion is deep within us and round us everywhere; we feel it, see it, and hear it always; it is in the sight of the first rose of late spring and in the last rose of summer; it is in the sight of the cradle and the coffin; in the wind and the rain; in the stone of Salisbury Cathedral and the steel and glass of Radio Centre Building; in the sound of a Beethoven Symphony and the monotonous and insistent beat of the Rock 'n' Roll; and it is in these things and in all others because it is deep in the human heart and forever active in the human mind.

It is odd that people who wallow in the fantasy of revue and pantomime often shrink away from fantasy in a play. We shouldn't be afraid of the fanciful, for it is a gay part of life, and, after all, even the poorest play is fancy-bred; and Milton called Shakespeare Fancy's child, so we have nothing to be afraid of or ashamed of when fantasy fills a play. There is a deal of fancy in the plays that you will be listening to, and, when you hear them (if you are kind enough to listen), you can, if you wish, look back in anger at the plays or look forward in hope towards a newer and a braver theatre. Whether you like the plays or not, whether they be good or be bad in your mind, they have one good thing about them — they were the best that I could do.

O'CASEY ON O'CASEY

A WORD BEFORE CURTAIN-RISE (1954)*

O'CASEY has a good name in some places and a very bad one in others. No one can go through life without getting a bad name from someone somewhere. It is the vivifying lot of any-one who tries to do anything new: to paint his hall-door with a new colour; to learn to play a fiddle; or to write a new-mannered play. Old friends will shake sage heads, and say, He's going beyond himself; he is to be pitied; and if the play-wright says a word against, or ventures a laugh at, the commoner and cosiest thoughts of those who live around him, there is an agonised uproar, and vicious cries go up to God.

Those who try to do things mustn't let themselves be bothered overmuch by a bad name or a good one; mustn't let themselves be puffed up by a clap on the back or frightened by a knock on the snout. It isn't possible, of course, not to feel joy at a clap on the back; impossible not to feel some kind of pain from a knock on the snout. As a playwright, I have received knocks when the hair was brown and the face young-looking; and I'm still getting them when, as Yeats said, I am old and grey and full of tears. Well, not quite full of tears, for within me the laugh comes and goes and always comes again. As well, one can hit back, and land, at times, many a gregorian slashing blow on the conk of him who tries to trip, or on one who aims a blow below the belt.

The knocks mentioned aren't those taps given by the ac-credited critics of the drama whose integrity as regards the drama

* Written as a foreword to *Selected Plays of Sean O'Casey*, Braziller, New York, 1954.

must be equal to that of the playwright, and who are as eager as the playwright himself that the play shoved on to the stage should be worthy of the theatre when its best banner blazoned with the drama's honours is flying from its turrets. Indeed, few of them fail to notice, or even to praise, any quick rhythmic patter of steady feet even momentarily appearing through the clumsy action of a stumbling play. These are the opinions that the drama cannot do without, however we playwrights may wince at some of the comments, for they have been woven into long experience and a wide knowledge of the things belonging to the peace and war of the theatre, from Euripides winning first prize in Athens, through the circus, and on to the Globe Theatre showing Shakespeare's best by candlelight.

No, not these, but those yellowing, bellowing priests, peasants, proletarians, resentful of any harm to their petted humbug, closeted cliché, or pietistic stutter, frightened of losing their fear, who shout out under the name of God to shut tight the mouth that tries to utter some whisper of the truth. All sorts and conditions of men, all ranks, from a Lord Chamberlain of his late Majesty of England, who didn't like the theme of one play[1] to Mister Mike Gold up in New York, who didn't like the theme of another,[2] or the playwright either. Well, the only retort to a boo is a bah!

In a number of his plays, Yeats, the poet, brings in music from flute, zither, drum, and gong — elegant sounds, and beautiful too. I, too, have tried to bring in the music of the flute, the fiddle, and the drum; not in the actual instruments, not through them, but by an occasional song, and by the lilt in the dialogue; by weaving into the emotional action of the plays the shrill or plaintive notes of the flute and the reckless rally that the drums of life so often give.

Well, here are the plays, and, as the curtain rises, let me say quickly that they have had, at least, the grand quality of causing the commotion of clapping of hands, and the commotion, too, of hatred, fear, and loud cries to God for help to kill them dead from fanatics and fools; first in Dublin, Cork, Limerick, and

[1] *The Star Turns Red.*　　　　　　[2] *Within the Gates.*

Galway, then down in London, then up north in Newcastle upon Tyne; in America, in Houston, down in Texas, up in Boston in Massachusetts (Boston well forgiven because it was the cradle of the great prose-poet Emerson); across Europe in Vienna and Berlin. Strike up the drums! Come on, Yeats — sing out your song!

> *Those fanatics all that we do would undo;*
> *Down the fanatic, down the clown;*
> *Down, down, hammer them down,*
> *Down to the tune of O'Donnell Abu.*

THE PLOUGH AND THE STARS: A REPLY
TO THE CRITICS (1926)*

A SPACE, please, to breathe a few remarks opposing the screams
and patter antagonistic to the performance of *The Plough and the
Stars* in the Abbey Theatre. In her letter to *The Irish Independent*
Mrs Sheehy-Skeffington does not drag before us the parts of the
play that spread irritating thoughts over the minds of herself and
her allies, but a talk with some of the young Republican women,
which I had after the disturbance, enabled me to discover that
the National tocsin of alarm was sounded because some of the
tinsel of sham was shaken from the body of truth.

They objected to Volunteers and men of the I.C.A. visiting
a public-house. Do they want us to believe that all these men
were sworn teetotallers? Are we to know the fighters of Easter
Week as 'The Army of the Unco' Guid'? Were all Ireland's
battles fought by Confraternity men? The Staff of Stonewall
Jackson complained bitterly to him of the impiety of one of their
number. 'A blasphemous scoundrel,' said the General, 'but a
damned fine Artillery officer.' Some of the men of Easter Week
liked a bottle of stout and I can see nothing derogatory in that.

They objected to the display of the tricolor, saying that that
flag was never in a public-house. I myself have seen it there. I

* The following two letters were written at the time of the first production
of *The Plough and the Stars* in Dublin, when the play caused riots in the
theatre and angry letters to the Press. O'Casey respected Mrs Hannah
Sheehy-Skeffington, though not her supporters, and spoke highly of her in
later years. His tribute to her husband, Francis Sheehy-Skeffington, is one of
the highlights of 'The Story of the Irish Citizen Army', reprinted in
Feathers from the Green Crow. 'The Plough and the Stars: A Reply to the
Critics' was printed in *The Irish Times* on Feb. 19, 1926 and in *The Irish
Independent* the following day.

have seen the green, white and gold in strange places; I have
seen it painted on a lavatory in 'The Gloucester Diamond'; it
has been flown from some of the worst slums in Dublin; I have
seen it thrust itself from the window of a shebeen in 'The Digs',
but perhaps the funniest use it was put to was when it was made
to function as a State robe for the Mayor of Waterford.

They murmured against the viewpoint of Nora Clitheroe,
saying it did not represent the feeling of Ireland's womanhood.
Nora voices not only the feeling of Ireland's womanhood, but
also the women of the human race. The safety of her brood is
the true morality of every woman. A mother does not like her
son to be killed — she does not like him even to get married.

The Republican women shouted with a loud voice against
the representation of fear in the eyes of the fighters. If this be so,
what is the use of sounding forth their praises? If they knew no
fear, then the fight of Easter Week was an easy thing, and those
who participated deserve to be forgotten in a day, rather than be
remembered for ever. And why is the sentiment expressed in
The Plough and the Stars condemned, while it goes unnoticed
(apparently) in other plays? In *The Old Man* (written by a
Republican)[1] during a crisis, the many fall back; only the few
press forward. In *Sable and Gold* (played by the Republican
Players)[2] a Volunteer, who is a definite coward, is one of the
principal characters, and yet no howl has proclaimed the representation to be false or defaming. And are the men of Easter
Week greater than those whose example they are said to have
followed? Were they all unhuman in that they were destitute
of the first element in the nature of man? 'Upon the earth there
is not his like,' says Job, 'who is made without fear.' Even the
valiant Hector, mad with fear, was chased around the walls of
Troy. And do the Republicans forget the whisper of Emmet to
the question of the executioner, 'Are you ready, sir?' — 'Not
yet, not yet.' I wonder do the Republicans remember how

[1] By Dorothy Macardle, first produced at the Abbey Theatre on Feb. 24,
1925.
[2] By Maurice Dalton, first produced at the Abbey Theatre on Sept. 16,
1918.

Laoghaire and Conall, two of the champions of the Red Branch, ran, as rabbits would run, from what they believed to be the certainty of death; and how Cuchulainn alone remained to face death, with 'pale countenance, drooping head, in the heaviness of dark sorrow'?

One of the young Republicans whispered to me in admiration the name of Shaw, inferential to my own shame and confusion. Curious champion to choose, and I can only attribute their choice to ignorance; for if ever a man hated sham, it is Shaw. Let me give one example that concerns the subject I am writing about. Describing, in *Arms and the Man*, a charge of cavalry, Bluntschli says: 'It's like slinging a handful of peas against the window-pane; first one comes; then two or three close behind him; then all the rest in a lump.' Then Raina answers, with dilating eyes (how like a young Republican woman!) 'Yes, first one! — the bravest of the brave!' followed by the terrible remark: 'H'm; you should see the poor devil pulling at his horse!'

As for vanity, I think I remember a long discussion in *The Volunteer* over the adoption of the green and gold, scarlet and blue, black and white and crimson-plumed costumes of the Volunteers of '82' for the Volunteers of '13'; and though these were rejected — they had to be — there was still left a good deal of boyish vanity in the distribution of braids, tabs, slung swords, and Sam Browne belts. And how rich (to me) was the parade of the stiff and stately uniformed men, 'the solemn-looking dials of them', as Rosie Redmond says in the play — and they marching to the meeting, were serious, very human, but damnably funny.

I am glad that Mrs Sheehy-Skeffington says that the demonstration was not directed against any individual actor. As Mr F. J. McCormick told the audience, the author alone is responsible for the play, and he is willing to take it all. The politicians — Free State and Republican — have the platform to express themselves, and Heaven knows they seem to take full advantage of it. The drama is my place for self-expression, and I claim the liberty in drama that they enjoy on the platform (and how they do enjoy it!) and am prepared to fight for it.

The heavy-hearted expression by Mrs Sheehy-Skeffington about 'the Ireland that remembers with tear-dimmed eyes all that Easter Week stands for' makes me sick. Some of the men cannot even get a job. Mrs Skeffington is certainly not dumb, but she appears to be both blind and deaf to all the things that are happening around her. Is the Ireland that is pouring to the picture-houses, to the dance-halls, to the football matches, remembering with tear-dimmed eyes all that Easter Week stands for? Tears may be in the eyes of the navvies working on the Shannon scheme, but they are not for Ireland. When Mrs Skeffington roars herself into the position of the dramatic critic, we cannot take her seriously: she is singing here on a high note wildly beyond the range of her political voice, and can be given only the charity of our silence. In refutation of a story going around, let me say that there never was a question of a refusal to play the part of 'Rosie Redmond' (splendidly acted by Miss Ria Mooney). The part declined by one of the players was the character of 'Mrs Gogan'.

NATIONALISM and *THE PLOUGH AND THE STARS* (1926)*

In a letter on 15th inst. [Feb. 15, 1926] Mrs Sheehy-Skeffington said that 'the demonstration was not directed to the moral aspect of the play. It was on National grounds solely'. Yet in her letter of 23rd she viciously affirms what she had before denied, and prancing out, flings her gauntlet in the face of what she calls the 'obscenities and indecencies' of the play. She does more: in the righteousness of her indignation, she condemns, by presumption, what she has neither seen nor heard. This is her interpretation of the Rights of Man. Evidently the children of National light in their generation are as cute as the children of National darkness by placing a puritanical prop under the expression of National dissatisfaction, even though the cuteness requires an action that can be called neither fair nor just.

We know as well as Mrs Sheehy-Skeffington that obscene and indecent expressions do not make great literature, but we know, too, that great literature may make use of obscene and indecent expressions, without altogether destroying its beauty and its richness. She would hardly question the greatness in literature of Shakespeare (somebody a year or so ago wrote asking if Shakespeare wrote thirty plays without a naughty word, why couldn't O'Casey write them), but in the condemnation of an O'Casey play the great cloak is concealed by the puritanical mantle. Indeed, her little crow over the possible horror of the censored part of the play seems to whisper that the wish is father to the thought, and that, when the play is published, nothing less (or more) will satisfy her than that the united church bells of

* Letter to the *Irish Independent*, 26 Feb. 1926. The title used here is supplied by the editor of this volume.

Dublin, of their own accord, in a piercing peal will clang together — 'This is a bad, bad, bad, bad play!'

There is no use of talking now of what Mr Arthur Griffith
thought of or wrote about *The Playboy of the Western World.*
Now the world thinks, and I think so, too, that *The Playboy*
is a masterpiece of Irish drama. If these Greeks knew not
Mr O'Casey (how the devil could they), O'Casey knows the
Greeks, and hopes that the Republican Players will one of
these days produce one of their own works dealing with ancient
gods and heroes. At present he himself is interested in men and
women.

Mrs Skeffington's statement that 'every character connected
with the Citizen Army [in the play] is a coward and a slacker'
is, to put it plainly, untrue. There isn't a coward in the play.
Clitheroe falls in the fight. Does Mrs Skeffington want him to do
any more? Brennan leaves the burning building when he can do
nothing else: is she going to persist in her declaration that no
man will try to leap away from a falling building? Will she still
try to deny that in a man (even in the bravest) self-preservation
is the first law? She may object to this, but, in fairness, she
shouldn't blame me. Langon, wounded in the belly, moans for
surgical aid. Does she want me to make him gather a handful of
his blood and murmur, 'Thank God that this has been shed for
Ireland'? I'm sorry, but I can't do this sort of thing.

She complains of the Covey calling sentences of The Voice
dope. Does she not understand that the Covey is a character
part, and that he couldn't possibly say anything else without
making the character ridiculous? Even the Greeks wouldn't
do this. And it doesn't follow that an author agrees with everything his characters say. I happen to agree with this, however;
but of these very words Jim Connolly himself said almost the
same thing as the Covey.

The Tommies weren't represented without fear; but isn't it
natural that they should have been a little steadier than the Irish
fighters? Even Mrs Skeffington will not deny that the odds were
terribly in their favour, and that they were comparatively safe.
Sixty or more to one would make even a British Tommy feel safe

The people that go to football matches are just as much a part of Ireland as those who go to Bodenstown, and it would be wise for the Republican Party to recognise this fact, unless they are determined to make of Ireland the terrible place of a land fit only for heroes to live in.

THE PLOUGH AND THE STARS
IN RETROSPECT (1960)*

IT is strange how simple things and simple incidents weave a
way into a life and often shape its ends; or is it the Destiny that
Shakespeare says 'shapes our ends, rough hew them how we
will'? Well, I suppose that things and incidents are parts of that
Destiny that raises us up or knocks us down. An odder thing is
that Destiny's knockout may, after all, happen to have been a
good thing; whereas Destiny's uplift may, in the end, prove to
have been the sorriest thing that ever happened to us. So in
Destiny's knockout — courage; within Destiny's uplift — an
occasional remembrance that what happens to every golden
lassie and every golden lad happens to us; and that after Destiny's
everlasting knockout we shall be where our brightest success
doesn't mean a damned thing.

Well, the play called *The Plough and the Stars* came into
existence in an odd way; and the effects of its living presentation
on the stage gave Destiny an opportunity to shunt me from the
way I went on to another and stranger road altogether. I, of
course, lived in the midst of all the events described in the play.
There I was part of them, yet subconsciously commenting on
all that was said, much that was done, to be coloured afterward
(though I had no inkling of this at the time) through my
imagination, seeing at the same time, the sad humour and
vigorous tragedy of this historic time to Ireland.

I had been one, with Jim Larkin, to welcome the flag [which
gives the play its title]; to unfold it and fix it to the staff; to

* Published in *The New York Times*, Dec. 4, 1960, as 'Memories of a
Farewell to Ireland'. *The Plough and the Stars* was being revived in New
York at the time. The title used above is the editor's.

95

expose it, like a sacrament to the Citizen Army members, who gave it a great cheer, and from every point of view the flag deserved one. It was this flag that fired in my mind the title for the play; and the events that swirled around the banner and that of the Irish Volunteers, the tricolor of green, white and orange — now fading to an incoherent yellow — that gave me all the humour, pathos and dialogue that fill the play.

Another odd incident gave me an urge to the writing of it: after *Juno and the Paycock* I wrote two one-act plays, *Kathleen Listens In* and *The Cooing of Doves*, which I sent in to the Abbey Theatre for consideration. I doubted about any acceptance of the first play, but was quite confident about the second one. A few weeks later a letter came when stars were failing, to say that *Kathleen Listens In* had been welcomed, but the other play, *The Cooing of Doves*, wasn't considered to be a sparkler and was herewith returned with thanks. A shock! Two shocks! One for the rejection itself; the other for the bad judgment of the directors in thinking the accepted play better than the one rejected. Hints before in letters and conversation, now a definite realization that Abbey Theatre judgments were hooped with fallibility, like all other opinions of error-garlanded man.

However, *Kathleen Listens In* had an amusing and extraordinary experience in Abbey theatrical production: when the play ended its first performance, the audience seemed to be stunned into a dead and fearful silence; they remained mute; not a single pair of hands gave a single clap; none even attempted to give one; not one voice called out for the author, not one cursed him. The little really insignificant playlet seemed to have bitten deep into their vitals. They sat in their seats for what seemed a long time, then silently and cautiously rose, one by one, two by two, and gathered cap or cloak; then they folded their thoughts as Arabs fold their tents, and stole silently away.

This was something never experienced by any other play before, as far as I am aware, and many others, too. However indifferent or disappointed an audience may have been with any previous play expression, someone, a few, even the most, have clapped their hands, called, even if but faintly, for the author;

always behaved with a little tolerant politeness, save in this one instance of a silent audience, uncomfortable, embarrassed, whose only desire was to steal from the theatre and be safe on the way home. What a remarkable experience for little Kathleen as she listened in! In a few short weeks, what a change was to come from this dead silence to a mighty roar!

Meanwhile, I remembered that I had written a play about the Black and Tan period; about the period of the Civil War; but no play yet around the period of the actual Easter Rising, which was the beginning of all that happened afterward. So I set about illumining and ravaging my mind for a new play about the Easter Rising, setting down scene and dialogue, taking notes on any piece of paper that was handy when an idea or word struck me.

I never make a scenario, depending on the natural growth of a play rather than on any method of joinery. Things I saw, things I heard, flooded my mind, and the germ became the gist, with a title vaguely selected of *The Easter Lily Aflame*; but the Banner and its design came too often before my mind to be set aside, so the title eventually became *The Plough and the Stars*. Then it was that I began to know more about the artistic, middle-class and intelligentsia face of Dublin, and it wasn't so delightful as I had assumed it would be; brimstone and sulphur fumed out from the white flame. A most unhappy time at rehearsals; Lennox Robinson irritable, at times abusive; some of the Roman Catholic members of the company in revolt against the play, one of them declaring she wouldn't say that she never had a kid born outside the borders of the Ten Commandments — as if it were a sin, an occasion, even, of sin to be born within their borders; another aflame with fear and dismay at the song sung by Fluther in the pub scene; still another declaring in dressing room and in the wings that he would never, never say 'snotty', though it is an Anglo-Saxon word, meaning, according to Skeat's etymological dictionary, 'mucus from the nose'.

I was a little bewildered by the apparent agitation on the stage, not knowing yet all that was happening there, and troubled at the time with a painful bout of eye inflammation, I had too

much on my mind to bother. Then came the performance and
the great roar — a roar that shook the homes of Dublin and the
corn waving in Ireland's four beautiful fields! Scholars, saints,
hurlers and bards shouted down O'Casey; and in spite of the
herculean defiance of the indomitable poet, Yeats, I felt as Ruth
felt among the alien corn; I was an alien in my own land. The
next day, angry and abusive letters against the play shone darkly
from the Dublin papers, and O'Casey was told by many symbols
in speech and letter that the shamrock wasn't for him to pluck.
It was time to go.

All the time, there was hovering in my mind that *The Cooing
of Doves*, the play rejected by the Abbey Theatre, now formed
the much-praised second act of the play: the stone the builders
rejected, though not a cornerstone, was an essential part of the
building; the Abbey was fallible. (Lady Gregory, alone of the
others, remembered, and when I went to visit her she mentioned
how happily *The Cooing of Doves* welded into the heart of
another play. It went in with but a few minor changes.) Besides,
a telegram rustled in my pocket: *Juno* was being transferred
[from one London theatre] to another, and the telegram said I
must come over if the new production was to be a success. Yes,
it was time to go; I would take the cash and let discredit go. So
I left for England, a soul-saving change, for London, through
Within the Gates, introduced me to New York, and gave me
many American friends who will be — if God be good to me —
my dear friends forever.

W. B. YEATS AND *THE SILVER TASSIE** (1928)*

Dear Mr Yeats, — There seems to me to be no reason to comment upon whether you read my play in Rapallo or Dublin, or whether you read my play before or after reading your fellow-directors' opinions, or whether the Abbey owed or did not owe its prosperity to me — these things do not matter, and so we'll hang them up on the stars.

And we'll send into exile for the present the 'dogmatism and splenetic age', and have a look at the brood of opinions these have left behind them.

You say — and this is the motif throughout the intonation of your whole song — that 'I am not interested in the Great War.' Now, how do you know that I am not interested in the Great War? Perhaps because I never mentioned it to you. Your statement is to me an impudently ignorant one to make, for it happens that I was and am passionately and intensely interested in the Great War. Throughout its duration I felt and talked of nothing else; brooded, wondered, and was amazed. In Dublin I talked of the Great War with friends who came to see me, and with friends when I went to see them. I talked of the Great War and of its terrible consequences with Lady Gregory when I stayed in Coole. I have talked of the Great War with Doctor Pilger, now the cancer expert in Dublin, who served as surgeon at the front. Only a week before I got your letter I talked of the Great War to a surgeon here. And yet you say I am not interested in the Great War. And now will you tell me the name and give

* Letter written in answer to Yeats's letter of Apr. 20, 1928, published in *The Letters of W. B. Yeats*, edited by Allan Wade, pp. 740–2. The full correspondence between O'Casey and the Abbey Theatre directors was printed in *The Irish Statesman* (Dublin), June 9, 1928, pp. 268–72.

me the age and send me the address of the human being who, having eyes to see, ears to hear and hands to handle, was not interested in the Great War?

I'm afraid your statement (as far as I am concerned) is not only an ignorant one, but it is a silly statement too.

You say 'you never stood on its battlefields'. Do you really mean that no one should or could write about or speak about a war because one has not stood on the battlefields? Were you serious when you dictated that — really serious, now? Was Shakespeare at Actium or Philippi? Was G. B. Shaw in the boats with the French, or in the forts with the British when St Joan and Dunois made the attack that relieved Orleans? And someone, I think, wrote a poem about Tir na nOg, who never took a header into the Land of Youth. And does war consist only of battlefields?

But I have walked some of the hospital wards. I have talked and walked and smoked and sung with the blue-suited wounded men fresh from the front. I've been with the armless, the legless, the blind, the gassed, and the shell-shocked; one with a head bored by shrapnel who had to tack east and tack west before he could reach the point he wished to get to; with one whose head rocked like a frantic moving pendulum. Did you know 'Pantosser', and did you ever speak to him? Or watch his funny, terrible antics, or listen to the gurgle of his foolish thoughts? No? Ah, it's a pity you never saw or never spoke to 'Pantosser'. Or did you know Barney Fay, who got field punishment No. 1 for stealin' poultry (as Estaminay cock, maybe) behind the trenches, in the rest camps, out in France? And does war consist only of hospital wards and battlefields?

You say: 'You illustrate these opinions by a series of almost unrelated scenes as you might in a leading article.' I don't know very much about leading articles, though I may possibly have read them when I had the mind of a kid, so I don't quite get your meaning here. And do you know what you are thinking about when you talk of leading articles, or do you know what you are talking about when you think of leading articles? Surely to God, Mr Yeats, you don't read leading articles!

I have pondered in my heart your expression that 'the history of the world must be reduced to wall-paper', and I can find in it only the pretentious bigness of a pretentious phrase. I thank you, out of mere politeness, but I must refuse even to try to do it. That is exactly, in my opinion (there goes a cursed opinion again), what most of the Abbey dramatists are trying to do — building up, building up little worlds of wall-paper, and hiding striding life behind it all.

I'm afraid I can't make my mind mix with the sense of importance you give to 'a dominating character'. God forgive me, but it does sound as if you peeked and pined for a hero in the play. Now, is a dominating character more important than a play, or is a play more important than a dominating character? You say that 'my power in the past has been the creation of a unique character that dominated all round him, and was a main impulse in some action that filled the play from beginning to end'. In *The Silver Tassie* you have a unique work that dominates all the characters in the play. I remember talking to Lady Gregory about *The Plough and the Stars* before it was produced, and I remember her saying that *The Plough* mightn't be so popular as *Juno*, because there wasn't in the play a character so dominating and all-pervading as 'Juno', yet *The Plough* is a better work than *Juno*, and, in my opinion — an important one — *The Silver Tassie*, because of, or in spite of, the lack of a dominating character, is a greater work than *The Plough and the Stars*. And so when I have created the very, very thing you are looking for — something unique — you shout out: 'Take, oh, take this wine away, and, for God's sake, bring me a pot of small beer.'

It is all very well and very easy to say that 'dramatic action must burn up the author's opinions'. The best way, and the only way, to do that is to burn up the author himself. What's the use of writing a play that's just as like a camel as a whale? And was there ever a play, worthy of the name of play, that did not contain one or two or three opinions of the author that wrote it? And the Abbey Theatre has produced plays that were packed skin-tight with the author's opinions — the plays of Shaw, for instance.

Whether Hamlet and Lear educated Shakespeare, or Shakespeare educated Hamlet and Lear, I don't know the hell, and I don't think you know either.

Your statements about '. . . psychological unity and unity of action . . . Dramatic action is a fire that must burn up everything but itself . . . the history of the world must be reduced to wallpaper in front of which the characters must pose and speak . . . while an author is writing he has no business to know anything that isn't a part of the action . . .' are, to me, glib, glib ghosts. It seems to me they have been made, and will continue to be spoken forever and ever by professors in schools for the culture and propagation of the drama. (I was nearly saying the Gospel.) I have held these infants in my arms a thousand times and they are all the same — fat, lifeless, wrinkled things that give one a pain in his belly looking at them.

You say that after the first and second acts of *The Silver Tassie* there is . . . nothing. Really nothing? Nothing, nothing at all? Well, where there is nothing, where there is nothing — there is God.[1]

Turning to your advice that I should ask for the play back; that I should tell the Press that I want to revise it, and so slip aside from the admonition of the Abbey Directorate, I refer you to what I have written already to Mr Robinson.[2]

I shall be glad for the return of the script of the play, and a formal note of its rejection. — Best personal wishes,

S. O'CASEY.

19 Woronzo Road, St John's Wood.

[1] 'Remember always where there is nothing there is God.' Line spoken by Paul Ruttledge in Yeats's play, *Where There is Nothing*.

[2] 'If W. B. Yeats had known me as faintly as he thinks he knows me well, he wouldn't have wasted his time — and mine — making such a suggestion. I am too big for this sort of mean and petty shuffling, this lousy perversion of the truth. There is going to be no damned secrecy with me surrounding the Abbey's rejection of the play. Does he think that I would practise in my life the prevarication and wretchedness that I laugh at in my plays?' (Extract from O'Casey's letter to Lennox Robinson, published in *The Irish Statesman*, June 9, 1928, p. 269.)

THE SILVER TASSIE (1928)*

Dr Starkie in Dublin is in literature what one would call a toff. He is a professor in Dublin University, a director of the Abbey Theatre, and a big thing in the Dublin Drama League. These powers have laid their hands on his head, and he wears a stole of authority from the literary apostolate and epistolate of Dublin, so that everything he writes is stamped with a scholarly image and superscription. Tired but proud of the tidy literary fold of Dublin, he has gone out to instruct into order and quietness some who decline to bleat with his baa-lambs. He starts his little exercises with a criticism of the plays of the celebrated workman dramatist Sean O'Casey.[1] We all must admire Dr Starkie for struggling towards new values and cheer him as he starts on a wonderful involution as a critic. But he must learn to classify his ideas, and work his criticisms up into a synthesis. Though his movements are often jerky and sometimes vertiginous, he shows many fine attitudes as he skips la, la, la over the pages of *The Nineteenth Century*.

Dr Starkie is a director of the Abbey Theatre that was concerned with the rejection of *The Silver Tassie*, and since he wrote about the play in this Review, it is natural that I should be interested to show that upon examination every one of his

* Published in *The Nineteenth Century*, Sept. 1928, under the title 'The Plays of Sean O'Casey: A Reply'.

[1] 'The Plays of Sean O'Casey', by Walter Starkie, appeared in the Aug. 1928 number of *The Nineteenth Century*. In this article Dr Starkie is highly complimentary about the first three full-length plays but cautious and equivocal about his latest one, *The Silver Tassie*. In his first paragraph, O'Casey turns some of the critic's own words like 'involution' and 'synthesis' against Starkie. It is perhaps only fair to add that in later years the two men became good friends.

criticisms is empty-headed. In his official criticism Dr Starkie said that 'in order to prepare his mind for *The Silver Tassie* he read over again the three published plays of Sean O'Casey'.[1] He read over again three old plays in order to prepare his mind for a new one. He thought that he must read *The Silver Tassie* cautiously, carefully, and thoroughly, so he sat down to read, not the new play, but the three old ones. What is one to think of a critic who thinks that the best way to prepare his mind for a new play is to sit down and read three old ones. This action of his thunders out the suggestion that, if at all possible, a flaw would be found in the new play. But the silliness of the preparation got a shock, for, having read the three other old plays, he finds in the new one 'a new departure, a new art, a new technique'. But then he does a worse thing. After priming his criticism with incapacity by reading three old plays to understand a new one, he paints his criticism with incapacity by criticising the new departure, the new art, the new technique, of the new play, by the old manner, the old art, the old technique of the old plays! Dr Starkie says that 'the fault of *The Silver Tassie* is that it is too vague and indefinite'. He does not say where it is vague and where it is indefinite. He hints at the last two acts. There is not a docker who is not a duffer (the percentage of duffers among dockers is low, and far less than the percentage of duffers among dons), who would fail to understand a single sentence or fail to feel a single emotion that is spoken or manifested in any one act of the play.

He says, writing about the second act of the play, 'It is difficult to imagine such scenes when we read the play'. Well, if he cannot, he has lost all that was left of his imagination. He says, 'Poor Harry has not half the personality of poor, pale little Mollser sitting outside the tenement in *The Plough and the Stars*'. Best to tell the Doctor that Harry has not any of the personality of poor, pale little Mollser sitting outside the tenement simply because he was not meant to have it. He says: 'The prayer-meeting, Bible-quoting Susie of the 1st act evolves into a frivolous V.A.D., but we are not shown any gradual trans-

[1] *The Irish Statesman*, Dublin, June 9, 1928.

formation.' If Dr Starkie had read the new play as often as he said he read the old ones, he would see that no gradual change is shown because no change takes place. Susie can show a leg in the 1st act as well as she can in the last. And if he had read the new play as often as he says he read the old ones, he would see that her sturdiness and decision in the 1st act function as strongly again in the last act of the play. And if he imagines that in the music of a jazz band a V.A.D. would hear only the moans of many patients, then one day Dr Starkie may become a plausible critic, but he will never be a playwright. Writing of the 2nd act, he says, 'The crude realism of the words does not suit the chant.' What does he mean? Is not one word as real as another? Is there a different kind of realism in different words? Or the same kind of realism in different words? Or a different kind of realism in the same words, or what? He says, 'The 2nd act is a queer, fantastic scene.' The act is built up of words, and if the words be crudely realistic, how can the act be queer and fantastic? He says again in one place that 'it is hard to imagine such scenes when we read the play', and in another place that 'the author has introduced a grotesque chanting in doggerel verse that haunts the imagination'. And this is the critic that says that O'Casey in this play is vague and indefinite, and must learn to classify his ideas! In criticism it seems that Dr Starkie does not know his right hand from his left. Again, 'The excellent 1st act, which suggests *Juno and the Paycock*.' Excellent, mind you, because it reminds him of *Juno and the Paycock*; the rest of the play not so good because it does not, mind you, remind him of *Juno and the Paycock*. He does not like the new play because it is not like the old ones. The change was nothing to O'Casey but it has huddled Starkie into corner-cowering criticism.

Starkie says again, 'He makes his opinions and theories fit into the framework of the bourgeois play, and thus he is not an innovator in drama. . . . He is still dominated by the well-made play.' Go on again, Dr Starkie. 'In *The Silver Tassie* he has left behind him the plays of a former manner and is groping towards new dramatic values.' In the *Irish Times* he called this new manner 'a technique touched with genius and standing out above all'. He cancelled his criticism before, and he can cancel it again. How can O'Casey be still dominated by the well-made play if he has left behind him the plays of a former manner? How can he be groping towards new dramatic values if these new dramatic values are touched with genius and stand out above all? And the fact that Starkie read over again the three old 'well-made plays' in order to prepare his mind for *The Silver Tassie*, and the fright that the new dramatic values of this play gave him, show that it is the critic rather than the dramatist that is dominated by the well-made play.

Dr Starkie says again, 'O'Casey has not lost any of his power in writing or his vivid imagination.' Will Dr Starkie tell me for my own good what I have lost? Perhaps the will or the stamina to transform a play into a synthesis. Or is it that O'Casey has 'left the scenes of his impressionable years and has ceased to see intensely'? This opinion of Dr Starkie, as well as being a Yeatsian echo, is a puny prod at the play when we remember that the critic spent his novitiate in the comprehension of new values by the hot-blooded study of old ones. But it is more than this — it is a mean and underhand method of trying to shoulder a prop under his opinions. In the first place, it would be impossible to lose in 2 years the impressions of 40; in the second place, a good deal of those 2 years has been infused into the production of my old plays, and the rest of the time has been spent in the writing of *The Silver Tassie*, so that about a lunar month remains in which I must have lost the 'power to see intensely'. At its worst there seems to be something spiteful in this contention; at its best it stands adjutant to the opinion of Mr Yeats. There would be something in it if all other opinions stood in the porch with Starkie's; but, if he wishes, I will send him opinions given by those as clever as he, Irish as he, far more experienced in the drama than he, which will tell him, saucy to his face, that the intensity and reality of the last two acts of the play endure to the end.[1] Let Starkie try to hit it off fairly, without imagining that others must be as he himself is — able to see only the things in his

[1] Here O'Casey is almost certainly referring to Bernard Shaw's opinions of the play.

own and his neighbour's garden. And if Starkie bets, and he is game, I will take a bet with him that he himself during his life has spent more of his time out of Ireland than I have. The fact is that Starkie's *leit-motif* of separation from Ireland is a veil over the conceited opinion that there must be a loss in the wider separation from that little Irish league of letters who have joined hands and dance continually round the totem pole of their own opinions.

It would be a weary thing to climb over the whole pile of his opinions, but there is one that Starkie has thrown in which deserves to be lifted out and laughed at. He says: 'O'Casey is not the dramatist of a new nation full of hope in its future progress. In this respect he is a contradiction to the optimistic spirit which has prevailed owing to the wise government of Mr Cosgrave and his colleagues. Let us not see too many of such plays, for in an epoch (great word, Starkie!) of reconstruction all our energies should be set upon creating a new country.'

This smells of courage, resolution, and determination. Starkie wants things done. He wants plays of hope, plays of purity, plays of progress for his dear old country; plays that will play their part in the present epoch of reconstruction; plays to buck them up and give them peace. The Irish dramatist of the future will have to take his tips from the Irish Government. He can see everything, but the Government will show him what to look at. And Starkie thinks that this is dramatic criticism. You are a politician, my dear Starkie. Stand for the Dail,[1] and, if elected, you will learn more quickly of the things that belong unto politics than you will ever learn of the things that belong unto the drama.

[1] The Irish Parliament.

BLASPHEMY AND *THE SILVER TASSIE* (1935)*

THE most serious objection alleged against *The Silver Tassie* is
that a travesty of the Mass is to be found in some nook or
cranny of the play. Mr MacNamara has been particularly vocal
about it, but, like Father Gaffney, he hasn't told anybody where
the travesty is to be found. Is it to be found in the first, second,
third, or fourth act of the play? And will Father Gaffney or Mr
MacNamara tell us what part or passage in the play forms the
travesty of the Sacred Office? There is no travesty of the Mass in
the second act of the play. As far as I know, and I ought to
know, there is no travesty of the Mass, stated clearly or furtively
implied, from one end of the play to the other. The murmuring
or singing of part of the Service in the second act, which was put
in by me to imply the sacred peace of the Office compared with
the horrible cruelty and stupidity of the war, constitutes the only
irreverence in the play as touching the Sacred Office of the
Mass. If the portrayal of the infinite peace and mercy implied in
the Sacrifice constitutes an irreverence to the Catholic Faith as
conceived by Father Gaffney and Mr MacNamara, then it is an
irreverence and it will remain an irreverance; for I refuse to take
my conception of the Catholic Faith from the conception held
tight in the minds of Father Gaffney and Mr MacNamara, now,
or in any hour of the time to come.

Perhaps the travesty of the Mass may, in the mind of either
Mr MacNamara or the mind of Father Gaffney, be associated
with the words spoken by the crippled Harry Heegan in the
last act of the play. They are these: 'No, white wine, white,
like the stillness of the millions that have removed their clamours
from the crowd of life. No, red wine; red, like the blood that

* This article was sent to Yeats following attacks, led by Fr M. H
Gaffney and the playwright Brinsley MacNamara, on *The Silver Tassie* after
its first production at the Abbey Theatre. It was first published in an
inaccurate transcription in Saros Cowasjee's *Sean O'Casey: The Man behind the
Plays* (1963). This transcription is from a carbon of the article sent to Yeats.
The title is the editor's.

was shed for you and for many for the commission of sin.' Now the last sentence is taken — with an alteration of one word — from the Anglican Rubric of the Service of Holy Communion, and so cannot be a travesty of the Mass. The Eastern Rite of the Mass is recognised by the Catholic Church, but the Anglican Rite is not so recognised, and so the sentence cannot be an insidious insult to the Mass. Let me say here that, neither directly nor indirectly, is the quotation meant to be a stab at the Anglican Rite of Holy Communion. The sentence was introduced in an effort to convey a suitable symbol of the anguished bitterness that the unhappy Harry might conceivably feel for what he thought to be the fell waste of the war.

Father Gaffney tells us that he 'cannot give an adequate idea of the play's deliberate indecency and its mean mocking challenge to the Christian Faith'. What is the Christian Faith? Isn't it to be found summarised in the creeds, the Athanasian Creed, the Apostles' Creed, and that Creed that particularly expresses the faith of Catholics? Now is there one phrase in the play from the start to the finish that in any way, directly or indirectly, challenges any part of the Catholic Faith as expressed by the Creed of Pope Pius? If Father Gaffney had said that the play was a challenge to the faithful rather than to the Faith, he would have been nearer to the mark. Let me suggest to Father Gaffney that the Faith is a perpetual challenge to the faithful.

Father Gaffney says that 'plain etiquette will not tolerate indecency or blasphemy on or off the stage'. This is nonsense. He has his job cut out for him if he thinks plain etiquette will banish indecency or horror off the stage or out of life. There are many indecent things in life outside of sex, things more seriously indecent than the common language of the streets and the workshops. There are indecent things in politics, in home life, in business, even in religion, that we never or rarely hear a word about. Plain etiquette won't do very much to soften them down. The Seven Gifts of the Holy Ghost and the Twelve Fruits of The Holy Spirit have to do with mightier things than the paltry thing he calls plain etiquette. If I were a Christian priest I should put more trust in the Sword of the Spirit than I

E

would put in Father Gaffney's Etiquettical Catholic Catechism.

There were some who raved about a few naughty words in the play that were peculiar to the characters who spoke them. Some of them are to be found in the Bible, naked and unashamed. Turning to the Second Book of Kings, the Eighteenth Chapter and the Twenty-seventh Verse, we find this: 'But Rab-Shakeh saith unto them, hath my master sent me to thy master, and to thee, to speak these words? Hath he not sent me to the men which sit on the wall, that they may eat their own dung and drink their own piss with you?' We find this, almost word for word in the Gaelic of Bedell's Irish Bible. In the First of Samuel, Twenty-fifth Chapter, Twenty-second Verse: 'So and more also do God to the enemies of David, if I leave off all that pertain to him by the morning light any that pisseth against a wall.' And let all concerned have a squint at the Seventh and Tenth Verses of the Fourteenth Chapter of First Kings. Here is written, 'Thus saith the Lord God of Israel . . . I will bring evil upon the house of Jeroboam, and will cut off from Jeroboam him that pisseth against the wall.' Each, of course, appearing in the Irish Bible as translated by Bishop Bedell. Hot and biting words indeed. What do the two chancellors of the spoken word think of them? But there is something more to come: in a play called *The Satin Slipper*, written by a well-known Catholic, the words bastard, son of a bitch, and arse are flaunted in our faces. Worse still, these are translated from the French by a Catholic priest, the Reverend Fr. John O'Connor, and the book is published by a Catholic firm, Messrs Sheed & Ward. What have Father Gaffney, Mr Brinsley Sheridan MacNamara, Red Handed Cu Uladh, or the Doxological Professor of Galway, Mr J. Murphy, got to say to me now, and what have I to say to them? I have only to say this:

What to such as they, anyhow, such a poet as I? Therefore leave my works,

And go lull yourself with what you can understand, and with piano tunes,

For I lull nobody, and you will never understand me.[1]

[1] From 'To a Certain Civilian', by Walt Whitman.

FROM WITHIN THE GATES
(1934)*

WHEN *Within the Gates* was first performed in London, some of
the English critics began to run around in circles, rumble out
protests, and do everything but face firmly the form of drama
that had been impudently thrust upon them. It was over their
heads, and they immediately began to try to trample it under
their feet. They were perplexed, and then they were frightened.
Like the Bishop in the play, they called for a fuller manifesta-
tion of life, but when it came, they fled from before it and
hurried for refuge in the ranks of the down-and-out critics.
One highballed critic complained that the play was not 'a
study of the whole seething brew of life'. He murmured resentment against a bitter comment on a land 'trying to live according
to its ancient lights'. They are, indeed, ancient lights in more
ways than one. Another said, 'the character who arises out of
the ruck is called 'The Dreamer', and that's a pity, for if one
thing is more certain than another in these troubled times it is
that the day for dreaming is behind us — far, far behind us'.
This fool failed to see that The Dreamer is always the first to
rise out of the ruck of things. One of his own great poets has
said of the first Dreamer:

> *Thou from the first*
> *Wast present, and with mighty wings outspread*
> *Dove-like satst brooding on the vast Abyss*
> *And mad'st it pregnant.*

The first Dreamer is the Holy Ghost. But this fool had forgotten
all about that. These English critics have become old and

* Written for *The New York Times* on the occasion of the New York
production of *Within the Gates*, and published in the issue for Oct. 21, 1934.

doddering minds in the theatre acclaiming an ageing and withering form, and the marching drama is leaving them behind with their dead hope and their dead faith. They have pilloried drama too long to the form of dead naturalism, and all fresh and imaginatively minded dramatists are out to release drama from the pillory of naturalism and send her dancing through the streets.

We have become too clever by half. Our graceful and polished manner of playwriting has sucked the life and soul out of the drama. For a long time the drama was the most popular and most powerful of the arts. It was majestic in the days of the Greeks and magnificent in the days of Shakespeare. It is now — with a few exceptions — neither powerful nor popular, and has become the pretty chambermaid to the lascivious. Nine-tenths of those who write for the theatre are gigolo dramatists in whom is no vestige of honour and scarcely a vestige of life. The stage is fully furnished now if it bears on its breast a bottle of champagne, a box of cigarettes and a coyly covered bed. Not a bed for glorious love as in *Romeo and Juliet*, nor a bed for terrifying lust as in *Desire Under the Elms*, but a bed for a mean and half-hearted pastime. The pomp and circumstance of life have been degraded down to the pomp and circumstance of a bed. Imagination has been lavished on the sheen of silk stockings and short chemises, too. There is a place, of course, for a pretty woman in a chemise and silk stockings in a play, but that place is not an important one, and a woman is something above and beyond a camisole. And the cult of these things has banished power and fantasy, music and song and greatness far from the drama, so that she is no longer a matron or maid, but a cheap, ageing and bedizened harlot.

We must go back for help and inspiration to the good and the great men. We must bring back to the drama its one-time simple austerity, its swinging merriment, its beauty in music of word and colour of scene, and its tragedy too deep for tears. Drama must be great, or at least fine, whether she has the lance in her breast or the crown on her head, whether she dons the simple serge of the religious or sports the coloured cap of folly.

An honoured English critic,[1] now safely housed in the grave, who wrote a few good things buried miles down in a lot of junk, said that passion and imitation constituted the elements of drama. Passion in primitive times was expressed, he goes on, not only by the voice, but by rhythmic movements of the body. Now the drama, he says, has grown out of dancing quite as much as out of song. Well, we're out to put dancing and song back again where they belong and make the movements of the body express something quite as well as the sound of the voice. When a man, says he, spoke in verse, he spoke as no man speaks in real life. This desire for real life on the stage has taken all the life out of the drama. The beauty, fire and poetry of drama have perished in a storm of fake realisms. Let real birds fly through the air, real animals roam through the jungle, real fish swim in the sea, but let us have art in the theatre.

And even in the most commonplace of realistic plays the symbol can never be absent. A house on a stage can never be a house, and that which represents it must always be a symbol, be the scene ever so realistic. A room in a play, be it ever so realistic, must always remain a symbol for a room. There can never be any actuality on a stage, except an actuality that is unnecessary and utterly out of place. An actor representing a cavalier may come on the stage mounted on a real horse, but the horse will always look ridiculous. The horse can have nothing to do with the drama. I remember a play written round Mr Pepys, performed in London, and in this play was used the actual snuff-box used by Mr Pepys when he was head of the English Admiralty in the time of Charles II. So much was said of the snuff-box that I expected it to be carried in on a cushion followed by a brass band and hawked round for all to admire before the play began. Now this snuff-box added nothing to the play, and because of this commonplace spirit in the play, the play added nothing to the drama.

The closer we approach to actual life the further we move away from the drama. There is a deeper life than the life we see and hear with the open ear and the open eye, and this is the life

[1] Almost certainly William Archer.

important and the life everlasting. And this life can be caught from the group rather than from the individual. 'We can know a man only imperfectly,' says George Jean Nathan, in his *Intimate Notebooks*, 'for every man has an emotional, spiritual, philosophical and personal fourth dimension, of which no camera can catch a photograph.' So no dominant character in a play can give a full portrait of a man or a woman. Even Hamlet is not a picture of the whole man. Know a man all your life and you do not know him wholly, and how then can we expect to picture the nature of a man in the space of a couple of hours? True to life on the stage, as far as drama is concerned, really means true to death. So to hell with so-called realism, for it leads nowhere.

Within the Gates tries to bring back to the drama the music and song and dance of the Elizabethan play and the austere ritual of the Greek drama, caught up and blended with the life around us. It is a play written round life not from outside looking in, but from inside looking out. It shows organized religion, good-natured and well-intentioned, unable to find a word or invent an action that will give to life the help it needs. It's one half running out to meet life and the other half running away again.

'The Young Whore,' symbol of those young women full of life and a fine energy, gracious and kind, to whom life fails to respond, and who are determined to be wicked rather than virtuous out of conformity or fear.

'The Old Woman,' symbol of those who stand still, think the little world round was born to serve them, and that when they die, life dies too.

'The Gardener,' symbol of the multitude mind moving on head down, shrinking from thought, and finding inspiration in all things cheap and everything easy. Seeking the things that present no risk and leave no risk behind them.

'The Young Man in Plus Fours,' symbol of those young and old men whose whole life is an interest in the surface of women.

'The Scarlet Woman,' symbol of those women who think their legs are the pillars of the world and of wisdom, who giving, give not, and who live far away from life.

'The Evangelists,' symbol of those preachers who daub the glories of God with mockeries.

'The Chair Attendants,' symbols of life's wreckage who, with the Evangelists, are wasting life by living it.

'The Atheist,' symbol of those who, trying to get rid of God, plant Him more firmly on His throne.

'Nursemaids and Guardsmen,' symbols of those simple souls who take life as they find it, and, without much effort, make the best of it.

'The Disputants,' symbols of those who hear and give great arguments, but are none the wiser for it all.

'The Young Salvation Army Officer,' symbol of the coloured sob-stuff in organized religion that reflects no gleam from the mind of God, and brings no gleam to the mind of man.

'The Policewoman,' symbol of woman dressed in a little brief authority.

'The Dreamer,' symbol of a noble restlessness and discontent; of the stir in life that brings to birth new things and greater things than those that were before; of the power realizing that the urge of life is above the level of conventional morality; of ruthlessness to get near to the things that matter, and sanctify them with intelligence, energy, gracefulness and song; of rebellion against stupidity; and of the rising intelligence in man that will no longer stand, nor venerate, nor shelter those whom poverty of spirit has emptied of all that is worth while in life.

'The Down and Out,' symbols of all who are dead to courage, fortitude, and the will to power; of those to whom a new thought or a new idea brings terror and dismay; of those who turn the struggle of life into a whine; of those, young or old, rich or poor, who in thought, word and deed, give nothing to life, and so are outcasts from life even as they live; even so.

So much for the symbols; now for the new form in the play.

Drama is tired of the neat and trimly dressed plays that live their little day on the stage, stretch out their little hands for admiration and then sigh themselves down to the dead; plays that sprinkle us with scent instead of purging us with hyssop; that enthrone the sex force on a satin-sheeted bed in a room from which never issues the chant of unto us a child is born, unto us a son is given; plays whose high moments are movements with big bottles of champagne and little glasses of sherry; whose horizon of life is the regular ledges of a cocktail bar; whose ingenuity of technique consists of inventing obvious and commonplace excuses to get one character off the stage and bring another one in; plays in which the acting has become so refined that it has ceased to be acting at all; plays that have been dead a hundred years before they have been written. Poetry, passion, song, rhythm, rhetoric; exaggeration of emotion and gesture have been gutted out of the so-called modern drama; it has been purified out of existence. The wedding garments are shown to us, but the bride and bridegroom have been driven away. Prohibition has laid its heavy, fat and ugly hand on the drama; she has been made sober by the law of technique, and will never come to her senses till she takes to drink again.

Classicism, Romanticism and Expressionism have each given of their quality to the drama. Realism, the portrayal of real life on the stage, has failed, for the simple reason that real life cannot be shown on the stage; realism has always failed to be real. Nothing can be more artificial than the play that claims to be true to life. In setting out to gain everything it has lost all. Realism died years ago, and the sooner we bury the body the better.

The new form in drama will take qualities found in classical, romantic and expressionistic plays, will blend them together, breathe the breath of life into the new form and create a new drama. It will give rise to a new form of acting, a new form of production, a new response in the audience; author, actors and audience will be in communion with each other — three in one and one in three. If a play is what it ought to be it must be a religious function, whether it be played before a community of thousands or a community of ten. Gay, farcical, comic or tragical, it must be, not the commonplace portrayal of the trivial events in the life of this man or that woman, but a commentary of life itself. That is the main thing to be done if the drama of today is to be in the main stream of the great drama of the past. To achieve this, the veneration of realism, or, as Archer called it, pure imitation, must cease, and imagination be crowned queen of the drama again. If we are to confine the drama to a sober and exact imitation of life, then the drama is dead, for life itself is much more interesting than its sober and actual imitation. What realists take for life is but a faintly warmed-up corpse.

WITHIN THE GATES AND WITHOUT (1934)*

BROOKS ATKINSON has said in a recent number of *The New York Times* that the battle for and against *Within the Gates* still flames; and Mr Mason Brown has just sighed out a question asking if it is conceivable that *The Plough and the Stars* and *Within the Gates* were written by the same man. Mr Ruhl has shouted out that any mention of the death of realism in the drama (though no-one has said anything of the sort) is nonsense, and to be mocked into silence. Some bless the play, others curse it, so that we may all safely say that the play, at least, has the power of leaving lukewarm none who have ventured to read it or have gone to see it performed. Indeed it has had a strange effect upon some of the critics, provoking them to say things out loud without thinking. Recently in a short article boxed in a leading newspaper, Mr Sinclair Lewis has valorously stated that the critics have a perfect right to criticise rubbish by him, or rubbish written by Mr Elmer Rice, or, indeed, rubbish written by anyone else. Of course this right is theirs, but what about the right of others to criticise the rubbish written by the critics? Some of them are stunned stiff when anyone ventures to raise a shield and lower a lance as they go galloping round on their horses flinging out challenges and never expecting them to be answered.

Mr Mason Brown, in a recent article, gathers the group who hate *Within The Gates* and the group that love it, and turns them into two persons, calling one the Enthusiastic Champion, and the other the Conscientious Objector. Near the end of the same article (when he has probably forgotten what he said at the be-

---

* Reviews by Arthur Ruhl and John Mason Brown appeared in the New York *Herald Tribune* and *Evening Post*, respectively, in Oct. 1934; Brown's criticism was reprinted in his book, *Two on the Aisle* (New York, 1938). It is uncertain whether O'Casey's reply was published at the time.

ginning) he ridicules the idea that the form and method of the
play may have an influence upon future dramatists, but evidently
fails to see that the play has already had an influence upon himself, for he turns those who like the play and those who don't
into symbols. He tells us that the play condemns everything from
Genesis to Winston Churchill. The play condemns neither
the one nor the other. It makes certain characters say certain
things about them and that is all. Does he think that because a
character calls the intrusion of a politician's name into a discussion 'an irrelevant triviality' that the politician becomes one,
or that the dramatist agrees with what his characters say? That's
a curious way of criticising. I suppose because a character is
made to say 'I'm not responsible for what Einstein says', that
ridicule is being made of the great Jew who discovered a new
universe? If Mr Mason Brown fails to discover the meaning of
a simple thing like that, what are we to think of the rest of his
criticism? Not much, I says.

Again, Mr Brown says that 'the muddy attempt at symbolism
was so flat and tiresome that I began to feel a little more friendly
to the most trivial examples of realism', making him think back
longingly to the hopeless little plays 'dealing with regulation
characters who are, at least, doing recognisable things'; and he
'regrets the harsh words spoken against dialogue getting no
farther than saying "it's not the heat, it's the humidity".'

Well, there you are, and there I ought to leave you, but I
can't, for there is much more to say. 'The most trivial examples
of realism.' Not even trivial, but the most trivial examples of
realism. He got down low enough to find a comparison to
Within the Gates. I wonder has he ever really been antagonistic
to these trivial little examples of realism? I suppose there is
something to be said for these little lice in the lion's mane.
They are so easy to direct, so easy to act, so easy to criticise.
These trivial examples of realism please this critic so well that
he hopes they may stretch out till the crack of doom, so that
nothing new may disturb him. Tuck him up and sing him to
sleep with his heat and humidity plays. A harlot drama that
tricks herself out to please allcomers; a hireling drama that flees

away from the danger of doing anything worthwhile, and this critic is sorry for the harsh things that sometimes he said against them. It's not the heat, it's the humidity — easier to say that than to say, *oh, what a rogue and peasant slave am I*; it's not the heat, it's the humidity — easier to say that than to say *was this the face that launched a thousand ships*; it's not the heat, it's the humidity — easier to say that than to say, *the heaven o'er my head seems made of molten brass.*

Even in the printed page, says he, the play [*Within the Gates*] is a confusing affair in which the author has failed to make his purpose clear. Make his purpose clear! Considering that the play tries to make itself a microcosm of life as we live it today, it is not surprising that the play's purpose isn't quite clear to every eye that saw it, for the simple reason that life isn't quite so clear a theme as Mr Mason Brown evidently thinks it to be. But is civilisation as we know it today the world over quite clear to Mr Brown? As clear to him as the purpose in each of those trivial little examples of realism that he loves so well, but not so wisely? Is the purpose of life as lived today in his own great Republic quite clear to him? Is the purpose of life as lived in the City of New York — to narrow the circle a little — quite clear to him? Nay, is the purpose even of his own life quite clear to him? Is it nothing but the going on forever of seeing and enjoying trivial little examples of realism having in them no higher thought of life than it's the heat rather than the humidity?

He tells us that the play on the printed page has 'a lusty earth-sprung quality in its writing. It rises in some of its poetic outbursts as well as in much of its richly cadenced prose to an eloquence compelling in its force, as it is occasionally breath-taking in its lyric beauty'. He tells us this, yet in another part of his article he seems to deprecate the fact that I consider the play an important one (though I never said so). Well, if it has the qualities he himself says it has, one hasn't to dive down deep to find a reason for thinking it an important play. In the performance, he says, 'the eloquence is muffled to the point of non-existence'. Yet he says the performance was a good one. Well, I am not an actor, neither am I an elocutionist, but were I to recite the speeches given by Brutus and Mark Anthony in *Julius Caesar*, I'll give a guarantee that the eloquence in these speeches wouldn't be muffled to the point of non-existence. So the learned critic simply can't be right in his judgment.

Mr Brown goes on to say that 'O'Casey is not averse to mentioning the Greeks and the Elizabethans (for no apparent reason) in connection with his own drama, and in explaining their influence upon him.' Well, if I mention the Greeks and the Elizabethans in connection with my own drama, and in explaining their influence upon me, I give a reason, don't I, and a very good reason, too. But will Mr Brown tell us where and when and how I have explained the influence of the Greeks and the Elizabethans upon my work? Will he tell us how any artist can explain the influence of another artist, or a group of artists, upon his work in music, or painting, or sculpture? And if it can't be done — then, how could I explain it?

The critic further calls the symbolism ridiculous, and the thinking childish. He doesn't wait to tell us why or how, but simply states in a very dogmatic — and childish — way that the one is ridiculous, and the other childish. That is ridiculous criticism, and reminds one of the disputants in the Park saying, 'You've got your mind, O'Casey, filled with the dialectics of the Greeks and the Elizabethans, and all that sort of thing. We're dealing now with little trivial examples of realism, and not drama; heat and humidity plays, and not drama.' He tells us that 'it would have been greatly to the advantage of his play if he had characterised any of the types as definitely as he described them in *The New York Times*.'[1] Yet in another article, he says that this article only made matters worse, for the article 'was more pretentious than the play'. But he has already told us that it would have been well for the play had it been as clear as the article. But if, as he says, the play be pretentious, and the article more pretentious than the play, then, had the spirit of the article appeared in the play, the play would have been more pretentious still. It would be easier to explain the influence of the

[1] 'From Within the Gates,' *New York Times*, Oct. 21, 1934, reprinted in the present volume, pp. 111–17.

Greeks and the Elizabethans upon my work, than to explain the meaning of what Mason Brown is labouring to say.

He says that a play an author has to write about, and which does not explain itself is hardly a great play. I suppose that a heat and humidity play, readily understood five minutes from the rise of the curtain, must be a very great play indeed. He says that 'one may discover new treasures in a great play each time it is read or seen, but we can't think of a great play that does not say its emotional say to an audience or a reader when it is seen or read for the first time'. We may let this stand, for one end of the sentence makes a liar of the other.

Mr Brown's declaration — for it is a declaration — that O'Casey should go on writing plays similar to *Juno and the Paycock* and *The Plough and the Stars*, shows that Mr Brown doesn't know much about the art of the drama, or any other art, for that matter. For here the critic implores the dramatist to go on imitating himself, and that would be as bad as to imitate another. Directly derivative art is not art at all, and, though I might give another night's enjoyment to Mr Brown, I think too much of the drama to go on imitating myself simply to please him.

I think that some of the symbolism that he ridicules has a wider scope than he imagines. For instance, when he says 'O'Casey is at his best when he writes of the slums and the tenements that he has observed at first hand, and he is at his feeblest when he tries to write of England as he has in *Within The Gates*', we hear the Bishop speaking: 'Go home, O'Casey, to mother Ireland. Show her you realise what a mother really is. Cultivate the habit of thrifty observation, and in a few years you'll be able to write a play far better than the one you've just written now.' Here we find the critic, exactly like the Bishop, piping out of him the same old rot we've heard a thousand times.

He tells us the other day, when reviewing *The Plough and the Stars*, that 'it seems hardly possible that the same man wrote *Within the Gates*, and *The Plough and the Stars*'. Well, he's right here, for once in his lifetime, for the man who wrote *The Plough and the Stars* isn't quite the same man now as he was then. But while the man as he is today could possibly write another play like *The Plough and the Stars*, the man as he then was, could not have written a play like *Within the Gates*. Mason Brown evidently wants me to be the same yesterday, today, and forever, but I have no desire to claim that distinction. Mr Brown writes as if he could, but it isn't a sign of progress. Men may come, and men may change, but Mason Brown's the same forever. Mr Brown makes a valiant effort to push the play called *Personal Appearance* into the canon of drama. He says it pretends to be nothing more than what it is, and it succeeds in doing exactly what it sets out to do. And that is nothing. There's no chance of such plays developing into anything else than what they are. But the sin of Mason Brown is a double one, namely, of pushing *Personal Appearance* into the canon of drama, and of trying to push *Within The Gates* out of it.[1]

[1] This article in MS concluded, as did 'Blasphemy and *The Silver Tassie*', with three lines from Whitman's 'To a Certain Civilian'.

THE CHURCH TRIES TO CLOSE THE GATES
(1935)*

A BUNCH of high-steppers in thought and deed and decency, have banned the performance of *Within the Gates* in Boston. They have proclaimed themselves to be infallible, or almost infallible, judges of what is art in drama and of what is morality in men. They have spoken out on behalf of God, and have said things to provoke a clapping of hands among the angels. Four of these high-steppers are clergymen, and one is the Mayor of the city. Two of the clergy are Jesuits; the third is a member of what is called The Universal Church — whatever that may mean — and the fourth is a Bishop of the Wesleyan Episcopal Church. Let us take these learned and lofty gentlemen, stand them in a row for all to see, and put them through the first degree of asking questions, ordering them to speak up so that all may hear what they say.

First we shall dismiss the honourable Mayor as unimportant for our purpose, feeling that if we ventured to ask him a question, he would run over to someone for an answer. So stand down, Mr Mayor, and run along home, like a good little boy.

We call now on the Rev. Bishop Charles Wesley Burns to open the proceedings, assuring him that we shall listen carefully to what he says, promising not to keep him long, but to dismiss him with a question or two.

'While I was in Maine,' says Bishop Charles Wesley Burns, 'my preachers held a meeting, and when I got back I was told they had voted to protest against the play because of what they had been told about it by Father Sullivan; and so I added my

---

* *Within the Gates* was forbidden performance in Boston by the mayor, F. W. Mansfield, after representations from religious bodies. It is uncertain whether this article was ever published.

name to the protest.' Commending coos of the Methodist doves to the croak of the Jesuit raven. The Sheep driving the shepherd. Here we have a Bishop, a leader of organised religion, eminent in the great City of Boston, deciding a question of art and morals, not on first-hand, not even on second-hand, but on third-hand evidence. He decides a question on what his preachers told him of what Father Sullivan told them. Men of Boston, what think ye of this prime fellow? A case of the Irish proverb, 'a woman told me that a woman told her'. There was no witness for the defence at the meeting; no one to whisper a word for the author; only the accuser and a prejudiced jury were present when the vote of condemnation was given. Is this a sample of Christian controversial decency and fair play? Here we have a try-out of the fairmindedness of organised religion. We've nothing more to say to you, Bishop Charles Wesley Burns; you can go, and God speed you.

We call now on the Rev. Father Russell M. Sullivan, Society of Jesus, representing the Boston College of Catholic Organisations, and Head of the Legion of Decency — quite an imposing array of connections — and listen carefully to what he has to say. 'Any religious affiliation,' he says, 'would protest (he calls them affiliations, mind you, not churches) against the sympathetic portrayal of immorality, and all rightminded citizens, too, would protest against these things described in the play, and even more so the setting forth of the utter futility of religion as an effective force in meeting the problems of the world.'

Coming to the low realistic level to which this Jesuit has brought the play, we shall meet him on his own ground, sauce his sayings with a few remarks, and pepper him with a few questions. All 'rightminded citizens,' mind you, will [act] immediately in accord with the expressed opinions of this reverend priest. All those who refuse to be spooned into his opinion of the play must be wrong-minded citizens. There's considerate arrogance for you, blended with a little spiritual pride, if you ask me anything. He has gathered under his arm, as a hen gathereth her chickens under her wing, all the righteous and rightminded men in Boston. In all humility it may be mentioned that, in spite of the Jesuit's self-righteous regard for his own opinion, among those who think *Within the Gates* above smut and filthiness there may be some who are not far from the kingdom of heaven.

And where does the 'sympathetic regard for immorality' come in? Is it immoral for a young woman to desire motherhood? Or to want to earn a simple living without having to prostitute herself to her boss? Or even to go away with a young man who loves her and give to him what most women give to the men they love? Is sex in itself a sin? What these reverend gentlemen are terribly concerned about is that this thing may be done without their consent in writing. This Jesuit reminds me of a big-headed Irish policeman who went over to a group of young men and girls rollicking together in a Dublin Park, and shouted at them, 'Eh, you there; see here, this sort of thing'll have to stop!'

Is the life force which we call sex from God or from the Devil? From God, the priest would be constrained to reply, but this force in man can be perverted by the Devil and used to advance the confines of his kingdom. Right, but so, also, can the force invested in a man that becomes a member of the Society of Jesus. A play can be padlocked out of a theatre, but the Devil can't be padlocked out of the Church.

Let this question be answered: is it immoral for a man to take a woman for his wife, or a woman to take a man for her husband without the consent of a Jesuit, or a Methodist Bishop, or a member of the Universal Church? Let those with whom we argue say yes or no to this. And is 'thou shalt not commit adultery' any more a sin than 'thou shalt not bear false witness against thy neighbour'? Why, when priests speak of immorality do they only mean the things connected with sex? Finer minds may find many things as and much more immoral than sex. These priests seem to have an original conception of the moral law and of Christian ethics.

What immorality is there in the implication of the play regarding the Church's ineffectiveness in meeting the problems of the world, except the immorality of touching the conventional churchman on a sore point? We are always restless and angry when failure is pointed out to us. Sullivan barks and tries to bite when he finds himself cornered. What effective part is the Church taking in meeting the problems of today? In England today one word from Lloyd George takes up more attention than a rigmarole from a bench of bishops, simply because the bishops have nothing to say, and old Lloyd George has. The Catholic Fold meets the problems of unemployment, peace, war, financial collapse, political chaos, sex, by an encyclical on Communism and Contraception; founds the Legion of Decency, and bans a play. As if decency in life began and ended round a woman's skirt. This is the wide range that these religious 'affiliations' give to decency in life.

Let us listen to and reply to some of the things said by the Rev. Terence Connelly, the 'noted dramatic Jesuit critic', who, apparently, has forgotten more about drama than we ever learned.[1]

'We are told,' he says, 'it is symbolic. Symbolic of what? To me it is symbolic of the futility of religion. The truth of the matter is that there is in the world today a religion that is still as effective in salvaging the world's derelicts as it was in the days of Christ Himself.' What does he mean by religion? Is it the ecclesiastical cliques and Legions of Decency of Boston? Is religion what Fathers Connelly and Sullivan and the Boston Methodists think it to be? Can no wind of religion blow outside of their little gathering? The play is certainly descriptive of the religion as avowed by this clique. In its banning of the play it has demonstrated its fear and cowardice. In his avowal of the salvaging of the world's derelicts, and in its banning of the play it has definitely joined the ranks of the Down and Out. They love to be ever paddling and playing among the derelicts. By honouring and glorifying them, it has given them power to add to their numbers. Christ didn't come into the world to found a Church that was to spend its time salvaging derelicts. From all we know He didn't spend a lot of His time fondling the derelicts He met on His walk through life. But His followers now revel in this lust

[1] Drama critic of the Jesuit journal *America*.

for disease. The mean, the miserable, the crippled, the whining, all are petted and praised, and the world cannot be full enough of them to satisfy the needs of many Christian leaders. Salvaging of derelicts — a sorry way of meeting effectively the problems of the world.

'O'Casey,' goes on Terence Connelly, 'has written on immoral subjects frequently in the past'; and then he makes this statement: 'In art as in life the end does not justify the means.' As in life so in art the means of its creation can never be immoral. The sex force that creates life cannot in itself be immoral, and neither can the imagination of an artist in the creation of a work of art. Milton imagined a far greater figure when he created Satan in *Paradise Lost* than the figure of Christ he created in *Paradise Regained*. And many a naked woman was the 'immoral means' used in the creation of a beautiful picture. But I suppose we'll shortly have these gents hunting these pictures out of our National Galleries.

'The whole play,' says he, 'is drenched with sex.' Well, there's quite a lot of it in life, and, if Terence reads the records of his own Church regarding the enforcement of celibacy on the clergy, he'll find them drenched in sex too. 'Wholesome, cultured, and refined people are reticent on the subjects that St Paul says should not be mentioned among us.' St Paul mentions them a number of times himself, and the Bible isn't quite so reticent on these matters as Terence Connelly would lead us to believe. And some of us are too reticent about these things. I know from first-hand knowledge a young girl who suffered a dangerous breakdown because of the reticence of the nuns in the convent who had charge of her young life had it deep in their silly heads that nothing should be said about these things. Reticence, indeed, and these are the first to go about bellowing of lust, filth, and obscenity where there is only seriousness, courage, and a hatred of sanctimonious sham.

He tells us that the love song in the play is but a lyric of lust, and a symbol of death. Imagine him linking up love and life with death. Imagine a Jesuit blaming a play that sings of life, and calling it a symbol of death. And the members of his own

Church, rightly or wrongly, are fed on the symbols of death and instruments of torture. How often have I seen the poor people of Dublin forking out their weekly penny to keep up the membership of the Sodality of Bona Mors, every thought outside of their day to day needs a thought of fear; fear, fear, fear, never realising that how they lived was more important than how they died. And are they not now trying to get the glory of canonisation for a Dublin workingman [Matt Talbot] who was found dead with hoops of steel round his body that had been there for years, and that had eaten into the flesh. And this Jesuit talks of *Within the Gates* as a symbol of death.

Now listen to the last thing said by this gentle, charitable Jesuit: 'There are degenerates who delight in looking at raw human flesh. And in art there are those who demand life in the raw. But normal human beings swoon at the sight of human flesh exposed. They require the silken curtain of the skin to tone down the sight and give the human flesh the normal colour that is the symbol of life.' It seems to me that any man who sees an analogy of raw human flesh exposed to *Within the Gates* must have a twist towards the abnormal. But let that pass. If I were to put on the stage life in the raw as I myself have sometimes, often, in fact, experienced it, our critic would throw a swoon right enough, and would have excellent cause for it too. But this implication that those who do not swoon at the sight of human flesh exposed are abnormal and degenerate would be scandalous if it were not stupid. Why this Jesuit fellow has in his mind the more violent forms of cruelty and sadism. And he links these up with my play. Oh, Christians, Christians. Why, man, there are at this moment millions of men and women looking at human flesh exposed and they are calm and undisturbed, normal, healthy, and gentle, and a good job for the unfortunate injured that these people don't fall in a swoon. My own kid suffered a very severe burn on his hand some time ago; the sight was rather horrible, but I didn't swoon, neither did his mother, neither did the doctor who attended him, and neither did the kid himself. Were we all degenerates because we didn't fall down in a faint? And to think, looking at the question from another point of view, that skin covers the body because we'd be too sensitive to look at the flesh, is too funny altogether. I suppose a lot of animals have fur on them because they're far too sensitive to bear the sight of their skins! These persons either know nothing, or pretend that they know nothing, about life. Do they know anything about conception? Or anything about the agony and sweat of bringing a child into the world?

Father Terence tells us that the play is 'the story of a harlot and the life she leads'. How does he know that the play is a portrayal of the life a harlot leads? Has he had experience? The life of a harlot can be known only to the harlot herself. And as for expressing sympathy in the play, I must ask who am I to condemn? What she is and how she lives does small harm compared with the high hypocrisies of formal and sentimental religion or politics.

Father Terence says that 'O'Casey has often written on immoral subjects. It appears first in the incident of the betrayal of Mary Boyle in *Juno and the Paycock*'. Not a word about the killing of the young Republican by Free State followers, or the killing of the young Free Stater by Republican adherents. There's nothing immoral about killing, I suppose. No thrill in that. A touch of sex and his nose begins to sniff. Is this Jesuitical morality, or is it the morality of Boston's Legion of Decency? And what about the Church's sanctifying the union of eighty years with come and kiss me sweet and twenty?

Preaching on 'The Church and The Bond of Marriage', a priest told his congregation that 'if the husband interferes in the kitchen things will go wrong. The husband pays the bills, eats the food, and praises the cooking. If the pudding's like putty, don't say so. Do your best with it, and see the doctor quietly. The husband likes to hang pictures. The wife might hang them better, but she needn't tell him so. Put them straight when he's out. He won't notice.' This is some of the silly chat that tries to pass muster for ghostly advice to married people. A fat lot this fool celibate knows about the problems and anxieties of married life. Another — a Dominican — preaching on social questions says, 'a poor man is charged with stealing a loaf or something of that kind. The magistrate — confound his impertinence — rebukes him for having seven children, instead of fining him five shillings and having done with it.' Another bright example of the way these fellows understand the social problems of today. Fine him five shillings and be done with it. A poor man steals a loaf, and if he be only fined five shillings, the question is solved. Thank you, brother; you mean well, but you've a hell of a lot to learn yet.

And it is strange that the playwright who writes so often about 'immoralities' should be asked to write a story for a magazine to be sold for the benefit of a boys' school attached to the Order of St Joseph; or to give an autographed copy of his play to be sold to help provide funds for the Redemptorists; or promised a share in the Holy Sacrifice of the Mass if he sold a bunch of Sweep Tickets.

We have kept to the level fixed by the priests and the clergy that got the play banned, and have answered them according to their folly, neglecting to write about the new form, the music, song, and dance in the play, leaving these to be talked of with higher minds instead of wasting time with those who have got their noses so deep in smut that they smell it everywhere. However, we may give a hint to the General of the Jesuits that while Father Terence Connelly is, without any doubt, a true and faithful member of his Order, he lacks a lot as a dramatic critic.

But what do the men and women of Boston think of it all? The play does not chant of death, but sings of life, and that is the thing that these persons do not like about it. Are the citizens of Boston going to dance only to whatever tune may be chosen by these clerical quintuplets of Massachusetts?

BADTIME STORY (c. 1955)*

There are quite a few chaps who think they should be able to get all they want from a girl for a cup of tea and a wafer-biscuit, and are unhappy if they find they have to pay more than what they thought the right market-value for their pleasure; while *les girls* are ever on the *qui vive* to wheedle and pluck all they can get out of their clients; and the battle of wits creates many a laugh many a time out of the manoeuvres, as, I hope, it does in this little play [*Bedtime Story*]. The child of this world, Angela Nightingale, is far cleverer, wittier, and more alive, than the child of light, John Jo Mulligan. She is more honest, too, as wickedness is as often as virtue, for piety is often stained with pride, while wickedness is in too much of a hurry to bother about it. She is forthright about her fault, he bothered with anxiety about pretence; eager to keep, not himself, but his little name unspotted from the world. Angela's cleverness, her honesty, her gift of seeing through another, and her humour, are lost, ill-used, or not used, a condition happening to many another woman, too. (I have often wondered why no one has ever thought of suggesting that there should be a few women on every meeting between Heads of Governments, women like, say, Mrs Eleanor Roosevelt of the United States, Mrs Pandit Nehru of India, and Miss Josephine MacNeill of Ireland, at present in Sweden as Ireland's Ambassador. They might bring the loftier minds of the men down to a lower level of sober reality.)

To return to the bedpost: there have been, and still are, a

* This article was almost certainly written as a programme note for an American production of O'Casey's one-act comedy *Bedtime Story*; the date is unknown, though probably late in the 1950s.

multitude of bedtime stories on the stage, and beds and bed-rooms have often, too often, appeared as brief, but important, chronicles of our time, making, as it were, poor life look as if it were a monstrous habit of getting into bed and getting out of one. *Bedtime Story* is another, a short one as things go on the stage, but the characters in this little play wear their rue with in-difference. It shows what odd things may happen when a pietist ceases to pray for a moment; how bewildered and lost he becomes because of a first lingerieing glance at lace on a petticoat. As Helen's unto that of Faustus, so the lips of Angela nearly sucked his soul away; or, maybe, nearly brought a little life into the shrivelled one John Jo Mulligan had. There are many varieties of man, nationally and individually, displaying differing phases of grandeur and meanness; but all of us have one thing in com-mon — at some time or another, each of us succeeds in making himself or herself look ridiculous. We cannot escape it. It is as if God made us so that He could have a good laugh at us now and again; but He did the decent thing in giving us the grand gift of being able to laugh at ourselves; for when we laugh at others, we are laughing at ourselves. If we keep our eyes keen and our ears open, we can catch a glimpse of humour in all things, except in the first cry given by a new-born babe, adding a new voice to the voices of the world, and the last sigh given by a life leaving the light of the world to go into the darkness of death.

Here is a little play in which there are neither good nor bad judged seriously, with a laugh at the beginning and another at the end. It is recorded somewhere that Jupiter, becoming fed up with man whom he had made, thinking them all either rogues or vixens, set out to destroy them all, but Minerva halted him (the Woman again), saying, 'Nonsense! They're only ridiculous little creatures who have a vague aspect, seen far or seen near; if you called them bad, they would appear bad; if you called them good, they would appear good,' adding that there wasn't one among men who wouldn't puzzle her owl to know whether any one of the humans was fundamentally good or bad. So, if Minerva's owl couldn't make them out, who are we to judge the ridiculous little characters appearing in this little play?

So here is an unconsidered trifle in the fashion of a Schnitzler *Anatole* play in the O'Casey style; a play, not of the elegant and charming characters of an *Anatole* version, but about mean people doing mean things, but redeemed, let us hope, by embedding their meanness within a loud laugh.[1]

---

[1] *Bedtime Story* is subtitled 'An Anatole [sic] Burlesque', which is presumably a reference to the series of seven one-act plays by Arthur Schnitzler entitled *Anatol*. These sketches, using a small group of people, skilfully realise the problems and conflicts of love.

O'CASEY IN HUNGARIAN COSTUME (1957)*

I DID not know that a play of mine [*Juno and the Paycock*] was to be published in the tongue of the Hungarian people till a letter from the editors of the magazine, *Tájékoztató*, told me so, adding a request for a few words about the play, about other work, and about my plans for the future. It is delightful to know that a play of mine is to be changed into an Hungarian dress, and I hope that the play may wear the gayer colours well and proudly.

The play, *Juno and the Paycock*, concerns itself with the time of the calamitous Civil War in Ireland, a fight between two parties over a few words included within the Treaty made by one of them with England. The difference between the two parties was trivial, almost insignificant, not worth a fight with fists much less with cannon, machine-gun, and rifle. The alternative Treaty proposed by de Valera's Party (now governing Ireland, with de Valera as Prime Minister) consisted of a few differing words that added nothing and took nothing away from the original document. But they went to war about it, and devastated Ireland between them. The members of the contending parties, too, were all of the same Faith, all good Catholics, yet they tortured and slaughtered each other with vigour and venom, in the way that Christians do, have done, and will do again. During the fight, father was against the son, brother against brother, girl against her lover; all fighting it out for a cause no one understood, and for which very few cared; while the mothers, alone sensible and suffering, bore the brunt of it all among the workers, knowing, probably, that when it would be all over, they and their families would be living in the same old way,

* An introduction to *Juno and the Paycock* for Hungarian readers, published in *Tájékoztató* (Budapest), Oct. 1957.

denying themselves things that the rent might be paid, and uncertain where the food for the next day would come from.

In the play the impact is shown on two worker families, on two mothers each of whom has lost a son; and, if there be a message in the play, I imagine it to be that a Civil War should be waged only for a deep and a great cause, like the overthrow of tax paid without representation that evoked the American War of Independence, the overthrow of Feudalism as in the French Revolution, and the establishment of political and economic rule and ownership by the people as in the October Revolution of the Soviets. We should, however, be careful of personal idealism; good as it may be and well-meaning, its flame in a few hearts may not give new life and new hope to the many, but dwindle into ghastly and futile funeral pyres in which many are uselessly destroyed and enormous damage done to all.

Juno and the Paycock is now a faraway effort. Since its writing, I have written fifteen other plays and eight other books, so that this drama-star is away down on the horizon of a past life, and now, to me, shows so faintly as to be hardly visible. As for taking on any plan for the future, there is a very uncertain future for one on the verge of his seventy-eighth year — certain only that the future will bring the end. But like Tennyson, the English poet, we can say,

> *Tho' much is taken, much abides; and tho'*
> *We are not now that strength which in old days*
> *Moved earth and heaven: that which we are, we are;*
> *[One equal temper of heroic hearts,]*
> *Made weak by time and fate, but strong in will*
> *To strive, to seek, to find, and not to yield.*

We Irish do not know very much about Hungary; we have heard of and honoured Kossuth and Deák as great patriots, and, long ago, an Irish national leader wrote a book called *The Resurrection of Hungary*,[1] advocating a determination to unite all Irish Nationalists to wage the fight made by the Hungarian people, and secure for ourselves a Dual Monarchy; the English

[1] *The Resurrection of Hungary: a parallel for Ireland* by Arthur Griffith (James Duffy, Dublin, 1904).

King to be head of both nations, but each nation to have the making of its own laws, and the preservation of its own language and traditional institutions. So you see, we have heard of you; and one of the Irish, a lad named O'Casey, sends his warm wishes and an old man's blessing to Hungary and the great Hungarian people.

O'CASEY'S DRAMA-BONFIRE (1957)*

THE letter from Comrade Kholopov telling me that *The Bishop's Bonfire* was to be published in *Zvezda* came as a surprise to me. During my time, I have had many surprises, happy ones, and very sad surprises; but this surprise is to be reckoned among those which were pleasant and gratifying of them all.

The editor has kindly asked me to say a few words about my recent works, and the place occupied among these by the present play to be printed in *Zvezda*. The writing of the play is but one of the many activities that will go on in my life till Time says It is now the hour to fold those hands of yours, and go away into your long sleep. When I look back on the long view of seventy-eight years, focusing a steady stare on the work done, it all looks very small, and gives no call or warrant to go about with a flag in my hand.

I find it difficult, and have always done so, to talk or write about my work; what I have done, what I intend to try to do. I am what is called a shy fellow, dreading to meet a new acquaintance but, invariably, if the newcomer be anyway human, I make friends in a few minutes. As for the work I do at the moment, I am writing down thoughts on things I have heard, things I have read, and things that I have seen; thoughts in flashes and thoughts born out of slower meditation. I have written another long three-act play called, at the moment, *The Drums of Father Ned*; a play of comment and action, of hope and resolution, of young and fresh thought clashing with, and overcoming, the thoughts and worn-out ideals of the old and fading; all written against the background of the Irish 'Tostal', a yearly festival of promise in my country, Ireland;

* Article published in *Zvezda* (Organ of the Union of Soviet Writers), Leningrad, in the first issue for 1958.

a festival of drama, music, dancing, folk-art, national games, and films, lasting a fortnight within the month of May. Mixing with the work of writing comments and plays, I write many letters (though now I tire more quickly, and cannot answer as many as I should), then I do odd jobs about our flat easing a little the tedious routine of housework that seems to be forever in front of my wife to be done between sun-up and sun-down.

The play, *The Bishop's Bonfire*, was performed for the first time in Dublin, where I was born so many years ago. At first, I hesitated to give permission, for I knew the play would be abused by cleric and critic; but as it was a good Catholic, and a very intelligent man,[1] who asked for it, I gave consent, and it was done in Dublin's principal theatre for a suggested season of three weeks. It caused a great commotion, great crowds assembling outside the theatre, not to boo or to protest, but to cheer the name of the author — one of my astonishing and pleasant surprises. Those who had booked their seats had to fight their way through the throng, and many who wished to see the play found it impossible to get in, including the American Ambassador and Madame Pandit Nehru. As I expected, the Dublin drama critics, with one exception, denounced the play, and many Catholic clerics joined in the condemnation, and there was a raging controversy in the Dublin and other Irish papers. But they had no effect upon the success of the play, for, instead of running for the programmed three weeks, it ran for six to packed houses and great applause through the Catholic season of Lent, a seven-weeks' period when good Catholics are exhorted to keep away from amusements of all kinds, when all dance-halls are closed, and when everyone is expected to deny himself and herself all pleasure, pray for their sins, and devote themselves to good works — contributing to Catholic charities and the needs of the church. The play is still remembered vividly, and, I am told, that Dubliners look eagerly forward to another play from the same author. So during the Irish Festival for 1958, it may be that the new play, *The Drums of Father Ned*, will strut the stage in Dublin. The President of the Festival is eager

[1] Mr Cyril Cusack.

to read the play, and hopes to God (he says) that it may be the centre of Festival Drama in Dublin.[1]

The Bishop's Bonfire itself is an effort in the form of drama to picture Ireland's present condition, social, economic, and political. To weave in and out, mingling together, the many and bitter complexities of Irish life and thought; her religion which is formal, bent on power over everything the people possess, over what the people do, and over everything the people say on a platform, in novel, poem, or play. A Customs Officer, at the port, for instance, if he has a suspicion that a book may contain something either 'indecent or irreligious', can seize it and hold it till the censorship have read it, and made a declaration about it in one way or the other, a period of time that may run into over a year. My last book, *The Green Crow*, has been seized in this way, and still is kept from any possible sale in Ireland. I, however, am used to this, for most of my other books stay banned there. But I have many friends in Ireland, many more Irish friends who live in England, who find here, at least, a release from the suffocating interference of the clerics in all that they think or do.

The play tries to symbolise the conditions, the superstitions, the frantic obsession with sex (the church in Eire has made it the one sin), the fleeing from their country of the young (more than forty thousand flee from Ireland every year, and many country districts now have no one living there between the ages of eighteen and twenty-five), so that the population declines year by year, reducing it by half during the last ninety years — from eight millions to below four millions; the difficulty courting couples experience with the clerics watching their every movement (some time ago, a courting couple were each fined forty shillings or a month's imprisonment for kissing each other in a street); and the dreadful fear now stifling the Irish writers of saying anything critical about the serious things of life. Fortunately, so far (though it is often called for) there is no official censorship over plays, as there is on books, and so it is possible

---

[1] This hope was to be rudely shattered a few months later by the Festival Committee's fear of clerical disapproval: see 'On the Banks of the Ban', pp. 146–9.

to put in a play what one cannot put in a novel — that is, of course, if one can get the play performed. However, there is a great demand for a play of mine in Dublin, and all lovers of the theatre there look forward to one appearing, and so the clerics find it very hard to keep me from speaking to my Irish comrades in the form of a play.[1]

The intelligent and educated Irish are, I believe, becoming impatient with, and resentful of, the interference of priest and bishop in every phase of their life. Some of them have spoken out, and even de Valera (Ireland's present Taoiseach — Prime Minister) has publicly repudiated the Bishop of Galway on a question of religious intolerance. I try to show this awakening, this thrust forward in thought, this new resolution, in my latest play, *The Drums of Father Ned*.

Along with the work of letter-writing, housework, play-writing, and the making of another book, I have to think of myself, to learn a few more things before I go; to learn more of Science in all its varying appearances, of the curious beliefs that men hold about phenomena, natural, and what they call super-natural; about the flowers of the field, and about world ways in politics and social activities. And, above all, there is the work for peace; to do a little to help those who call for peace in our time, and for all time, till we learn that life in this world is for all to think and do to make it, life, more secure, more enjoyable, more productive in goods, in games, in literature, art, music, and theatre; the day when the banner flying over the whole world of life will be an everlasting peace, an understanding friendship, and joy and security for all.

Then there are my other friends — the birds. We have a tiny garden with a small grass sward, lots of bright flowers, and a few flowering shrubs. Here, I sit when the sun shines, and the birds come for fat that I save for them — a lovely bull-finch, a blackbird, a linnet, and an impudent robin who perches on the arm of my chair the moment I appear. I love them, for birds, too, are part of our lovely life.

[1] It would be extremely difficult to equal the unconscious irony of this passage.

F

COCKADOODLE DOO (1958)*

THERE is a little bi-monthly magazine called *Encore* dealing solely with the theatre, published here in England. Its last issue [Sept.–Oct. 1958] writes mainly about the newer English playwrights and what they have done. The leading article says: 'The minute a newcomer evidences the slightest talent, the red carpet unrolls, a dozen doors fly open, the options and contracts pour in. . . . Our playwrights, it would appear, have never had it so good. Yet, despite all the coaxing and cossetting the results, that is the bulk of the plays we finally see on the stage, are depressingly inadequate.' Well, England has never put down a green carpet for me, which doesn't shock, for the fact is that Ireland never did either, and won't, as far as I can see, hasten to set one down within any day to come. Recently, in a moment of mistaken enthusiasm, the Tostal Drama Committee took the green carpet out of its dark corner to lay it down for O'Casey and James Joyce, but my Lord, the Catholic Archbishop of Dublin, said No, shook a warning finger at the Committee, and the green carpet was hurriedly shoved back again into its dark corner before the Committee had even started to unroll it. Not that either green or red carpet matters a damn, for neither can add a cubit to a playwright's stature, or give him any additional inspiration, any quality other than what is innate and has been developed within himself.

There are eight newcomers to the drama in a photograph on the cover [of *Encore*] not numbering among them Mr Osborne, yet it is said that the bulk of the plays are distressingly inad-

* Part of this article was published in *The New York Times* on Nov. 9, 1958, under the title 'O'Casey's Credo'; it was intended as an introduction to the first production of *Cock-a-doodle Dandy* in New York.

equate — a polite way of saying that none of them has as yet written a striking play. Perhaps it is that the number should have been seven, for eight isn't a holy one. Why these plays are inadequate is a question I don't intend to answer for the simple reason that I don't know; adding the belief that a playwright has enough to do with his own work without bothering about the work of others. I am busy trying to make the plays I write striking, if I can; or, at least, give them an adequate dramatic quality that will make them worthy of the actors, the director, and the audience.

The first thing I try to do is to make a play live: live as a part of life, and live in its own right as a work of drama. Every character, every life, however minor, to have something to say comic or serious, and to say it well. Not an easy thing to do. These are the commonest things around us. We see them everywhere we go; see what they do, hear what they say; often laugh, sometimes wonder. But there are other parts, phases of life, and these, to my mind, should be prominent in the play. Above all, there is the imagination of man and that of the playwright; the comic, the serious and the poetical imagination; and, to my mind, these too should flash from any play worthy of an appearance on a stage; the comic imagination as in *The Frogs*; the sad imagination as in *The Dream Play*. Blake thought imagination to be the soul; Shaw thought it to be the Holy Ghost, and, perhaps, they weren't far out; for it is the most beautiful part of life whether it be on its knees in prayer or gallivanting about with a girl.

To me what is called naturalism, or even realism, isn't enough. They usually show life at its meanest and commonest, as if life never had time for a dance, a laugh, or a song. I always thought that life had a lot of time for these things, for each was a part of life itself; and so I broke away from realism into the chant of the second act of *The Silver Tassie*. But one scene in a play as a chant or a work of musical action and dialogue was not enough, so I set about trying to do this in an entire play, and brought forth *Cock-a-doodle Dandy*. It is my favourite play; I think it is my best play — a personal opinion; the minds of others, linked with time, must decide whether I'm wrong or right.

The play is symbolical in more ways than one. The action manifests itself in Ireland, the mouths that speak are Irish mouths; but the spirit is to be found in action everywhere: the fight made by many to drive the joy of life from the hearts of men; the fight against this fight to vindicate the right of the joy of life to live courageously in the hearts of men. It isn't the clergy alone who booh and bluster against this joy of life in living, in dance, song, and story (many clerics, even Bishops, are fair, broadminded, and help the arts; like the Catholic Bishop of Ferns and Leighlin, who is the worthy Patron of the Wexford Opera Festival); who interfere in the free flow of thought from man to man. Playwrights and poets have had, are having, a share in squeezing the mind of man into visions of woe and great lamentations. Not only is there none who doeth good; no, not one, with them; but also they seem determined to deny the right of man to a laugh. They labour hard to get us all down. Joyce said that 'God may be a cry in the street', and O'Casey says now that He may be a laugh or a song in the street, too. Political fellas in the U.S.A., in the U.S.S.R., in England, and especially in Ireland — everywhere in fact — political fellas run out and shout down any new effort made to give a more modern slant or a newer sign to any kind of artistic thought or imagination; menacing any unfamiliar thing appearing in picture, song, poem, or play. They are fools, but they are menacing fools, and should be fought everywhere they shake a fist, be they priest, peasant, prime minister, or proletarian. To discuss and argue about these things is fine, and if the discussion be sincere, can but lead to a wider knowledge of all things; but when hateful ignorance rushes out, and tries to down the artist with a bawl, it is high time to cry a halt!

The Cock in the play, of course, is the joyful, active spirit of life as it weaves a way through the Irish scene (for, like Joyce, it is only through an Irish scene that my imagination can weave a way), within the Irish shadows or out in the Irish sunshine, if it is to have a full, or, at least, a fair, chance to play. So the

Cock dances and crows, rousing up commotion among the young and the souls zealous for life, and consternation and hatred among those who demand denial, and the necessity to keep the mind well within the dark; rousing up controversy between the courageous and all who are afraid of others and equally afraid of themselves. In spite of the fanciful nature of the play, almost all the incidents are factual — the priest that struck the blow, the rough fellows man-handling the young, gay girl, the bitter opposition to any sign of the strange ways of a man with a maid, the old, menacing fool, full of false piety, going round inflicting fear of evil things on all who listen to him; and, above all, through the piety, through the fear, the never-ending quest for money. In spite, too, of the fantasy and the fear, there is courage, reason, and laughter in the play, and I hope that with its shape and form, and all that is within them, those who see it may have a gay and a thoughtful time. So, to end this explanation, I leave the play in the hands of actors, director, designer, and in yours, dear playgoers, turning my last words into a quotation from the poet Yeats:

> *Lift up the head*
> *And clap the wings,*
> *Red Cock, and crow !*

ON THE BANKS OF THE BAN (1963)*

I HAVE lived a troublesome life in Ireland, in my youth hard times in the body, and in my manhood years a hard time in the spirit. Hardship in my young days taught me how to fight hard, for if that characteristic wasn't developed then, it meant that one became either a slave or a lickspittle. So I learned how to resist all aggressive attempts to make me a docile one, and could hit back as hard as he who could hit hardest. This gift (for an earned gift it is) kept within me when I reached the world of thought as it had been in the world of hard labour — at times, I fear, fighting what I thought to be aggression where none was meant. Indeed, had I been Adam, I think I should have resisted the angel with his sword of flaming fire that drove him and his Eve from the Garden of Eden.

When the door of the Abbey Theatre opened softly to let me through to Drama's land of good pasture, I imagined I would find a land of Canaan, one flowing with milk and honey; but I found the honey to be often bitter, the milk sour, and that figs had to be plucked from spiky thistles. The first three plays, *Juno, The Plough and the Stars,* and *The Shadow of a Gunman,* always hailed in Ireland now as O'Casey's great plays, when they appeared on the Abbey stage, were received by poet, critic, playwright, and novelist with biting scorn and decided condemnation; but then the great Yeats stood behind the plays, so they sailed on and off the stage safe and smiling.

Then came the discontent of *The Silver Tassie,* when Yeats opposed, and I defended, and all the Irish hooted me and hailed Yeats as more than a Daniel come to judgment. But all this

* This article, written in Dec. 1963, was printed in *The New York Times* on Jan. 5, 1964.

eventually resolved itself, and poet and playwright were friends again.

Lady Gregory passed away, Yeats followed; the Abbey played the three 'great' plays, ignoring all the others. Ireland, to revive her falling spirit, decided to have a National Festival called the 'Tostal', of opera, films, music, and drama, along with the tidying of towns, the painting of door and window in gayer colours, the placing of window-boxes full of flowers on window-sills, the younger priests joining in, all of which I symbolized in a play with the title of *The Drums of Father Ned*. Hearing of this, the festival organizer, a courteous and good man, wrote to me appealing for the play. I sent the manuscript; he replied, saying enthusiastically that the play was an ideal one for the festival; and, hesitantly, I gave it for the festival. A first-class cast and production: all was enthusiasm. I sat back bright-hearted, but with a black spot of doubt in the bright centre.

Suddenly, one morning afterward, reading an English news-paper, I saw in big headlines: 'Catholic Archbishop of Dublin Bans O'Casey and Joyce Plays!' All the pietistic and sacred societies began to blast and bawl, yell and yelp; the Drama Council was frightened. It couldn't well send the play back, so the members handed it over to an insignificant group, whose directors wrote to me demanding written authority to be given to their producer 'to alter the play as he thought fit'. I withdrew the play, the Joyce play was abandoned, and the drama part of the festival sank beneath the dirty waters of the Liffey. No single intellectual in any of Ireland's three universities, Catholic or Protestant, made a single public protest against clerical censorship or the sly secular censorship by the Dublin Drama Festival Committee.[1] This is understandable, for a lecturer doing so might lose his job, or an undergraduate might lose an examination. So to show my resentment at this censorship of myself and Joyce, and my indifference to a clerical ban, I

[1] This statement is not wholly accurate. I know of at least one Catholic lecturer at University College, Dublin, who protested strongly in the Dublin Press at the time the Tostal was abandoned. Such public gestures, however, are lamentably rare in Eire today. *Editor*.

banned all my plays from production in any part of the Irish Republic nearly six years ago.

O'Casey has lifted this ban only for a special reason and a particular period of time lasting no more than five or six weeks. It happened this way: To honour an anniversary of Shakespeare's birth, the Stratford-upon-Avon Shakespeare Society decided to hold an International Drama Festival in the Aldwych Theatre in London. It asked Mr Peter Daubeny to organize it. First-class plays with first-class companies are coming from France, Italy, Germany, Poland, the Soviet Union, and from Greece, and two plays of mine, asked for by Mr Daubeny, are coming from Ireland. None of the [younger] Abbey actors had had experience in acting my plays, so the Abbey appealed to me to allow them to have this experience by public performances before they faced a London audience.

This was a very reasonable request, and O'Casey being a reasonable person, granted it. I gave permission for two or three public performances in Dublin, and this temporary concession has been misconstrued in some places as being a 'Lifting of the Ban'. It is nothing of the sort. I have but given a chance to Irish artists to be at their best among such rich and rare international companions, and a chance to Ireland to do honour to England's great poet and dramatist, William Shakespeare, to whom be honour and glory forever. The old ban remains as fresh and green as a dewy bunch of shamrock at sunrise on a St Patrick's morning.

There had been complaints to God and the Abbey Theatre, some vocal and vehement in the Press, others by younger play-wrights, that the Abbey directors doted on the O'Casey plays, and that they and the actors gave them a care and an attention above their importance; so I welcomed, as an undertone to the ban, that a withdrawal of my plays would leave the Abbey stage wide open for newborn playwrights to show the stuff their dreams were made on; but it didn't pan out that way yet. The plays so far shown by the newer playwrights have been epiphanies of second-rate or third-rate minds, and present Irish drama is a thing of shreds and patches torn from what was once a coat of many colours. It is hard to say whether this is caused by the lack of imagination in the minds, and of gusto in the bellies, of the younger playwrights; or by the decision of the [Abbey Theatre's] directors to produce only those plays they are sure will provoke a noisy rattle in the tills of the theatre's box office.

*

PART TWO

ON BOOKS AND WRITERS

WHAT THOU SEEST, WRITE IN A BOOK
(c. 1950)*

THERE are many kinds of literature, classical, romantic, realistic, or naturalistic, some forms blending with others so that sometimes we are hard set to know which is which, though that doesn't matter so long as the book is a good one. A lot think that anything fiery, fierce, or commonplace is realism, but realism is but a form of writing in which imagination has no place. It is a setting down of things and characters as they are, without change, selection, modification, or arrangement. Naturalism is that style in which man is arrayed against forces stronger than himself, completely beyond his control, and the characters are invariably set down on the animal plane. Meredith said somewhere of this kind of writer, 'He sees the hog in nature, and takes nature for the hog.' The trouble with readers who rail against the tougher (as they think) parts of 'realism' is that they refuse to see the hog at all, though he is as much a part of natuer as the bird of paradise, perhaps, a more important part. In Ireland, to be 'on the pig's back' is to be well on the way to success, or in the pink of prosperity. We forget that we are animals ourselves, even though we be tinctured with the grace of God. And, after all, most animals, all I daresay, did we know them well, possess some beauty or remarkable quality of their own; even those who haven't assumed what we conceive to be a comely physical form. There is beauty in the glittering eyes of an ugly monkey, and there is strength and resolution in the outward thrust of a hog's snout.

Setting aside the cult of taboo asserting that evil lurks in

* I have been unable to trace whether or not this article was published, or its date of composition. *Editor*.

certain words, which is plain superstition, giving an importance to a thing it doesn't possess, just as the cult of amulets to protect us from illness or danger is superstition, too; setting aside any attempt at a Freudian explanation (about which I know very little), let us try to look at the question of the use of 'vulgar, vile, or filthy words' in a broader and more generous way. There can be no doubt of the virility in a number of words that strike some persons with fear and an angry trembling. They are simple, vigorous, and direct; much more so than the genteel words woven to cover them up from view. We are weakening the lusty English language by rejecting them. The habit is becoming a dangerous one. Fowler says of what he calls 'Genteelism': 'the substituting for the ordinary natural word that first suggests itself to the mind, of a synonym that is thought to be less soiled by the lips of the common herd, less familar, less plebeian, less vulgar, less improper, less apt to come unhandsomely betwixt the wind and our nobility.' He gives a number of examples, of which these are a few: serviette for napkin; lingerie for underclothing; stomach for belly (we have genteelised this a little more now by calling it 'tummy'); mirror for looking-glass; perspiration for sweat; expectorate for spit; and many more. Here we have, not the passionate resentment of the artist, but the calm cold rebuke of the technician, the scientist, the scholar. George Moore in his *Hail and Farewell* complains of the same thing, telling how the word 'shift' has become chemise, and later on neutralised into shimmy. Some of you may remember the tremendous and long-lasting turmoil that sprang up in Ireland and America because Synge had dared to use the word in a very lovely play. The Abbey Company were put under arrest in America, and one 'lady', giving evidence in court, said that she would blush even to think of such a term; and a man-witness declared it to be a sin to mention the name of any garment that touched a woman's fair skin.

We are in danger even of losing the lovely word of 'woman', for we pride ourselves on having charladies to work for us instead of charwomen; and the theatre waives away the vulgar word of 'girl' by boycotting them, and getting chorus ladies to dance for it. We change servant into domestic, thus abolishing the grand phrase of 'He who is greatest amongst you, let him be your servant'.

When in a tremor of fear, or in a spasm of ridiculous self-righteousness, we turn up our noses at a 'vulgar' or an 'improper' word, we really repudiate, we even insult, quite a number of impressive persons. First, we assume a gentility that puts even God in His place; for if we believe that the Bible is an inspired book (as millions of us still do), that in it 'men and women spake as they were moved by the Holy Ghost', then we must hold Divinity responsible and accountable for the very 'bad language' that is so carelessly scattered about the book. The creature becomes more civilised, more genteel, than his Creator — for that is what it amounts to. We repudiate the lusty vigour of the great Elizabethans, and their lovely songs, music, and plays; and we repudiate the elegance, the wit, and brilliant ribald language of the finer Restoration dramatists. We provoke the laugh given at the big, burly policemen of Dublin, most sensitive and modest of mankind, who, whenever they have to give evidence regarding a woman with child, always refer to her as 'being in an interesting condition'. They are less shy in the Soviet Union, where two good seats in bus or tram are always reserved for the accommodation of pregnant women. We, in our stupid modesty, try to conceal the coming in of new life; doing our best to frighten life out of its existence.

When Christ's disciples turned away in disgust from the decaying body of a dead dog, their Master, tradition says, exclaimed at the beauty in the glistening whiteness of the teeth in the dead animal's gaping mouth. Isn't it strange, too, that He was so often found among the publicans and sinners? He was very sensitive, His stories and parables declare Him to have been an artist, and, like every artist, He was at ease in what many would have thought to have been very bad company for any respectable man to be seen with. He must have heard quite a number of hot and hostile things in his journeyings to and fro through Judea and Galilee, but there is no record of Him ever having given a personal rebuke for a vulgar phrase or a rousing curse. Perhaps, though, the Christians of today have become more respectable than their Master.

If we are to mingle with life, if we are to try to fulfil our purpose here, we mustn't be afraid to handle things liable to spot our fair hands and stain our purple and finer linen. There's no use of pleading our gentility or a higher sensitiveness: it won't do. Like the scented fop wrangling with Hotspur, sweating on a steamy battlefield, sniffing aromatic powder up his lordly nose to deaden the smell of burned-out saltpetre, and railing at the rough soldiers for bringing slovenly, unhandsome corses betwixt the wind and his nobility; and telling Hotspur that he himself would have been a soldier, but for these vilely-smelling guns. Florence Nightingale, who was as sensitive as anyone, disregarded the smell of powder, and didn't fear the look of slovenly, unhandsome corses; didn't fear the dreadful sights filling Smyrna and Scutari lazar-houses that the nicely-minded officials of that day called hospitals. She didn't even budge before the bad language spilled out by hot lips in the pain of wakefulness or the dream of delirium. A saint, dipping her fair hands in the slime of illness and festering wounds; unafraid in the midst of villainous sights and sounds; intent only on the saving of the fine qualities of bravery, honesty, and kindness hidden under a villainous veil. This I know, first-hand, for my own uncle lay on a dirty couch in Scutari, getting well, with her help, of a nearly-severed arm from the slash of a Russian sabre in the Battle of Balaclava. Was this woman, refined and delicate, astray there? No; in spite of the filth, the misery, the foul language, her delicacy, grace, and skill were in the right place.

The fact is that if we turn our haughtily-stiffened backs on bad language, we turn them on tens of thousands of our brothers and sisters, young and old. There are, I'm afraid, many more curses than prayers heard in heaven; but the good man isn't always good; nor is the bad man always bad. Profanity existed, I daresay, since man first found a tongue. In a Morality Play Noah uses it to get his wife into the ark; and she uses it to keep herself out of it. In times, or moments, of stress and strain, a prayer or a curse is a great relief, and through the terrible

blitz much bad language must have gone up to heaven to re-
lieve a dangerous tenseness; understood there, I've no doubt, for
profanity is no less than a crippled prayer.

We carry our bodies about with us; we can't get out of them,
and few of us have any desire to do so. And we should remember
that God made us from the waist down as well as from the waist
up. Our bodies do many wonderful, useful, and lovely things
for us; but they play strange tricks with us at times; and it is
good that the artist, or the writer, sees these things, and has the
courage to comment on them, or to laugh heartily at them, an
enjoyment in which we should all join, instead of lifting up our
voices in condemnation. The artist doesn't set down shame
for shame's sake, but sets down what he sees in sincerity and in
his own truth. He never wishes to turn glory into shame, but,
even in his vulgar language and his vile rhymes, rather tries to
turn shame into glory. Let us meet him bravely, join in his song,
story, or play, and promote the name of our country to the name
of honour among the nations of the earth. Be sure, if we don't
venture to join him, he will go on alone.

EMPTY VESSELS (1942)*

KNOWLEDGE of, and interest in, literature seems to be a faraway thing to many Socialists. They fight shy of anything in the shape of a book, other than what may be classified as a pamphlet holding often clumsy (and worse still, dull) expressions dealing with their daily life and meagre existence in the struggle to fill our bellies with bread. Of course we all know, some of us by bitter experience, that bread is the thing that gives us the energy to do all things, and the sensibility to enjoy the lovely things man's love of colour and beautiful sounds creates. We can't live lowly or highly without bread. Christian or Atheist, we have to forage for it, and woe unto us when it is unobtainable. So far, then, so good. But Labour, as a whole, allows the pageantry of life to pass by without turning a head or opening a window to have a look at it, as if afraid, like the Lady of Shallot, if they did, they'd immediately drop down stone dead. Those who carry on the battle for the workers, who lead them on, in major or minor roles, know nothing, seemingly, and care less, for the broader knowledge and keener strength and lovelier expression often to be found in the works of greater men and greater women. It is a very irritating thing to find men (and women) enthusiastic and unselfish, content to find all inspiration, or what they believe to be inspiration, for themselves and others, in self-imposed confinement to the material of elementary economics. Consequently, they are, for the most part, dull, unentertaining, and can never appeal to anyone whose imagination is above that of a mouse. They work, but they do not enjoy, and without enjoyment no-one lives. A knowledge of literature, of things said and sung by men gone, and men present, though divorced from actual

* Article published in *Irish Freedom*, May 1942.

and positive dialectical economics, is an important addition to knowledge and culture that every leader or would-be Socialist leader should have if he is going to be the force in everyday thought he wishes to be, and often, poor man, thinks he is.

As far as literature and general knowledge are concerned, the Trade Unions are a wide open bog of ignorance, and most of their leaders, and those of the Labour Party, prate and toil as if great human beings never had been born, and the human race, having no vision, was doomed to perish. We have often heard vehement scorn poured out on the Nazis for burning books; but for all the honour we give the higher examples of man's achievements, emblazoned in books, we, too, might as well make a bonfire of them, and warm our hands with the blaze, and go. In the course of the last few years, many young Socialists have visited me, and I have been shocked by either their awe of, or their totalitarian fear of books. In the transitional period of the Soviet Revolution (the early stages, note), the same fear was frantically shown of anything said or written by any one who wasn't, or hadn't been, a Proletarian; and what was called Bourgeois Literature sank under a wave, of bullying and scorn. Not for long, though: the Bolsheviks weren't fools; and soon a better education, given, of course, by the Bolsheviks, coaxed the people, first to admire, and then to love what they had once feared and then hated. And today, in the Soviet Union, Pushkin, Lermontov, Tolstoy, and a host of other great men are honoured as they should be honoured — by being read — from one end of the great Union of Soviet Republics [to the other]. But what of us? A little time ago, a group came to see me, and I found that just one of them had looked at the page of a great book, and he was looked upon as something of a Trotskyist because he liked Dickens. They were all content with a few little pamphlets, giving, here and there, a few words, as spice, from the great mass written by Lenin, though none of these extracts seemed to say, or give a hint of, a word about Lenin's knowledge, or the encouragement given to authorship and stage and music by this man and by Stalin, even in the midst of a bloody revolution.

Apart from the enjoyment ensured by the reading, there is

hardly a great writer who doesn't offer them a fruity sentence or remark to back up even their own opinions. Dickens, of course, is full of them, many remarkable, indeed, for a man to make eighty years ago. Listen to what he says about Shares (if we haven't any, we know what they are): 'As is well known to the wise in their generation, traffic in Shares is the one thing to have to do with in this world. Have no antecedents, no established character, no cultivation, no ideas, no manners; have Shares. Where does he come from? Shares. Where does he go to? Shares. What are his tastes? Shares. Has he any principles? Shares. What squeezes him into Parliament? Shares.' And what could be more delightfully sarcastic than his account of the pompous Podsnap's vision of Literature, Painting, and Music? Then again what could be more quietly effective than Goldsmith's indictment of riches in his 'The Deserted Village'? 'Ill fares the land, to hastening ills a prey, where wealth accumulates and men decay!' 'The wealth of a Nation,' says Stalin, 'is its people.' Thus this Irish poet of one hundred and sixty years ago said what Joseph Stalin said the other day. The slogan that appeared over Jim Connolly's *Workers' Republic* 'The Great only appear Great because We are on our Knees' came, if I remember rightly, from a speech of Mirabeau's during the French Revolution; and the phrase, 'Haves and Have-Nots' from Cervantes's *Don Quixote*. Here's what Kingsley says of the poor, addressing the rich: 'Worse housed than your hacks and your pointers, worse fed than your hogs and your sheep.' The great writers sparkle with these kind of thoughts, and Morris is packed with them. Every Socialist should read his *News from Nowhere*. Read what the Saint, Sir Thomas More, said of the Commonwealths of the world; and here's a comment on charity by an Irish rebel, J. Boyle O'Reilly: 'The organised charity, scrimped and iced, In the name of a cautious, statistical Christ.'

So you see, even from our advanced point of view, we do well to make ourselves acquainted with these great thinkers and poets. It will help us to be more assured when in the presence of those who have got a chance of a better education than we have. It will give us a power of dealing with the comments of all kinds of people. We must be able, like the great General in *Distant Point*, to deal with all manner of men, and, like him, be able even to deal sensibly and understandingly with comrades holding creeds that we think to be worn-out and perishing. And in no distant way, or self-superior way either; for what do the most learned of us know but a little knowledge gathered with great labour. Sure and steadfast, we must conduct ourselves with humility; and remember always that the coming of Communism is not the end, but the beginning of life. It is but the power and the way of life that will enable us to live.

CENSORSHIP (1945)*

MR MONK GIBBON's defence of Censorship is, it seems to me, a comic medley of fright, fear, superstition, faint piety, Greek fire, and a cool desire to keep on the lee side of the counts, knights, and esquires of the Holy Roman Empire. He starts out by conceding that 'a reasonable censorship is almost a contradiction in terms', and then proceeds to debate 'whether censorship is, or can be, justifiable'. This contradiction in terms seems to end the matter for Mr Gibbon, but he hurries on to defend the indefensible. 'A commonplace,' he says, 'is [that] every community defends its young, for what youth thinks matters at least as much as what it eats, perhaps more.' Oh? Thirty years ago, or more, when I was speaking at meetings about 'Meals for Necessitous School-children,' there wasn't much of a sign about of communities defending the young; and only the other week, an article in *The Economist* said that an inquiry among many homes in Crumlin, among families in the favoured position of having the head of the house in permanent employment — that is in a position better than thousands — eighty per cent of the children showed definite signs of under-nourishment. Curious way of protecting the young. To me, the mind

* In 1945 the Editor of *The Bell*, Dublin, initiated a debate on Censorship in Ireland with the words:
    'We now have, here, a Literary Censorship, a Film Censorship, the Censorship of the Common Law, the Censorship of the secret reports of the Librarians' Association, and the private censorship which any citizen irrespective of class, education, age, or sanity may exercise over any book in a public library merely by objecting to it.'
In Jan. 1945 the poet Monk Gibbon published an article, 'In Defence of Censorship', in the journal, to which G.B.S. and S.O'C. replied in the Feb. issue. The above article was O'C.'s contribution to the debate.

that thinks thought as important, or more so, than food to the young is away behind the back of beyond. Food was, and is, and will be, life's first need, always. And as for thought, children for a good many years drown their minds in the thought of their elders. That is why it is so hard to make the Irish language the common tongue of the people. And it is a mistake to associate a change in community life with deterioration. It is nonsense to connect the corruption of the controllers, the grandees, the kings, the courtiers with the virile, everlasting life of the people. The change from tribal life to feudalism (changing thought too) wasn't deterioration; it was a step forward. So, too, the change from feudalism to mass production, to capitalism, wasn't deterioration; it was another step forward; and so, too, will the change — taking place now — from the control of the means of life by the few, to the ownership of these things by the people who created them. We are a little too fond of harking back to the Greeks and the Romans as ones selected by God to show the way to the world. Our life, socially, scientifically, and even morally, is altogether different from that of Roman or of Greek. We might as well look back to the life of Aztec or Inca. What is it to present-day man or woman in field, factory, or workshop that Ovid was sent away, while Virgil stayed at home? We're getting a bit tired of this three hundred men and three men business. Even the Brehon Laws wouldn't fit our social life now. And what has all this got to do with Magennis [Chairman of the Board of Censors] and his crew determining what book must be pooh bahed out of Ireland?

Mr Gibbon tells us that 'writers influence current mentality, if not current morality,' thereby hinting, though he won't say so definitely, that they do influence what he thinks to be morality. But he doesn't tell us what influenced the writers to write as they do. They take, in their writing, their cue from the life around them. Those two fine men Shaw and Wells, who have written numerous books, haven't influenced thought and life one ten-thousandth part as compared with Hitler, who has written but one. But even that is an illusion, for it wasn't Hitler's book that did the damage, for only when he became unpopular did the crowds start to read it. It was the thought in the man's own mind that was crowned with power and potency by the big business men, and their allies, here, there, and everywhere, to bring about a condition of things in Church and state which would leave them sitting on top of the world. It nearly succeeded, but the people were just too much for them, and business men and clericals are passing through a very anxious time of it. Not 'impure literature', but cupidity and fear brought about the world's apparent undoing. But only apparent, for the people are coming out of the debacle stronger and more determined than they ever were before. And may I ask was it Joyce's writing brought about the civil war in Ireland?

Mr Monk Gibbon says, 'Two realistic institutions, the Roman Catholic Church and the U.S.S.R., have consistently made it plain that in their opinions certain authors and certain books are better left unread.' As far as the Catholic Church is concerned, this is true enough, God knows; and not only the Catholic Church, ex officio, but every bishop, priest, deacon, and confraternity man, from the centre to the see, is bursting with anxiety to have special books banned from the sight and sense of all other man — having first read the books themselves. But where did Mr Monk Gibbon get his news about the U.S.S.R.? I have reread a week ago the History of the U.S.S.R. Communist Party (Bolshevik), which is mainly the history of Russia from 1917 to 1940, and I have seen no reference whatever to the censorship of poem, play, or novel throughout the whole of that historical period. I myself have been in touch with the U.S.S.R., regarding literature and the drama, since 1925, nearly a year before I left Dublin, and I am still in touch, closer touch, today, and I have never yet heard a whisper of the banning of play, poem, or novel by the officials of the U.S.S.R., good, bad, or indifferent. On the contrary, just a year ago, I put in a lot of work writing to all the British publishers, and the American publishers, too, appealing to them to forward all the books they could to Moscow and to Leningrad. Indeed, at the request of Moscow, I wrote a long article on Irish Literature,[1] and was

[1] 'Literature in Ireland,' see pp. 170–81.

surprised in the acknowledgement to read that they were surprised I hadn't mentioned Phelan's *Green Volcano*. So, at least,
I have some reason for asking Mr Gibbon where he got the
news that officials in the U.S.S.R. have declared that some books
are better left unread?

The case of the young girl who became 'hardboiled',
she had 'read practically nothing but Maugham for a whole
year', may be passed over. That attitude of mind was fixed, not
by dangerous literature, but by the aftermath of the First World
War. It has passed away, and even Maugham, himself, has
changed. To me, it doesn't seem a question of what we have
lost or gained in Ireland by the censorship (most of those who
read have read the books that have been banned); but a question
of how long intelligent people are going to stand this pompous,
ignorant, impudent, and silly practice that is making Ireland a
laughing-stock among the intelligent of all lands?

Signor Benson's (is this Monsignor Benson, one of the champions of wholesome literature, in the same row with Belloc,
Chesterton, and Noyes?) monologue on the novel, quoted by
Mr Gibbon: 'Fiction in the hands of new and distinguished
authors was undergoing a corresponding sea change . . . it made
its studies of morality in the monkey house and it followed its
heroines to the water-closet. The mirror which it is the function of Art to hold up to nature (as if the water-closet wasn't
part of poor human nature) seemed to be always adjusted to
reflect to what lies below the belt; the heart and the brain (with
the exception of the department of the sexual urge) were outside
the field of vision . . . and the most unsatisfactory feature of these
coitions was that the partners in them seemed to care for the act
so much more than they cared for each other.' Well, that's
Benson failing to see anything in the works he read save what a
gentle soul like his should keep away from. But this criticism
is mainly a lie; a mean, desperate lie, uttered with forethought
to bolster up the silly and demoralising literature so firmly
sponsored by the professional Catholic author. No distinguished
author would, nor could, make the water-closet, and its spare
parts, a main, or semi-main, theme in a novel, play, or poem.

Such a thing would be impossible in the first place; and, in the second place, were it possible, such a work would knock the author off his claim to be distinguished. As for the morality of the monkey house, to go by a lot of the clergy, that kind of morality is to be found rather in a dancing-hall than in a book. It is a remarkable and enlightening thing that the clericals and their followers concentrate so ardently and so persistently on these kind of thoughts, more so by far than the worst writer with which they themselves are acquainted. At least, no author whom I have read, and I have read a few, made such things the theme of his work; but possibly Benson, keen on the track of these things, nosed them out more successfully than I did.

But why all this frightened rage against 'that part of the body below the belt'? Isn't it half of life? Wasn't it (according to Benson, Chesterton, Belloc, and the rest) moulded by God just the same as that part of the body above the belt? And imagine calling the sexual organs 'the department of the sexual urge'! The basement stores! However we may try to hide it in silk or satin or snowy clerical linen, we can't do without this part of the body, for it is an essential part of life just as important as that which we may, with Benson's permission, [call] the upper storey. More important, for from the belly proceeds all the energy that keep the senses whole and the brain of man going, and from 'the department of the sexual urge' comes the fire and fury that preserves the world alive. And apart from sexual ecstasy, as irresistible as hunger, there are the physical pleasures that the legs give — walking, running, playing hurley and football. Oh, pride and vanity! These transcendental souls are in low rebellion against the manner of God's creativeness.

And how are we going to satisfy the 'need for protecting adolescence against a warped mental bias'? The protecting angels themselves may have a warped mental bias, and so the adolescents will have to have an additional protection against these, and so on, *ad infinitum*. But surround youth with protectors, as the Light Brigade were surrounded by guns, yet no power of wisdom, age, or piety can dam a physiological urge;

and books, or no books, it will have its way, as strong in those who cannot read as in those who can, for life comes first; and a good and fine thing, too, provoking in man the urge to create some of the most beautiful things in art and literature that have justified the ways of man to God.

Mr Gibbon, assuming the mantle of censorship, says to Anatole France, Rousseau, Voltaire, and Maupassant: You can go out to play, boys; your marks are good; and to Strindberg, he says: You must stop in — you are really a bad boy. This of a man who is one of the greatest playwrights of his time and ours. And why? Strindberg frightens him. He finds the playwright a little spurious, a little windy, and a little rhetorical, just as each of us is at some time or another of our little day of life. Well, Mr Gibbon has a perfect right to banish Strindberg out of his own life, but none whatever to banish him from the life of others. Besides, if the others got away from Gibbon, someone would seize on France, another on Rousseau, and a third on Maupassant, leaving Voltaire to the clericals, who, when Noyes wrote a book about him, came rushing and roaring together, till Noyes took the book back to hide it from the sight of men. I notice Joyce wasn't mentioned — too far down for Gibbon to reach. Joyce, the bravest and finest soul in literature Ireland has had for many years; who made of Dublin a dancing Hecuba, and, at the last, wrote the most extraordinary and wonderful Everyman the mind of man could conceive. But, if not mentioned by Gibbon and the rest of them, the stars themselves move over the Dublin sky to figure out the name of Joyce there. Mr Gibbon complains about the 'propagandists' dismissing religion with 'The great mythologies of the past (including the Church) are deprived of enough façade even to launch good raillery against.' But surely one ought to be free enough to say a thing like that; and isn't it the clerical who is the biggest propagandist of them all? Not alone in matters of religion, but in politics (see the Catholic Press for Poland, Yugoslavia, and Greece; and we all remember the hullabulloo for Franco), literature, art, family life, schools, and what not; each of them insisting that he, and he alone, has all the truth there is to be found in what he says about anything whatsoever. It's a bit of a cheek to hear the princes of propaganda complaining about the humble yeoman. And Mr Gibbon forgets that Chesterton is full of the very remarks he condemns in his writings about those who challenge the creeds. But Chesterton's a privileged person.

And where did Mr Gibbon pick up the brilliant thought of 'The artist goes his own way. He is content, if necessary, to wait for recognition.' Content to wait, eh? There isn't an artist who hasn't, or who doesn't, make a fight for recognition, in one way or another. Mr Gibbon should read the Introduction to the American edition of Joyce's *Ulysses* (perhaps the bravest and proudest artist of them all), where he will learn something of the fight Joyce made for the publication of *Dubliners*. Not only for recognition do artists strive, but, willy nilly, for a living too. But then Mr Gibbon believes that 'literature in our time almost ceased to think in terms of art. Writers are not artists, they are propagandists for a particular point of view. Poets tend to be communist firstly and poets, if at all, secondly.' There you are! Saying exactly of art what he condemns writers for saying about religion. But a poet always remains a poet, though he be an aristocrat poet like Byron; a democratic poet like Burns; a middle-class, grandiloquent poet like Yeats, or a communist poet like Mayakovsky.

Authors must always fight these enemies of free thought be they publicly commissioned censors or self-appointed guardians of morals, like the National Organization for Decent Literature, presided over by the Catholic bishop of Fort Wayne, Indiana; the Watch and Ward Society of Boston; or the Society for the Suppression of Vice in New York. There they are being licked in one fight after another, and let us hope they will soon disappear from Eire. Mr Gibbon seems to agree with his officer friend about rapes and murder in literature, while forgetting that he will find both in the Bible and Shakespeare; plenty of murder in the poet's best plays, and the plays of his Elizabethan comrades; and, to me, the vilest story of a murder I have ever read appears in the works of the Christian bravo, G. K. Chesterton. It is just as well that Mr Gibbon decides to stand aside. He would be a responsibility rather than a help to sturdier writers determined to fight rather than be submerged under the standard set up by the Eire Censorship Board, or the Legions defending Decent Literature scurrying about the streets of Boston and New York.

LITERATURE IN IRELAND (1939)*

To write about literature in Ireland is a complex job. At present, and for some time past, Irish literature has been the core of several controversies. What is and what is not Irish literature is dividing the country into two clever camps. There are those, few in number, but loud-voiced and a little bitter, who say that it can only be whatever of value in prose and poetry that is written in the Gaelic language, the national tongue of the Irish people; that all the works, written in English, be they never so great or so beautiful, fail, by any true test, to be considered to form part of Ireland's literary heritage. There is a good deal to be said for those who hold this view, that Irish literature can only be Irish when it is written out of the heart and mind of the Irish, that is, the Gaelic language. The weak point is that the English language is still the tongue of the vast majority of the people. The Irish language was, of course, the language of the people for many centuries, and, even today, the idiom of that language is heard and felt in the English at present spoken by the people. For many centuries the Irish language was the tongue in which the people said their say, sighed their sorrows, bought and sold in the market place, sang their songs, prayed to their gods, blessed their friends, and cursed their enemies. In this language is written all the sorrows and most of the glories of the older ages in Ireland; and the language in the works of the poets and scribes, was thrusting itself forward to a fuller strength and higher beauty, when the first English invasion interfered, and started the long drawn out and bloody conquest of the people. As soon as the English had the power they began to put an untidy end to Gaelic

* An article originally written for readers in the U.S.S.R.; it was published in *International Literature*, Dec. 1939.

scholarship and to hunt the poets from their high places, hanging them, if they couldn't tame them; to dragoon the people, having first, of course, robbed them of their patrimony. From the day this alien power settled itself to rule Ireland from Dublin Castle, every effort was made to destroy the language, customs, and characteristics of the people, but it was only about one hundred and fifty years ago that the language ceased to be the language of the majority of the people, and it was never entirely lost.

In the days of long ago, prechristian times, when Ireland was probably the centre of a Celtic civilisation stretching from her own shores to the shores of the Black Sea (Dr Dwyer Joyce in his *Irish Names of Places*, mentions the close connection between the Irish and the Georgians), many things were written, but because of the destructive invasions of the English and the Danes, all, or mostly all, were lost forever, though, it is thought, many lie scattered about in the world unhonoured and unknown.

The present Irish Government are doing something, in compilation and translation, to bring before us, through the mass of MSS left, the light of other days, for Ireland never gave way before the denationalising influences of the Roman Empire; and, even when Christianity came, Ireland for many years was too far from Rome to be dominated by her, the national language remained practically untouched, and it flourished in the literature that then arose. It is, indeed, thought that it was the Irish influence in Northumberland, England, that taught and encouraged the Anglian scribes to preserve and cultivate the national literature.

The Danes, in their various forays, set fire to anything that would burn, and thousands of MSS perished in the flames. So terrible was the fear of the Irish before these invaders, due, I think, to the softening of the martial fibre of the Irish by their new Christian practice of prayer and fasting, that a poet, thinking of the terror, wrote:

> *Bitter is the wind tonight,*
> *It tosses the ocean's white hair;*
> *Tonight I fear not the fierce warriors of Norway*
> *Coursing on the Irish Sea.*

Far better the spirit of

> *Ye people of great Murrough,*
> *Against which neither forest nor wild moor prevails,*
> *Ye that before your Norse battle-standards of sun-bright satin*
> *Have routed the heathen hordes as far as the Boyne!*
> *Blood breaks like snowflakes from their noses*
> *As they flee across Aughty in the late evening*

when the invasions broke all patience down, the whole country uniting, and finally defeating them in a great battle on the outskirts of Dublin.

It is often thought that we Irish are a dreamy people (we, of course, have our dreams), and that the faery atmosphere, as set down in so many stories and sayings about us, and the forawhile cult of what was called the Celtic Twilight, is redolent of the whimsical, mystical nature of the Irish. But many of the things written by the Celt show that he was a practical thinker as well as one who had a vivid imagination. For instance, the Triads, typical of one form of Irish thought, show how wise and practical the Gael or Celt could be. Here are a few:

> *Three slender things that best support the world: the slender stream of milk from the cow's dug into the pail;*
> *The slender blade of green corn upon the ground;*
> *The slender thread over the hand of a skilled woman.*
> *Three glories of a gathering: a beautiful wife; a good horse; a swift hound.*
> *Three laughing-stocks of the world: An angry man; a jealous man; a niggard.*
> *Three things that constitute a physician: A complete cure; leaving no blemish behind; a painless examination.*
> *Three candles that illumine every darkness: Truth, nature, knowledge.*
> *Three coffers whose depth is not known: the coffers of a chieftain; of the Church; of a privileged poet.* (Today we have the capitalist, the Church — as ever — and the venal best-seller).

But, on the whole, apart from some fierce songs by some fierce poet, and many lovely love songs, Irish literature, after the conquest of Christianity, became a thing of patience, penance, and prayer, and weakened the Irish terribly in the fight to regain their own again. As, for instance, in this song called 'Eve's Lament', showing Christianity's strange unnatural dread of woman:

> *I am Eve, great Adam's wife,*
> *'Tis I that outraged Jesus, of old;*
> *'Tis I that robbed my children of heaven,*
> *By rights, 'tis I should have gone upon the cross.*
> *There would be no ice in any place,*
> *There would be no glistening windy winter,*
> *There would be no hell, there would be no sorrow,*
> *There would be no fear, if it were not for me*

and many more of this kind of ringing of church bells, so mocked at by Oisin, the great Fenian poet, in his argument with St Patrick.

After the defeat of the Confederation of Kilkenny, the flight of the Earls, owing to party ambitions, personal greed, and religious nonsense, Ireland's fetters were set firmer on her feet. Then Cromwell came blasting a way through the country; and, after him, the flying Stuarts whose cause the Irish stood by, the common people foolishly following a royal name and a royal coward, Sheamus a chaca, Sheamus the shit as he was afterwards called by the people who suffered in his cause. The fate of the people grew worse, and anyone who had anything had to conform to the law and established religion, or lose all or the little they had. The literature is now full of hopes for the restoration of the Jacobite line; visions of a beautiful girl, symbolical of Ireland, telling her woes, often ending in the wish fulfilment form of the overthrow of Ireland's foes, and her own rise to wealth, comfort, security, and jubilation. We have the lovely lyrical strains of Eoghain O' Ruaidh O'Suilleabhain, the vigorous chants of Aodhagain O'Rathaille, and the not so vigorous, but more gentle (though he could be fierce enough at times) verse of Sean Clarac O'Domhnaill. In 'Ata an Speur 'sa Cuallacht', the vasty sky's in sore affliction, and a windswept downpour's falling ceaselessly, O'Domhnaill paints a vision in which he sees despair, misery, and want, change to glory, with wine and corn and dancing in plenty for all in Ireland. So it went on in most of what

G

was written down by the impoverished and hunted poets, a never-ending hope for the future, and an endless curse on the foreigner holding down their country. But the English tongue kept getting a firmer grip on the people pushed hard out of the fair places in the land to the parts where the land gave little, and the life was stern. There had ceased to be any law for them; they were outcasts and beggars, living on less than husks in their own land; but the clergy still preached patience and the love of God.

We come to later times when the English find the language they forced on the people getting used against themselves in the writings and ballads of the men of '48', a stream of song that dried up only when the present President of Ireland, Eamon de Valera, sounded the cease-fire that ended the civil war. Although many of the old Gaelic poets had written fierce satires about individual clerics, they were narrow and isolated. Now began a stiff challenge to the commonplace and tear-appealing cry for patience sent up by the crowd following fast on the heels of the clergy, all of them looking sturdy and each of them feeling faint.

On this scene of processional patience burst the patriotic ballads of Thomas Davis and the fiery denunciations of John Mitchel in a paper called *The Nation*, read by all who could read, and listened to by all who could not. In the midst of famine and disease, took place the scene described by Mitchel:

> a 'model' communal kitchen was turned into a gala, one of the ghastliest galas ever exhibited under the sun. There in the Esplanade, before the Royal barracks, was erected the national model soup-kitchen, gaily bedizened, laurelled, and bannered, and fair to see; and in and out and all around, sauntered parties of our supercilious second-hand 'better classes' of the Castle offices — fed on superior rations at the people's expense — and bevies of fair dames and military officers, braided with public braid and padded with public padding; and there, too, were the pale and piteous ranks of model-paupers, broken tradesmen, ruined farmers, destitute sempstresses, ranged at a respectful distance, till the genteel persons had duly inspected the arrangements, and then marched by the police to the places allotted them, where they were to feed on the meagre diet with

chained spoons — to show the gentry how the pauper spirit could be broken, and the pauper appetite could gulp down its bitter bread, and bitterer shame and wrath together.

Mitchel's voice rang out from one end of the land to the other in *The Nation*, but the people were too soaked with the advice to submit and be patient to hear the cry that

> the railways were better dispensed with for a while than allowed to become a means of transport for invading troops. Troops transported by rail might be conveniently met with in many places. Not even Hofer and his Tyrolese could have desired a deadlier ambush than a good deep railway cutting. A few hundred men could lie in wait with masses of rocks and trunks of trees ready to roll down; and a train or two advancing with a regiment of infantry, and the engine panting nearer and nearer till its polished name may nearly be read: Now, in the name of the Father, and of the Son, and of the Holy Ghost! . . . Now!

This sort of literature didn't go down with the clergy or the authorities, and Mitchel was hurried away in chains to serve a long sentence of transportation, writing his fine *Jail Journal* in the convict hulks, leaving a flame in many Irish hearts that finally overthrew the main force of alien rule in Ireland.

Here, at this time, too, wrote Fintan Lalor, the Lenin of his day, the most advanced thinker of his period with his Irish Communistic Manifesto of the time, declaring in *The Rights of Ireland*:

> The principle I state and mean to stand upon is this, that the entire ownership of Ireland, moral and material, up to the sun and down to the centre, is vested of right in the people of Ireland; that they, and none but they, are the landowners and lawmakers of this island; that all laws are null and void, not made by them, and all titles of land invalid, not conferred or confirmed by them. In other, if not plainer words, I hold and maintain that the entire soil of a country belongs of right to the entire people of that country, and is the rightful property, not of any one class, but of the nation at large.

But these declarations, unfortunately, were not seized on by the other leaders, and never reached the host of people who would have acclaimed them, and as surely fought for them; and it was not till another generation that these things were made plainer by Michael Davitt, and plainer still, later on, by Jim Larkin and Jim Connolly.

Then came the wide, energetic, and tremendous struggle for security of tenure under Parnell and Davitt; Parnell's betrayal by the debauched members of his party; and literature sank down into the wearisome platitudes preached by the leaders of the party after Parnell's death. Then, suddenly, a great renascence of literary and dramatic activity sprang into being in the midst of the pseudo-political life of the people. The Gaelic League, a society for the revival of Ireland's language, songs, dances, and customs, became strong and prominent; and the Abbey Theatre was founded in Dublin by W. B. Yeats, George Moore, and Lady Augusta Gregory. From these two fine and pulsing movements have sprung all the literary and dramatic activities that stir up Ireland today. The greatest of these big figures was, undoubtedly, Yeats, the strange, dreamy, faraway poet, who could, all in a moment, be so practical in the affairs of the theatre. He is the great poet of the period, and so far, possibly (to me, certainly), the greatest poet writing in the English language. At the first go-off, and, indeed, for some time, Yeats built all, or almost all, his poetry on the legends and romances that sparkle in the literature of the Gaelic past, though, to no little extent, he fled too far away from the common people, turning the poet into a cold aristocrat who turned his head up to the heavens, looking at no-one below the altitude of a star; failing to see that many, especially among the workers, were themselves, in their own way, seeking a vision, more roughly, perhaps, but no less deep than his own.

In London, Yeats mixed with Lionel Johnson, E. Dowson, John Davidson, T. W. Rolleston, John Todhunter, and others. 'There,' says Horace Reynolds, in a preface to *Letters To The New Island*, 'Yeats could talk poetry to his peers.' But these weren't his peers, not by a long chalk, and they surely did him some harm by interesting Yeats too much in the tiny importance of the talk of cliques (much less majestic than the scorned roar of the mob) who loved, before all else, their own imagined importance, and thought that what they wrote down would be printed in the book of books. This literary giant spent far too much of his time blathering to poetical pygmies. Again, he sought too much the weblike fellowship of theosophy and the Hermetic Students (whatever they may be) as they sat pensively on the Cabala (whatever that is), trying to make a cat jump by imagining a mouse under her nose. All these things were a waste of time to Yeats, and gave a slant to a good deal of his work, which, but for the great poetry in the man, would have turned him completely away from the life that lived so abundantly around him. When he stood upon the Lia Fail, Ireland's Stone of Destiny, he was great; when he perched on the Cabala, he was foolish; when he sang of love, he was beautiful, for Yeats has written the loveliest love lyrics in the English language, such as:

> *Had I the heavens' embroidered cloths,*
> *Enwrought with gold and silver light,*
> *The blue and the dim and the dark cloths*
> *Of night and light and the half light,*
> *I would spread the cloths under your feet:*
> *But I, being poor, have only my dreams;*
> *I have spread my dreams under your feet;*
> *Tread softly because you tread on my dreams.*

In spite of his dreaming, his holidaying after the symbolic, Yeats knew in his deep heart that there were many things wrong with the world, and longed that it should be brighter for all men:

> *All things uncomely and broken, all things worn out and old,*
> *The cry of the child by the roadway, the creak of a lumbering cart,*
> *The heavy steps of the ploughman, splashing the wintry mould,*
> *Are wronging your image that blossoms a rose in the deeps of my heart.*

Yeats, in the beginning, challenged what he called 'the Davisisation of poetry', saying, trenchantly, that poetry and literature must be freed from politics; and the then Irish Literary Movement swung towards what was called a pure art expression; but deep in his fine heart was a deep doubt, for he wrote a political play called *Cathleen ni Houlihan* (symbolic name for

Ireland) that became a trumpet-call to the Irish Republicans in the struggle for National Independence. This terror of immersion in the things that belonged to the people was, I think, due to the pure and precious literary groups with whom Yeats mixed and talked; little themselves, they wanted to make Yeats a little less than he was, and while they plucked away at their one-stringed instrument, Yeats couldn't help sometimes pouring out strains on the literary and national warharp of the nation.

There was a lot to be said for opposition to the Davisisation of Irish poetry, for Davis, though a fine singer, was not a poet, and he was followed by a stream of poor and infantile imitators. But Davis wrote many fine rousing National songs, one of which I partly give here:

> *Oh, for a steed, a rushing steed! And dear Poland gathered round,*
> *To smite her circle of savage foes, and smash them upon the ground,*
> *Nor hold my hand while in the land one foreigner foe was found,*
> *One foreigner foe was found!*
>
> *Oh, for a steed, a rushing steed! on the Curragh of Kildare,*
> *And Irish squadrons trained to do what they are willing to dare;*
> *A hundred yards, and the English guards, drawn up to engage me there!*
>
> *Oh, for a steed, a rushing steed, in any good cause at all!*
> *Or else, if you will, a field on foot, or guarding a leagred wall,*
> *For freedom's right, in flushing fight, to conquer, if then to fall!*

Yeats, too, was a fine and fearless fighter, raising himself against the intimidation, the stupid intolerance, the ignorant opposition of the religious societies, anxious to make sure that nothing outside of their own seedy, senseless, and lackalight lumber should be said or sung in the land.

In the last years of his life, Yeats became much more human, drew nearer to the world's needs, and, as he told me himself, became intensely interested in the new voice of the resurgent working-class speaking in its own way, and demanding the earth and the fullness thereof. He is gone now, and Ireland will miss him sorely, for he was Ireland's greatest poet, and a great warrior to boot.

Following him, and often trying to move a little in front of him, came George Russell, writing under the title of 'AE', who, for many a long year, was looked upon as a great poet, a great painter, and a greater seer. Possessing many good qualities, he was far from being a great poet; looking at painting from a serious point of view, he was a wretched painter; and his quality as a seer was, I think, largely built on the qualities of others. But we remember one thing: in the great strike of 1913, when the workers of Ireland were battling for their rights under the leadership of Larkin and Connolly, George Russell and Yeats wrote splendid letters defending the workers, and this was done when there were very few who dared to stand out openly and say a fair word for the workers.

Over all this cloud of poetry and mysticism shone out the piercing sun of G. B. Shaw's wisdom in preface and play, dissolving a thousand and one shams that went with the gold-guarded respectability of religion and life; and, through him, eyes became keener to see, ears became keener to hear the shaded lies that pretended to harmonise the smell of the workers' sweat with the perfumes of the well-to-do.

In an article, it is not possible to go into the things written by these men, and we must be content to mention them only, as Joyce mentions some things in *Finnegans Wake*, 'From dark Rasa Lane a sigh and a weep, from Lesbia Looshe the beam in her eye, from Suffering Dufferin the Sit of her Style.'

So now we reach the day we stand in, and look around to see what we can see: around the Abbey Theatre, a group of play-wrights, old and young, going round the building continually, and sometimes finding the door open; the best of them, Paul Carroll, with his *The White Steed* and *Shadow and Substance*; with Synge and Lady Gregory still holding their own; and all the new ones, I think, commenting on the life of Ireland that was and that is today.

Next door to these are some young poets, F. R. Higgins and Seumas O'Sullivan, who have written well; a newcomer, Patrick Kavanagh, who, in his *Songs of a Ploughman* and *The Green Fool*, bids fair to become a name in Ireland. There was, some time ago, a brilliant young promising poet, Lyle O'Donaghy, but I haven't heard of him for ages. Then there is a group of novelists, mostly young, Liam O'Flaherty, Sean O'Faolain, Frank O'Connor, Francis Stuart, Francis MacManus; and that, I think, about ends the list of novelists worth considering.

Most of these are to be found in the land of realism, mainly critical or commenting or simply describing of the moods, manners, and methods of their own people; and this is not, on the whole, liked by a large section, who like to think that the life of the Irish people is altogether fair and fruitful and faultless, especially those whose poor minds reflect the trend and altitude of thought mirrored in the common and cheaper sections of the Press that is called Catholic and, of course, by those who know that their way of livelihood depends altogether or to any great extent on the approving smile of the clergy.

This element is, in Ireland, growing in main strength and ignorance, and has formed an official censorship in the country, and, at the moment, hundreds of books have been banned. If it continues much longer, nothing will be tolerated above the understanding of the cheap and tawdry piety of the average member of the confraternities and Young Men's Catholic Associations busy daubing the face of Ireland with their own ignorance. Those writers who have already gained an extra-national public don't, and needn't, care about it; but the writers, as yet unknown outside of Ireland, will wilt before it, will have to cry a halt to their thoughts, will have to say everything in the name of the Archbishop of Armagh, and in the name of the Archbishop of Dublin, and in the name of the Archbishop of Tuam, amen.

Many things have been written round the war between the English forces and the Irish Republican Army, the best of them being, I think, *On Another Man's Wound*, by Ernie O'Malley. And the left wing of the Labour Movement in Ireland has undoubtedly produced a fine writer in Peadar O'Donnell.

For her size, Ireland has done more than well in the world of literature, and the daddy of all those who write, a genius standing alone on a high and lonely peak is undoubtedly him who is called James Joyce with his *Dubliners*, *Ulysses*, and, now, *Finnegans Wake* lying at his feet; the last a judgement on the world's life as it was and is; a Sinai spouting flames of scorn, with the thunder changed to peals of laughter.

Ireland's life has been a life of rich literature; and she moves on; but, if she is to go farther, she will have to strike down the thick and clumsy hands that are trying to quench the three candles of truth, nature, and knowledge.

IRELAND'S SILVERY SHADOW (1946)*

IT shines still, all over Ireland and over many other places — the silvery shadow of W. B. Yeats, the Irish poet. He came into Irish life neither too soon nor too late, but just in the nick of time; just when his strange and magnificent genius was most needed to influence and direct; when Ireland, artistically, politically, and intellectually, had ebbed almost into insignificance. Since the death of the great Parnell, Ireland had been separated from the colour of movement and the form of intelligence. Irishmen and Irishwomen who read something more than a newspaper were wagging their heads and saying that Patriotism was the last refuge of a scoundrel; and, in Ireland, so it was. She had been caught in a Laocoön of despair, of nullity of thought and imagination in literature, of common vulgarity in art, of mean idealism even in things holy; and though, occasionally, a murmur was heard of a better past, Ireland was submitting to the squeezing decline and fall without apparent resistance. No action, few thoughts, little work among the people was worthy of what had been done by great men and women of the past, so long dead, now, that their very graves were sinking out of sight of the people. The Keen of Kilcash, written by a long dead Gaelic poet, was indeed true of Ireland then: 'What shall we do for timber to build? The woods of Kilcash are all fallen!'

Then, like a bright cloud in a dark sky, no bigger at first than a man's hand, came Standish O'Grady with his *Heroic Tales*; T. W. Rolleston, who founded the Celtic Literary Society; the Gaelic League grew stronger, and suddenly the Irish people

* This is the text of a talk written at the request of the B.B.C. Spanish Service for broadcasting in Spanish; translated by J. L. Plaza, it was broadcast in 1946.

found themselves among Lady Gregory's Gods and Fighting-men. Not merely looking on, but fighting with them; and among the fighting for higher thought, finer literature, and fairer art, none bore a tougher shield, a brighter sword, or a loftier crest, than W. B. Yeats, the poet. I would liken him to one of his own linnets, with the darting flight of a swallow, and the soaring quality of a falcon; though George Moore, the Irish novelist, when he saw Yeats with his long black hair, his dangling black tie, and his long, flowing cloak, thought Yeats looked like a rook. In youth, Yeats was a tall, thin man, clean-shaven, with a sombre lock of hair always falling over his eyes; eyes dark, deeply-set, having in them the smouldering fires of many troubled, and many lovely, thoughts. In middle life, he broadened out, his mass of black hair beginning to grey, and the restless movements of his youth grew into a mature and convincing dignity; arrogant at times, not always wise; but vigorous, poetic, and of unbreakable integrity. Yeats had become a powerful and pervading influence in Irish life and letters.

By many, and for a long time, Yeats was looked upon as a dreamer, nothing more, nothing less; and a lot think of him as such to this very day. Indeed, in one of his lovely poems, he exposes his mind by making Fergus the King exchange his king-ship for the grey hair, the hollow cheeks, hands that couldn't lift a sword, and the trembling body, in return for a little bag of dreams given him by a druid. Says Fergus the King:

> *A wild and foolish labourer is a king*
> *To do and do and do, and never dream.*

But Yeats, dreaming his life away, did and did as heartily as any king. He was a dreamer who strove to handle the lovely illusions of his dreams, even when death came to look earnestly into his face. But he often wakened to pull beauty, like a divine conjuror, from the tawdry things of life. This strange man, seeking the excitement of supernatural knowledge, and, in his visionary life, casting but a careless thought or two on the practical things which concern the moments of man's mortal existence; this man probing himself into the mystery of the why and wherefore of what man called life; loving the dream far more than the thing to do, or the thing done; yet spent far more of his life in doing things than in dreaming about them. He proved splendidly in his life, if not in his philosophy, that a man to live must do as well as dream. To do and never to dream is worse than to dream but never to do; for to dream and never do is to at least live in a rich state, even though it be an unnatural condition to striving humanity; but to do, and never to dream, is to humiliate that humanity into insignificance, and to dishonour the colour and form in that arrangement of things by God which man calls life.

What man, a doer among doers, ever did more than Yeats in the Irish conditions which surrounded him? If there were any, they were very few. It is amazing the number of active things that this man crowded into his dreaming life. The creation of the Dublin Abbey Theatre, its plays, its acting, its simple, but suggestive, and often lovely, scenic effects, in which Yeats was always the inspiration, and often the practical man. To bring forth such a theatre, world-famous, would have been achievement enough and to spare in the life of one man. He, with the help of Lady Gregory, created a new style of acting, never seen before on the English-speaking stage; he read plays; he rehearsed his own, and helped in the rehearsals of others; he edited a magazine that he filled with his own wonderfully-worded comments on his own theatre and the theatre of Europe; he was one of the founders of the Celtic Literary Society; he spoke eloquently at many meetings, literary and political; he wandered over the United States lecturing to the Colleges about the theatre in Dublin, and about drama in general; he defended Synge against the silly puritanism of Ireland and America; he defended himself against the attack on his play *The Countess Cathleen*; and faced the crowd who tried to shout down *The Plough and the Stars* when it was produced in Dublin; and he defended Hugh Lane's efforts to make art more widely known and more generally honoured throughout the land; in fact Yeats spent a good deal of his time fleeing from crowds, and a greater part of his time facing them, like a true son of what he himself called 'the indomitable Irishry'. On a visit to Paris, he met Synge wasting his time trying to write criticism of French literature, and persuaded him to return to Ireland, so giving Ireland and the English-speaking world one of the finest dramatists they have ever had. He entered the Irish Senate, and became a notable figure there; and, in between these activities and many more, he wrote his beautiful poetry and his exquisite plays. So you see, Yeats was a doer, and a hearty one as well as a dreamer. He did not blaze, as Shakespeare did, like a noonday sun in summer; but he sailed the Irish sky like a lambent moon, giving an exquisite silvery glow to everything beneath it.

Yeats was born in Dublin of a middle-class family, in the best house of an avenue, with plate-glass windows and steps going up to the door, but most people think of him as a Sligo man — a beautiful county on the west seaboard — and, I think, he thought of himself as of Sligo too. There his family had its origin, a long ancestry, going back — as Yeats himself says — to the Butlers, Dukes of Ormond, who were, according to the poet, 'half-legendary men'. Yeats had a curious, but steady, desire for family connection with the old aristocracy, perhaps because he could claim none with the older and more aristocratic Gaelic stock. Of Dublin, where he was born, he seems to have thought little, passing it by indifferently, sometimes almost with a gesture of scorn; but Sligo he loves and thinks of often. Sligo where the old myths are as plentiful as blackberry blossoms on the hedges; where dolmens, cairns, cromlechs, and stone circles silently tell of a past, not only human, but superhuman too. Here on the top of Knocknarea, the Hill of the Kings, though some say Hill of the Moon, for Rae is the Irish genitive for moon — towers the cairn where Maeve is said to be buried; Maeve, legendary Queen of Connaught, a character in fierceness, in courage, and in stature, far excelling the Boadicea of Britain, or Brünhilde of Germany. Here, too, wandered, fought, and died the legendary Fenian warriors; and here Yeats wandered, brooded deeply, and filled his dreaming thoughts with the epic memories of Sligo's past. As Wessex was Hardy's country, Warwickshire Shakespeare's, Cork Spenser's, so was Sligo

Yeats's natural home and haunt. Here a young lad's mind was wakened to the magic of literature by his father reading to him Thoreau's *Walden*; here the boy Yeats walked thirty miles to a dry rock in the wood of Slish where he lay down throughout the night to see the dawn break over his beloved Isle of Innisfree, where he thought midnight was all a glimmer, noon a purple glow, and evening full of the linnets' wings.

Of Yeats as a poet, there can be no doubt that Yeats was the greatest poet of his generation, and of many generations before writing in the English language. He wrote some of the loveliest love lyrics in the language, perfect and exquisite; though sometimes one would like to change their intellectual beauty for a deeper love-cry, like unto the one uttered by Robert Burns in his 'My Love is Like a Red, Red Rose.' A number of his poems and some of his plays were disliked by the clergy, for these do not encourage familarity with a past that, while it was beautiful in legend and myth, was distinctly pagan; and Yeats found himself criticising the clergy who were sinking into satisfaction with vulgar decoration in their churches and indifference, spiced by opposition, to the finer things in literature and life. But, as far as Yeats is concerned, that is all passed by now, and the poet is received and honoured by cleric and laity in Ireland who welcome his memory now as another banner of joy and achievement over the people: a banner of silvery sheen giving an exquisite glow to even dull things of life in the land.

When Yeats turned for a rest from poetry to prose, he set down beauty in an unembroidered dress, in a form more simple, but laced with a strange grace and dignity of its own, reminding one of a prose, less splendid, but more quietly-exquisite than that of Shelley. All who have the English language naturally or who have acquired it should read *Reveries, Plays and Controversies*, and the account of his life he gives in *The Trembling of the Veil*. They will indeed reward anyone who reads them.

Yeats lies buried in Roquebrune, in France. It was his last wish to take his last sleep under the shadow of Ben Bulben, Sligo's mountain, ringed with a thousand legends. The war prevented his quiet return home. Ireland waits the chance to bring her great man back again so that he may sleep where the noon is a purple glow; where evening is full of the linnet's wings; where peace comes dropping down from the skies; disturbed only by the gentle lapping of Loch Gill's waves, holding tight to her bosom his own loved Isle of Innisfree.

MELPOMENE IN IRELAND (1947)*

A BIG book this, the biggest ever seen about the Irish theatre; all about it since the first day an Irishman began to have a dispute with another, or one with himself. A long and a varied history, beginning with God and ending, I daresay, with the devil. The jacket tells us that 'it is a monumental and exhaustive history of every facet of the dramatic movement in Ireland'; and, by and large, so it is. So full of facts about plays and players that it almost frightens one to think of the work Dr Kavanagh must have done to gather them all together into one estimable and historic book. Here indeed is the gathering of all Ireland's dramatic clans. Though the book is far too big to be carried about in a pocket, it is one that should be in every public library and on the private shelf of everyone who is desiring to know something of the vagabond actors and their plays who paved the way for the modern Abbey Theatre and the Gate.

It is a sad thing to have to say that nothing whatever is known of a Gaelic theatre; nothing even resembling one is shown anywhere, nor does the drama seem to be mentioned in any of Ireland's old books, which chronicle all the things that happened since Noah's children first landed in Bantry Bay to the time the Normans put an end to the Gaelic civilization, and the clans were scattered over the world. Dr Kavanagh gives two reasons for this; one, that 'Even in the great age of learning in Ireland, the country was for the most part wild and uncultivated, with no towns, and communications between different parts of the country most difficult.' I'm afraid that this story of an age of learning is a little exaggerated; that Ireland [at] this time wasn't really a place where every lad was a Latin scholar and a Greek

* Review of *The Irish Theatre* by Peter Kavanagh (The Kerryman, Tralee, 1946), published in abbreviated form in *Tribune*, Jan. 31, 1947.

student. The peasant at the time couldn't have been any better than the peasant on the Continent, and that peasant's lot was a very hard one. What learning there was must have been confined to the monasteries, and, in them, to the monks who were earnest and diligent enough to use their time with profit. The peasant and whatever workers there were, serving the chiefs, the abbots, the priors, and the monks, must have been hard put to it to earn a living, and every day must have been a day of heavy toil either for his master or for himself, so that, at the end of it, it wasn't Latin he desired or wanted, but a long drink and a merry dance to drive away from his memory the illpaid labour of the day. This seems to be proved by the warning issued by the Church authorities: 'All parish priests of our diocese and province are distinctly ordered to announce publicly in their churches that no-one is to presume to hold a dance, wrestling match, or other disgraceful games in our churches or cemeteries, especially on the vigils of saints. The priests must also forbid such theatrical games and frivolities by which churches are dishonoured, and warn them under suspension, and order them in future to abstain from such acts, and cease from them, under pain of greater excommunication.' Puritanism before the Puritans! The Chesterton–Hilaironian dream that the peasant and worker in the Middle Ages had a merry and melodious life of it was about as substantial a thing in Ireland as it was anywhere else. Their dream was a dream forever expanding, and ever going backwards. No roads and no towns does not speak very highly for an age of learning. Ireland misses the Roman road. But even where they were, even where the Romans had left a sense of method and order, the worker and the peasant had a hard and a scanty time of it. In those days, in Ireland as well as other countries, the great monasteries dictated the life of the community, and it wasn't a very good life for poet, peasant, or worker. It was only at the coming of the Dominicans and the Franciscans that the Church Orders took a definite step towards democracy. The lack of roads, the absence of towns, and the opposition of the Church were the main two reasons why there never was a drama in the Gaelic tongue. Anyway, even

had there been roads, and even had the Church refrained from
condemnation, life was so uncertain, that no time could be given
to gather a company together for anything save to go into a
battle. So there was no Gaelic theatre in the days of the chief,
the abbot, or the poet, and there is no Gaelic theatre yet. But
on the whole, I am inclined to believe that it was neither the
lack of roads, nor even numerous calls to battle, but the invasion
of Ireland by St Patrick that ended any hope of an Irish drama,
till enough of centuries had passed to allow of evolving the
liberal mind ready and independent to produce it.

In 1637 an Irish theatre came into genuine life when a
theatre was built in St Werburgh Street, Dublin. Built by a
Scotsman (as Divilin was built by the Danes), its first dramatist
was the English poet, Shirley, whose second play for the theatre
was called *St Patrick for Ireland!* Curious the dust that has
gathered on the streets of Dublin. St Werburgha — who was he,
who was she? No-one prays to this saint now. There still
remains a church dedicated to this holy person, and in its vaults
lie two of the United Irishmen, the Brothers Sheares, who were
executed for rebellion in 1798, and whose bodies lie there 'in a
perfect state of preservation'. Dust, all the same, and a dimming
memory too. Shirley's sojourn in the city is dust, and the very
play he wrote is but dust on the stage of the world's theatre.
But some of it was flecked with gold, for Shirley's visit and
Shirley's play, though it tried to glorify a saint who was a symbol
of rancorous opposition to those things likely to strengthen and
enliven the hard life of man, brought a new idea to Ireland; an
idea that was to grow into a great movement destined to have an
effect on thought and outlook on Irish life, changing it in mind
and manner so much that old things passed away, and many things
became new.

In his play, Shirley gives a fine sketch of the saint. One of the
Druids relates a dream he had in which

> *We saw a pale man coming from the sea,*
> *Attended by a tribe of reverend men,*
> *At whose approach the serpents all unchain'd*
> *Crept into the earth.*

And dancing, merriment, and the natural joy of life were three of them. Pale-faced St Patrick (the Patrick who gets all the kudos, for there was another who did all the work) and his tribe of reverend men are still among the Irish people, busy banning serpentine books and plays into the earth's centre or the sea's broadest bosom; while the playactors, Chesterton and Belloc, sing that where the Roman Church is, there is freedom of thought. Shirley must have been caught in Shaw's Irish climate, for he makes Patrick say of Ireland to King Leary's son,

> This nation
> *Shall in a fair succession thrive, and grow*
> *Up the world's academy, and disperse,*
> *As the rich spring of human and divine*
> *Knowledge, clear streams to water foreign kingdoms;*
> *Which shall be proud to owe that they possess*
> *In learning, to this great, allnursing island.*

Well, Up the world's Academy! And de Valera in his gorgeous robes as the lord-god Chancellor of the world's Academy with Professor Magennis's ghost murmuring over his shoulder, Mind you keep in the right way, Dev; remember that everything — even a play — has a beginning, a middle, and an end. For this piece of Shirley's innocent prophecy alone, the book deserves its life.

Then others than Shirley ushered themselves into the theatre, Sir John Denham, Richard Flecknoe, and Henry Burnell, who were ushered out again by the audience as quick as they had ushered themselves in, for as playwrights they were so bad as almost to incriminate the theatre forever in the minds of the people. Flecknoe must have anticipated the modern men of decency in the theatre, for he, who in his early life had been a priest, the book tells us, tried to carry the discipline of the seminary on to the stage, earning from Dryden, for his piety, the resounding title of King of Dullness. Priests seem to be poor hands at any kind of literature, and they should never try to write a play. We have had a few shocking examples in Ireland, for priests (and professional lay Catholics for that matter) streak their work with that timidly-bombastic piety which sounds so ridiculous on the stage, or over the wireless, or anywhere outside the walls of church or chapel, where the audience is ever ready and resigned to accept anything that may be said to them. Of one play, a critic wrote, 'Flecknoe's is a dramatic piece full of excellent morality; written as a pattern for the reformed stage . . . Whether the play answers the title page (*Love's Dominion*), or whether Mr Flecknoe have so regularly observed the three Unities, I shall leave to the critics . . . It had the misfortune to be damned by the audience.' The audience of the seventeenth century evidently had a sharp and final power, and rightly so when the play happened to be such a bad one. Often now the efforts of an audience seems to be to keep a bad play going, for we are more merciful (or more ignorant) now; then the people put a crippled thing out of its agony; now we give it a crutch, and critics often send round the hat to provide means to keep it comfortable. It was hard to drive the laugh, the love of a glass of wine, a woman's kiss, and general vigour of life from the stage; as hard as to drive them from the desire of noble, peasant, and worker; as hard as to drive them from the practices of the cloistered monks of the Middle Ages.

We learn from this history that of all people the Jesuits provided the drama as part of their educational course at that time; but their plays were written and performed in Latin, and as the Gaels had presumably lost their earlier scholarship, they didn't benefit thoroughly by their exhibition, and had to be content with a brief resumé of what the play was all about. One example given shows that they didn't miss much, for it seems to show that the dignified carefully-cut clerical cloth was no better than the gaudy fustian worn by the lay dramatists. The title of the play, *Titus; or the Palme of Christian Courage* comes near enough to let us guess the kind of play it was, and the full synopsis, which Dr Kavanagh gives, shows that the play well deserves the flaunting crown of its title.

The book brings us through the period of the Heroic Plays, centred by the towering figure of Dryden, and as Dublin depended on London for its plays (as she did, generally, up to the beginning of the First World War), most of these plays were performed in the new theatre of Smock Alley. From the Heroic Play period, we are led through the cynical, laughing avenue of bewigged, laced, and scented gentry of the golden days of good King Charles, with Congreve head and shoulders over the rest of the dramatists. This chapter gives some quiet and concise comments on Congreve's dramatic genius. There are a few amusing entries, such as the collapse of the Smock Alley Theatre roof on the Lord-Lieutenant, his sons, and the audience, followed by the Dublin puritans acclaiming it as An Act of God. From the point of view of the welcome given to bad drama, it's a pity that roofs do not fall oftener. Again, because an actor refused to repeat some patriotic lines in a play, when Sheridan came to the theatre the next morning he found that the anger of the audience had left no more than the shell of it for him.

A lot of space is wasted on Lord Orrery and others who don't deserve a line. Pepys sums them all up in a comment on the Lord: 'The play, though admirable, yet no pleasure in it, because the very same design, and words and sense and plot, as every one of his plays have, any one of which done, would be held admirable, whereas so many of the same design and fancy do but dull one another.' Pepys let Orrery down easy, but his implied advice, which Orrery didn't take, is good, though present-day playwrights won't, I daresay, take it either.

The fact is that the Irish theatre comes to life only when Congreve sits down to write a play. All who have gone before are of no value whatever, be they playwrights religious or secular. They have been so long forgotten till now, that now they should be forgotten forever. After Congreve, the theatre goes to sleep till George Farquhar shakes her into wakefulness again; then she dozes off deep till Goldsmith and Sheridan tempt her to get up, dress, and have a good walk in the open air; developing into a sprightly dance in the sentimental, but brightly-coloured melodramas of Dion Boucicault. (By the way, the villain in *The Shaughran* is not Harvey Duff, but Corry Kinchella, the Squireen, who aims at depriving the Fenian hero of his property and his girl; and in *The Colleen Bawn*, it is Mrs Cregan, and not

Hardress Cregan, who gives a glove to Danny Mann as a token that Eily O'Connor is to be put out of the way.) Then the theatre comes to life wittily in Wilde, sinking into torpor once more till the agile Shaw sprang on the stage to frighten, madden, or cajole the people into decency and commonsense towards life on the one hand, and the theatre on the other. And here we are as far as thought can go, with the Abbey Theatre on our right, and the Gate on our left.

When one looks at the innumerable play titles, and the long, steady list of poor playwrights, with but a few fine names almost hidden among them, one wonders at such an intolerable amount of sack for such a tiny spot of bread, the good play — the theatre's sacrament. But all activities have the same tale to tell: even in the apostolic succession of the old theatre of the Church there are as many duds, and more, than there are in the new church of the theatre. This is a book for the old, hardened sinners of the theatre. The young saint about to write his first play should keep well away from it: it is not for him. It is not easy to read, but it will make a first-class reference book of the Irish theatre. It is well and sturdily turned-out by the printers.

G.B.S. SPEAKS OUT OF THE WHIRLWIND
(1934)*

BERNARD SHAW stands pilloried in his play of *St Joan*. Immediately after he had completed the work with its bold lines, its critical humour, its delicate beauty, its tapestried tragedy, all those who saw and admired, seized the artist and imprisoned him forever in his own drama. When he writes another play the crowd cry out, not this thing, not this thing, but another and another *St Joan*! The most dangerous thing for an artist to do is to please the people, for they will never be satisfied till he pleases them again in the same way, which, of course, no artist can do. *St Joan* may or may not be the most beautiful thing Shaw has done; it is certainly not the most important. His *Back To Methuselah* is, to me, as beautiful as *St Joan*, and much more important than *St Joan* ever was or ever can be, for it stands a Postscript — and what a majestic and inspiring Postscript — to the Gospel of God! Bernard Shaw himself says that *St Joan* is but a play built out of official documents, and, though realising its strange beauty and wonderful charm, we ignore that modest repudiation of a great work, yet all who know the man through his works will unhesitatingly agree that to measure Shaw by *St Joan* is to measure a mountain with a tailor's tape.

Neither of the two major plays in this volume[1] may be as attractive in pattern or as rich in colour as *St Joan*, but though the forces in these two plays carry no banners, they are more terrible than the army that carries them. The flags here are

---

* Book review printed in *The Listener*, Mar. 7, 1934.
[1] *Too True to be Good* and *On the Rocks* in *Three Plays: Too True to be Good, A Village Wooing, and On the Rocks*, by Bernard Shaw (Constable, 1934).

flames of courageous thought, which some day, sooner or later, will burn to ashes the hay, straw, and stubble of cod mercy and truth and righteousness and peace that find their vent in the singing of hymns, piling of law upon law, and the pampering of the useless and the unfit.

Mr Shaw tells us in a preface that he thought he felt an unusual resentment in the attitude shown to *Too True to be Good*. Resentment is an unpleasant thing to a dramatist, yet it is a testimony to the fact that the barbed thought in the play went home. The irony within the irony is that every barb that struck another sank into Shaw's own breast, for he is the last man in the world that would wish to hurt another human being.

The English can stick *St Joan* because all that happened to her happened so long ago. The play, to all who came to see it, was like an illuminated Book of Hours that one can finger and fondle, and be amused by the quaint pictures, thanking God all the time that we are not as other men were. They like Shaw and they cheer him when he is content to be a Pursuivant dramatist with a play like a blazoned tabard; but they resent what he says and forsake him and flee when he elects to become a prophet of God. People can weep with St Joan for St Joan isn't 'The Patient'; they can condemn the Cardinal, for the Cardinal isn't the 'Clerical Burglar' and has nothing to do with an Anglican Episcopate; they can laugh at 'The Dauphin', for the Dauphin has no relationship with the British Premiership: his name is Louis and not Chavender.

Mr Shaw asks in the Preface to *Too True to be Good* to be told 'who have pictured the idle rich or really believed that they have a worse time of it than those who have to live on ten shillings a day or less, and earn it?' I, for one, have believed it for a long time now. For a long time I have believed that the first state is worse than the last. Not only the idle rich, but the vital and energetic rich, the good and the gracious rich, share sharply in the artificial sorrows and trials brought about by the system under which we live. I have often said that I am a Communist, not only out of sympathy for the poor, but also out of sympathy for the rich. The well-off, no less than the poor and the needy, need the savour of salvation that a sensible change of life can bring. The rich have to wage a never-ending battle against the advance and threats of poverty, combined with a never-ending battle with the confusion, the weariness, and the toil of doing all the things that wealth must do. They can escape from their riches no more than the sinner can escape from God. The temptations that the poor have to meet are small compared to the magnitude of the temptations that beset the rich. The poor stand as a picket outside the gates of heaven and refuse to permit the rich to enter, each the eternal enemy of the other. It is as bad, if not worse, to be born into great riches as it is to be born into bitter poverty. Looking back on my own life, when, in my infancy, the few things needed were not to be had, and that need unsatisfied meant many years of great pain coupled with the inability to do things done brightly by others; ending at last, but leaving behind forever irritating and incurable defects: looking back on all this, and thinking of them long and deeply, I unhesitatingly say that these terrible handicaps of poverty were no worse, if they were even as bad, as the handicaps, different, but none the less terrible, than those who are born to riches have thrust upon them. It wasn't for nothing that the Church put in her Litany a petition for deliverance in 'all time of our wealth' beside the petition for deliverance in the hour of death and in the day of judgement. And we all remember — or do any of us remember now? — the story of the young man who had 'great possessions'. He wasn't an ignorant or a careless or a vulgar or a selfish young man; no, no; far from that, for we are told that he had kept the law from his youth up, and that Jesus beholding him loved him. He loved the rich young man as much as He loved the poor; more, maybe, for we are told that as He looked upon him He loved him, and after the young man had departed, grieved because he could not do what Jesus had asked him to do, Jesus used an expression second only in sadness to those He used in the Garden and on the Cross. And the irony of the system under which we live is that now the rich cannot sell all that they have and give to the poor without making damn fools of themselves. If they did, they would not benefit the bodies of the poor, and they would lose the one chance of saving their own souls, namely, to use their intelligence to make life more healthy and sensible than it is, and to use their money to add power to their persuasion.

In *On The Rocks* and in the preface before the play, the old warrior has raised the flaming banner of the right to exterminate. At present but a corporal's guard has rallied to the colours, but this corporal's guard one day will be an army; for, sooner or later, the problem of the extermination of the unfit, the useless, who keep an army idle attending to them, and of all who find it impossible to fit into the mass that makes the nation, must be faced and must be solved if life is to lift itself a little higher than dogs who bark as we go by them. There must come a development of political wisdom which will ensure that the 'percentage of irre-claimable scoundrels and good-for-naughts that every human group contains ready to wreck any community' shall be cheaply exterminated, and not retained to be a worry and an expense to the rest of rational humanity. 'The notion,' says Mr Shaw, 'that persons should be safe from extermination as long as they do not commit wilful murder, levy war against the crown, or kidnap or throw vitriol, is not only to limit social responsibility, unnecessarily, and to privilege the large range of misconduct that lies outside them, but to divert attention from the essential justification for extermination which is always incorrigible social incompatibility and nothing else.' This is the problem that must be solved soon. We can't go on bolstering up and covering with down the hopelessly unfit and the incurably useless, but rather must we learn to eliminate the waste products of humanity. Intelligence is a little sick of a sham mercy running round with a hanging rope in one hand and a prayerbook in the other. The neglect of the potentially fit in their youth, the heaping up of worry and unnecessary expense upon the already fit and useful in the care of those who can never be any better, but will prob-ably become worse, is a sin against mercy and a violation of commonsense. The present-day talk about the sacredness of life is a sham. The healthy young among the mass of the people, under the present system, must sink into ruin before they can magnetise attention to themselves; while the unfit and the useless are not only cared for, but pampered with the attention of philanthropic and Christian Societies and people. To get sensible help one must almost always first be in a condition when help is practically useless. To keep the fit fit and the healthy healthy must be the first care in an intelligent community. And to do this less time or no time can be wasted on the hopelessly unfit, and the incorrigibly incompatible. Critics will cry out, who are going to judge, who are going to be the judges? A scientific, humane, and sensible judgement will eventually be evolved out of trial and error. Out of here a little and there a little fuller development will come. There is no other way of learning. We must not fly in terror from a mistake, or from the fear of making one. No mistake can ever be so bad as that which sent the best of men to the grave in shoals. The fear of making a mistake is a besetting sin with the English. They are sheep who have never gone astray. This fear of making a mistake will always keep them separate from God.

'We must', says Mr Shaw, 'have a common faith as to the fundamental conditions of a stable human society.' No community can be governed and no-one can govern a community without it. A national standard of life must be formed. A standard of efficiency, of usefulness, of courage, and of faith. The unity of one faith, one lord, one baptism, will no longer do, for in religion as it is, even here at home, we have too many lords, too many faiths, and too many baptisms. One is all we need, but one is vital. We must have a standard for the common good of all. If a man or a woman sink below this standard, then he or she must be eliminated. Should a man or a woman rise above it in efficiency, in usefulness, in daring, then a bigger place will be found for the functioning of that fuller efficiency and greater courage, and the result will be a double gain to the standard of life of the whole nation. We are already beginning to realise that national life is something more than a Parliamentary conversation picture piece, or an occasional jump into an adventure that we call 'the balancing of the budget'.

I praise him or her or them with a loud voice who ventured

to change the colour in the format of the volume containing Mr Shaw's latest plays. The colour has been changed from an unsightly and sickly greenish-yellow to a dignified maroon. In this new shelter of maroon linen, with the titles in gold on the spine, the book is delightful to look at and charming to handle.

The short play, *A Village Wooing*, with all its wit and sex-sense, is, to me, but an instance of a gigantic intellect unable to let an idle moment pass in an idle way.

SHAW'S PRIMROSE PATH (1952)*

LETTERS, letters, and letters! What a man Bernard Shaw was for sending his blasts and benedictions everywhere, falling over the land like the thistledown from a blown-out dandelion. And for a long time, busy hands will be gathering them up to scatter them widely again, for most of them have the core of wisdom's wheat in them, and a few, more than a few, the heady laughter hidden in the barley-grain. Here, a number are scattered among us by the English drama critic Alan Dent,[1] bringing before us musty glimpses of a lost theatre, a world nearly gone, a war swallowed up before it had time to grow old by a worse one, and ghosts of men and women forgotten by the young who are busy looking for new surprises on another peak in Darien. These letters set a door ajar into a corner of the private life of Shaw; not that the great man had much of a life that wasn't public, for as long as his legs held him up, he stood four-square before all men; and shortly after his legs failed him, he died. He couldn't stand the strain of having to be helped.

Well, it is interesting to watch Shaw gallivanting about with a plume in his hat, throwing a loose leg, snatching a little bout of wildness from the regularity of life, and doing a dance with the hilarity of a monk fortified with a tall glass of potent wine taken after a long season of fasting. Here, amid the fluttering of ribbons, the waving of fans, the presentation of bouquets, we run about after him in his curious courtship of the dazzling Mrs Patrick Campbell. We see him abandon the back of the gallop-

* This review was published in *The New York Times* on Nov. 9, 1952, under the title, 'With Love and Kisses from Mr. Shaw.'

[1] *Bernard Shaw and Mrs Patrick Campbell: Their Correspondence*, edited by Alan Dent (Alfred A. Knopf, New York, 1952).

ing pooka, and, for a rest, go gaily trotting about on the back of
O'Flanagan's mare; the time that Shaw had his Stella too.

Mrs Campbell was a very remarkable actress, and a much
more remarkable woman, fiery with vitality, beset with a streak
of irresponsibility, brave and bubbling with a sense of roguish
humour that maddened Shaw. The gay, irresponsible laugh was
a thing that Shaw hated, though it is good for the health, and at
times good for a too solemn world. To be touched up by her
saying, 'What a dear man you are', when he was in a critical
mood, was hell for Shaw; and into this hell he was plunged time
and again by the letters from Mrs P. Campbell.

The whole correspondence is like a hasty, rowdy rhapsody,
with a furious finale and a dignified, resigned coda. It begins,
from Shaw's side, with a quiet 'Dear Mrs Patrick Campbell'
and flowers fulsomely later on into 'Ever blessedest darling'.
Shaw for once was forgetting himself. Yet the very fantasy of
the rich endearments gave a secret sign that it could be thought
Shaw wasn't serious: he ran forward to love, then his caution
led him away from his love again with a jingle of bells. One
minute he says, 'You've only to whistle for me to come to
you,' and the next minute, up in London, where she is, he writes,
'I dine with Lena Ashwell Thursday afternoon, two committees
Friday evening, then *Caesar and Cleopatra*. Saturday, back here.'
Whenever he came to London, and so got close, he seemed to
pack himself into appointments so as to keep at a safe distance.
He follows the tale of commitments with

> *Oh these fine spring days!*
> *But what are vernal joys to me?*
> *Where thou art not, no spring can be.*

And hurries back to Ayot St Lawrence and to the sour looks
of Charlotte Shaw, resenting the attachment, wanting to know
all about it, though fearful, and wishing she could forget it: and
so to bed.

It reminds one of the English captain in one of Boucicault's
plays, who, deceived by a girl for the sake of her escaping Fenian
brother, sees her weeping, stretched out on the ground, says,

'This way, love; that way, duty,' and, after a second's pause, flings his shako into the air, and exclaims, 'Duty be damned, I'll follow the girl!' Shaw turned the exclamation about, saying, 'The girl be damned, I'll follow the duty!' And, more or less, he sticks to duty all through the correspondence. Why, I wonder? Like many another brave Irishman (present reviewer included) Shaw had a hard core of timid caution in his mind, always running into risks, always running to escape them.

His description of *Androcles and the Lion* as 'a bellowing, roaring business, that would uproot your house and leave you naked under the stars' is a timid description of a quiet, sensible, orderly play. Again, in his description of *The Apple Cart* as 'of the red-hot poker order; wildly disgraceful', followed by the statement that 'Orinthia never loses her distinction and beauty even when she rolls upon the floor. If she did, I would amputate her without hesitation, and be ashamed of her' is another sign of Shaw's core of timidity. Orinthia is so different from Shakespeare's aunties tumbling in the hay.

There was Mrs Charlotte Shaw to think about, too, sitting at home beside the harpsichord, jealous of Mrs Campbell, and hating the dame who had cast such a spell over her great man. She could be bitter and biting, as Shaw himself grimly mentions in some of the letters: 'After two perfectly frightful scenes with me, in which she produced such a case against my character, at a moment when murder and suicide seemed the only thing left to her, she suddenly recovered her amiability, and became once more (after two years) the happy consort of an easygoing man.'

Two years of unamiability from the amiable Mrs Shaw must have cornered Shaw into many utterances of secret blasphemy. Mrs Shaw was good and she was dowdy, surrounding him with dames dowdier than herself, and it is no wonder that the sage sanctioned an episodic companionship with a woman sparkling with vivacity and go.

The strange aspect and odd tenor of the letters at times leads the reader to imagine that they are gaily bluffing one another. But was it bluff? Hardly, though it is hard to know which was the hunter, which the hunted. She was the only one who could jab through his dignity with a nickname, and he was the only one who could call her names, and still affectionately hold her hand in his. In the letters, he has most of the wit, but she has her share of it, and she has all the humour. She has most of the poetry, too, and all the sorrow, though it comes and goes with a laugh. Here are all the kisses he blew, all the slaps he gave her. They are at rest now, Charlotte, the good and kind woman, with all her faults, between them.

Mr Dent has done the editing quietly and well, bringing into our street the exciting figure of Bernard Shaw trotting, terrillirril, past, a lady's favour pinned to his well-burnished armour.

A PROTESTANT BRIDGET (1946)*

HERE in this book, recording the hasty memories of Lady Gregory, we have another of the stories brought by Bridget. Impatiently put down, as an artist usually does with notes to be arranged and tidied up at leisure, they are rough, terse, and often irritating in that by telling so much, they tell too little; but they will be very interesting to all those who know something, and wish to know more, of the life in Ireland as seen by this strange lady of the Victorian mind, brightened with Picassian patterns of modern thought and dealing.

There were two triads in Lady Gregory's life, and these form sombre and brilliant patterns through all that she did, and all that she thought of in her persistent and courageous way through life. Her three sorrows of storytelling were the tragic death of her son, Robert, who as an airman lost his life in the First World War on the northern borders of Italy; the equally tragic death of a beloved nephew, Hugh Lane, who went down in the *Lusitania* off the Irish coast, almost in sight of his own old home in the county of Cork; and the third was the despicable robbery of the Lane Pictures by the political and art-minding authorities of Britain, who, to this day, hold the loot, and, like good Christians, have blessed and legalised the theft. Her three joys of storytelling were her House of Coole, her three grand-children, and the Abbey Theatre. So she says, 'With all the anguish of Robert's death, I have lost my one great fear of losing his affection.' She never could have lost it, but it was a cold comfort to her to think she might, and that his death sealed it to her forever. 'Desire for Society went with the death of Hugh

* Review of *Lady Gregory's Journals*, edited by Lennox Robinson (Putnam, 1946), published in *The Bell* (Dublin), Feb. 1947.

Lane,' she tells us, and 'so I passionately wish for the children's love and their happiness; for the return of Hugh Lane's pictures; for the government of Ireland in the hands of Ireland; and for the increased worthiness of the Abbey Theatre till we hand it over.' These fine wishes show the goodness of her soul and the wide generosity of her nature.

But the garden of her soul wasn't all trim and neat and tidy. There were some rough paths, some spiky, flaunting weeds that hindered a quiet walk in either its shade or sun. 'We drove over to Roxboro', our old home. The house — the ruin — is very sad, just the walls standing, blackened, and all the long yards silent, all the many buildings, dairy, laundry, cow-houses, coach-houses, stables, kennels, smithy, sawmills, and carpenters' work-shops empty. Some of the roofs falling in. I am afraid the house will never be built up. The garden is grass and weeds. All silent that had been so full of life and stir in my childhood, and never deserted till now.' Good Free State Catholics and equally good Catholic Republicans were busy showing what they could do for the glory of God and the honour of Ireland. And now Coole Park is just as silent, just as dead as Roxboro'. The house where she was born is gone, and the house where she lived so long is gone too. The first burned down by the Republicans, in a time of passion and mad foolishness; the second removed, calmly and quietly, stone by stone, by the god-fearing, highly-respectable, legally-formed de Valerian Government. As an act of grace, these vandals left the copper beech standing, I am told, whereon the names of great Irishmen and artists are carved, that of Yeats, and G. B. Shaw, and Augustus John. Not a sign now of this great woman, this Protestant Bridget left in Clare–Galway; not a sign of her left anywhere in the whole of Ireland, for, from all accounts, her spirit has departed even from the Abbey Theatre. Any Government with a tiny sense of honour for the rarer things in life, with any tendency towards a sense of admiration for God's gift of imagination, with even a sane sense of bestow-ing a dignity on Ireland, would have preserved the home where this woman had lived in the same way the Soviet Union has preserved the home of their great citizens, Tolstoy, Chekhov,

Lermontov, and Gorki, altogether irrespective of the class from which they had sprung.

It isn't as if Lady Gregory had given the back of her hand to Ireland, and had left her for another land, as Shaw had done with a laugh, and as Joyce had done with a scornful curse; she had stayed there to the last, doing what she could, mourning when her people mourned and rejoicing when they rejoiced, till the worn body coveted a long rest and till the same land that had given her birth had caught it to her breast. She rests among her own, and her dust now is Irish earth, a sanctified sod where she lies to all who have ever had a fine thought or two about good- ness of heart, or about the glories of art and literature. But a complacent Irish Government hacks in everything but the conception of their own peculiar vanities, took the roof of this home off, removed the walls, and levelled the place where it had once stood, rubbing it away from the breast of Ireland forever. Oh, rough and cowardly Philistine hands that would pluck a jewelled cross from Ireland's bosom. Only the tree, the copper- beech still stands, a symbol of her who made a symbol of it. As the shadow of the tree falls on a small spot of Coole, so the shadow of her life will fall over many a mind in Ireland, and many an Irish mind in other lands.

> *This learned I from the shadow of a tree,*
> *That to and fro did sway against a wall;*
> *Our shadow-selves, our influence may fall*
> *Where we ourselves can never be.*

What does this book do? Well, it shows, in hasty and dim lightning-like flashes, Lady Gregory doing too many things, linking herself up with too many people to allow perfection in the work that she could do so splendidly herself. It shows her using her own powers lavishly to infuse others with its influence; dropping one thing for a moment to find room in her hands for something else. Here she is with her face covered in grease paint, 'white, with black under the eyes, and red inside the lids — dreadful!' waiting trembling in the wings of the theatre to go on in the part of Cathleen ni Houlihan: it shows her reading

play after play, trying to pick one out good enough for production; it shows her bringing Yeats down to Coole for a rest,
where he can think out some new verse in perfect peace, while
the evening is full of the linnet's wings; it shows her going
around among the wealthy, trying to get them to spare a penny
or two for her Abbey Theatre so that the bank may be pacified
about the overdraft at a time when to buy an india-rubber ball
and a coconut for a play was a desperate expenditure and a
gamble; it shows her trudging England in search of Dublin's
Lane pictures; it shows her trying to get between Cosgrave and
de Valera, slashing at each other with knives whose hafts are engraved with the Sacred Heart, shouting as they cut at each other
the righteousness and truth of Tweedledee and Tweedledum;
it shows her conducting rehearsals of *John Bull's Other Island*,
snatching an odd minute's rest in a handy armchair, or, tired and
anxious, after a full day's work, crawling into bed for a real rest
at last.

In her spare time, she did the housekeeping of Coole, working
savagely to preserve the place for her grandchildren, ever praying
that they might be kept from the evil that is in the world, while
in between she listened to the winding words of the Kiltartan
peasants telling their woes the way they tell their beads, and
trying to find a focus into which she can suddenly dive a wrinkled
hand to help them, then trotting out in the pouring rain to pull
the last remaining tulips so that the altar of a church with which
she has no attachment may look bright and fair for a morning
service. Never-ending work, never-ending anxiety, never-ending
exasperation, softened by the snatching of a sweet text from one
of the Gospels, crowned by her three sorrows of storytelling, the
loss of her son, Robert, the loss of her nephew, Hugh Lane, and
the loss of her beloved Lane pictures. Her face crinkled, her
body grew stiff, her hair turned white, but she went on bravely,
always hopeful, ever sure, her luminous eyes keeping their
daring and laughing gleam in them to the last hour that God was
willing to give her.

God gave her many gifts, but denied her one thing, most
necessary, most precious to her — time. God didn't give her

enough time to do the things she wanted to do. Troubled about finances, about her grand-children, about Yeats's cough, about the Lane pictures, using a lot of her royalties to hurry out to plant new trees in the Seven Woods of Coole, worried about the squirrels eating her best apples, she hurried from task to task, full of vigour and hope, getting stiffer in her joints month by month, she went on doing things for herself, for others, for all, till at the end she found that God hadn't given her enough time to do all that needed to be done. Her day was too short and the night came when the woman could work no longer. She hadn't time even to set down her journals properly. But they are valuable, containing the brief and abstract chronicles of the time, and those parts of them left out may well be as interesting and as important, even more so, than the extracts here presented to us in this volume. Some time in the future, when Ireland has a National (or Labour) Government ready to bring dignity into the land, these *Journals* will be published by the State in full, as the Journals of Chekhov and Stanislavsky have been published in the U.S.S.R., for they have an importance and a meaning quite as rare and valuable as many things delivered to the nation by the Irish Texts Society. But that time is not yet, for the present Government's interest in literature and art is about begun and finished when de Valera shakes hands with Jack Yeats to bid him the top of the evening.

The hot time of the Black and Tans, followed by the hot times of the Civil War, pulled many a valuable year from Lady Gregory's life. But she went on, practising the art of living right within range often of the mouth of machine-gun and rifle; still having resolute hope when Ireland's newest banner was a shroud, thinly bordered with the colours in the tricolor. Lady Gregory, like a lot of others, sometimes, still in the quietness of her bed, found herself listening to the purring of a lorry, while she listened for the heavy knocking on the door. These parts of the *Journals*, though picturing many a rough scene and anxious moment, are too numerous, and too sketchy for such a trouble-some period. The recital of raids, the receiving of wounds, the burning of houses, the burying of the dead, are so similar in colour and line as to become monotonous. Here again, Lady Gregory lacked the time to tell of these things well. But these doings disturbed the gentleness and peace of Clare–Galway, and this was well, for the place can never be quite the same again. Even Clare–Galway has had to enter into the turmoil-changing of the world.

The most pathetic and interesting part of the *Journals*, to me, is the half-conscious account Lady Gregory gives of the fading from Ireland of the Big Houses. She seems to have a semi-clear idea that old things are passing away, and that, though all things are not becoming new, all things are becoming different. This may be symbolised in the brief account she gives of a visit to Lady Ardilaun, one of the richest lasses in the country. She writes, 'Lady Ardilaun is a lonely figure in her wealth, childless, and feeling the old life shattered around her. Macroom has been burned, and Ashford is a barracks, and she laments the loss of Society and "those nice young officers who used to write their names in our book", and she speaks with violent complaint of the Free State Government and its opponents, adding "our class is gone, and who is there to replace it?" ' The new one, dear lady, that is rising up under the one which has already replaced it.

We are told that this rich lady, near lost in her huge house of St Anne's, with its hundreds of rooms, found 'solace in kindness, and showed me a glasshouse containing a quantity of geraniums in pots that are grown for poor women of the tenement houses who come to tea sometimes. Lady Ardilaun gives each poor tenement woman that comes a geranium in a pot to take away.' She may well have asked who is to replace the class that gives away to a poor woman in the tenements a geranium in a pot. Such evangelic charity isn't easily replaced. But its brightness is darkened a little when we remember that it was these poor women of the tenements and their kin, who, by drinking Guinness's beer, gave this rich lady the wherewithal to possess this huge house, with its widespread gardens, displaying wonderful flowers, with hosts of dahlias and the glory of many roses. Again Lady Ardilaun complained to Lady Gregory of the change that had come over the Royal Garden Parties in London in 1924. One of the Labour Ministers came in a tweed coat, and the King had to speak to him about it. But the 'tweed coat' has grown more numerous, for the world largely depends for its life on the tweed coat and the cloth cap. And the tweed coats and the cloth caps know it now. The world that Lady Gregory knew was dying fast when she died herself.

Mr Robinson, the editor, I think, makes two mistakes in his comments on Lady Gregory's achievement and upon her nature. He says, 'The half-tones of Chekhov would have bored her, they lacked vitality'; and 'Her place in Irish Literature depends upon her achievement as a dramatist'. I'm quite sure [the plays of] Chekhov wouldn't have bored her, if they had been well played, for they don't lack 'vitality', and they are not so subtle as all that. Some of her own plays go along quietly enough. I think she admired the plays of Yeats, though they lack the 'vitality' that is manifest in the plays of Chekhov. And the beings in Chekhov plays are surely as 'fated' as the characters in most other plays. One of her greatest favourites in authorship was Hudson. While she would ply her hurried strength through the bustle of London and Dublin, we must not forget that she could sit calm and pensive in her still garden of Coole under her own catalpa tree. Mr Robinson, I imagine, has a bad habit of assuming that no one can be quite so subtle as he.

Living her own life with insistent intensity, Lady Gregory lived, at the same time, ardently, a life among the plain people. She knew Curley the Piper as well as she knew Yeats, and Ardrahan Church better than Westminster Abbey. Stately and confident in a train, she was quite at home among the peasant third-class passengers. Though far from being well-off, she gave of what she had, and added a large part of herself to the gift; never content to make her union with the people anything more than the presentation of a geranium in a pot. 'She never aspired to be a Maud Gonne or a Countess Markievicz,' says Mr Robinson. Sensible woman that she never had any desire to be like the Countess, whom she saw for the last time in O'Connell Street, when the traffic was being held up by a procession, in which, high up on a wagonette, stood the Countess, cheered by a watching crowd. The Countess was content when she was high over a crowd, if the crowd happened to be big enough to satisfy her; but she couldn't be at rest in a cottage by the fireside of the people. Shy and sensitive before a crowd, Lady Gregory was quite at ease and happy before the sparkle of firelight in the people's homes.

Well, here in this book is a sketchy profile of Lady Gregory; a kind of dark magic-lantern in which the slides are pushed in and pulled away too quick, but colour and light flashes from the picture often enough to make the book a thing to have and to keep till her country gives her the meed of praise and honour she so richly earned. The format of the book is bad, in my view. The jacket is a black-displayed reproduction of the Abbey Theatre's sign-manual. The focus of Lady Gregory's life as Ireland knew her was not the Abbey Theatre, but Coole House, and this house should have been shown rather than the insignia of the theatre. The cover, too, is rather forbidding, and altogether more wretched than the big price of the book would warrant it to be.

A SPRIG OF ROSEMARY AMONG THE
LAUREL (1962)*

IT is odd to let the imagination dwell on the group of hog-politicals talking together for a few minutes, and then deciding with an ignorant Irish hey ho nonny O, that the historic House of Coole should be pulled down and rooted up from the roof down to the cellar, and the stones to be scattered far and wide so that the house dwindled down to a place where no one came. They tried to tear asunder, leaf by leaf, the wreath that the poet Yeats had placed upon her head, failing to realise that this was far beyond the reach of apathy, ignorance, or spite. This was the house that nourished Yeats, giving him wine, if not from the vineyard, then from a vineyard just as good; wine from abroad and honey from her own bees, honey I and she ate when break-fasting together. This was the house that gave him great woods, a fine river, a wide lake, the majestic whirr of wild swans in flight, and evenings of peace full of the linnet's wings.

It was Lady Gregory who opened to the poet the warm welcome, spiritual and practical, of an Irish soul; it was her sympathy and help that gave the poet to Ireland, and Ireland who willy nilly gave the great poet to the world: she should be remembered forever.

In her book, *Cuchulain of Muirthemne*, Lady Gregory says: 'If there was more respect for Irish things among the learned men that live in the college of Dublin, where so many of these old writings are stored, this work would not have been left to a woman of the house, that has to be minding the place, and listening to complaints, and dividing her share of food.'

* Foreword to *Lady Gregory: Selected Plays*, chosen and introduced by Elizabeth Coxhead (Putnam, 1962).

In my opinion, Lady Gregory, if not a great writer, was a first-class one, and a prolific one, too. She wrote many plays and a number of books. (I wonder, at times, why Ireland's National Government, such as it is, does not re-issue such books as *Gods and Fighting Men, Saints and Wonders, Poets and Dreamers,* and the one about Cuchulain — presenting the hero in a far more vivid way than the figure now standing in Dublin's Post Office.) Hampered as she was with the many burdens she carried about with her — her little theatre, her home, orchard, woods, the anxiety she felt for Yeats, and, worst of all, the burden of bringing safely back the Lane pictures to Dublin — considering all these it is more than a wonder this indomitable woman squeezed out the time to leave behind such a fine amount of first-class literary work. Lady Gregory was the last but one (if we count Yeats as a Christian), and since she left, the present-day Irish Protestants in the Irish Republic have ceased to be indomitable, and aren't even interesting, for they aren't even the ghosts of those who went before them: most of them like the *siogaidthe* mentioned in Art MacCooey's song of 'One-eyed Mary'.

Since she died, there has been no whisper of remembrance given, as far as I know, to Lady Gregory; the Abbey Theatre and the Irish Academy of Letters seem to look upon her as a poor has-been; no one even has placed a laurel wreath round the brows of the bronze head of the gallant lady in the Dublin Municipal Gallery. Perhaps it is just as well, for she was no kind of spirit to be admired by our intellectual and artistic group shivering at the shake of a clerical finger.

One gallant group, led by Michael Scott, the architect (in more ways than one), has managed to set up a lasting memento to James Joyce. A Martello Tower where Joyce once lived, bought by Mr Scott, is being made into a museum of many things close to the life and work of the great writer. That, at least, can be set against the scabby destruction of Coole House. No sign remembering Synge, Stephens; Yeats has his grave, and now a Summer School in his honour is held yearly in Sligo; but still none remembering Lady Gregory or George Moore.

Perhaps, some time, an Irish Government will issue stamps remembering them all;[1] and if they don't, never mind — they will be remembered, not so much for what they handled or owned, but for what they did; which things are not writ down in water, but engraved deep on the everlasting tablets of Irish history.

Miss Coxhead has already written a fine life of Augusta Gregory, and this book is another tribute to the great gifts which were within the body, mind, and spirit of the gallant one we recognised and knew as Lady Gregory: I commend it to all Irishmen and Irishwomen (and English and American) wherever they may be. It is a fine sprig of rosemary among the Yeatsian laurel.

Lady Gregory, mother of many books, daughter of Ireland, daughter of wise words, of good deeds, of great humour, lover of tree and sweet herb, of beast and bird, we hail thee still! We do not wish, nor can we afford, to murmur farewell to thee for a long, long time to come.

---

[1] A start was made in this direction in 1965 with stamps commemorating the centenary of W. B. Yeats's birth.

THE GAELIC BLACK-HEADED BOY (1945)*

AND translated well, too. It's worth getting for its own sake. Here's a poem you'd hardly find in Dr Douglas Hyde's *Love Songs of Connacht*. Gay as it is, it isn't quite in the jovial and Gaelic-gushing style of Hyde's line of poetry. Not a thing to be read in church, though as near to God, and more lively than most of the Keys of Heaven and Gardens of the Soul.

During my long experience of the Gaelic League, I couldn't get out of any other member a word, save that Merriman was a poet, and that he had written a thing that jarred and scarred Ireland's innate modesty and reticence. Mention his name to a Gaelic Leaguer, and muttering 'must go', he'd hurry off to keep an oppressive appointment. Yet I never met a native speaker who didn't know it well but one, who hadn't read it, though he was seeking to find it high up and low down.

Merriman wouldn't expect to be allowed to walk arm in arm with Professor Corkery and Thady O'Donoghue (not the O'Donoghue who killed the yeoman captain with a skelp of his smith's hammer); this novelist and this poet are part of the stock of wholesome and clean-minded Gaeldom. This stately gander and this demure goose cast but occasional glances at the wild swan on wing overhead; but the hissing of the stately gander and the demure goose will die down, and be forgotten, and the life-song of the wild swan will linger long in many ears, even though some of the ears will have to stretch out in secret to hear the swing and gaiety of the wild song.

Another Irish novelist and critic, Aodh de Blacam, while

* Review of *The Midnight Court*, poem in Gaelic by Brian Merriman, translated into English by Frank O'Connor (Fridberg, 1945), printed in *Our Time* (London), Nov. 1945.

giving the poem a fair measure of cautious praise, tells us that 'unhappily, the theme and the mood of this supreme piece of colloquial Gaelic verse forbid its popularity'. And later on, says: 'Merriman had the mediaeval frankness, like Chaucer; and, like Chaucer, he will lead no one very far wrong.' But Chaucer isn't hidden away; he is there for everyone to read him; while Merriman has long been thrust into an inner cell of the Hidden Ireland, the black sheep of the fair, holy-shining flock.

It is one of the wonders of Ireland that this saucy, savage poem has been preserved. The poem that vehemently and gloriously strikes at the humbug and hypocrisy of what was called marriage in his day, and is still called by the same name in our own. Of the charms of womanhood, and the right those charms have to a full recognition and enjoyment with life that is equal to making a full use of them. I agree with O'Connor when he rebukes Professor Corkery for referring to Merriman as a coarse jester. He was no more a coarse jester than Shakespeare was; far less, indeed, for in his sincerity, he shows, as O'Connor points out, he wrote this way because he was shocked at what he saw going on around him in the life of love. And, indeed, in this respect he is up-to-date. I remember as a young man in Dublin how a relatively wealthy old fellow of sixty sought the hand of a buxom, handsome lass of little more than twenty, who was in love with a young laddie as hale as herself. But the parents, aided by the priests, badgered the lass into the arms of the old man; for the clergy were enthralled with the idea of a maximum wedding-fee, forgetting the withered power of life and limb that went with it. After a few years of married life, the young woman, too fearful, or too virtuous, to take on the young man as a lover, took to drink, and, after a spell of drunken misery, ended her days in a lunatic asylum. I knew them both, and sometimes worked for the useless but lecherous old villain. And, today, the young women of Ireland could cry out, as did the lass in Merriman's poem, that to sleep with a spade or a bolster is the only choice they can have for a bedfellow. Haven't I read somewhere that forty per cent of the Irish people under forty have no husband on the one hand, or any wife on the other?

It would be no wonder for the lasses to call out again for the removal of the vow of celibacy from the clergy. The Gaelic poet McGrath, wrote bitterly about this practice, too. One day, he met a young woman weeping bitterly, and asking her why, she told him that she was forced by her parish priest to wed, for the sake of his wealth, an old man, whose coldness of age had near destroyed her:

> *A priest bade me marry 'for better or worse',*
> *A wretch who had naught but his money and years—*
> *Ah! twas little he cared, but to fill his own purse.*

The clergy like a purse stuffed so that it doesn't jingle.

We are told in the preface that, after *The Midnight Court*, Merriman wrote nothing else. It isn't surprising. He would hardly escape the vigorous hostility of the very rev. Jim canon this, or the rev. father John that; and as he couldn't sing quiet, he ceased to sing at all. And Ireland lost a greater and more musical Robbie Burns. The British Government aren't altogether to blame for the arrest of thought in Ireland.

This publication is very welcome. It is a good thing that the English (among others) should see something of the hidden Ireland; and in this charmingly printed book this can be done. It shows us a side of Ireland other than the romantic one displayed by Yeats, which is only partly true; or of that of de Valera's Ireland, which is hardly true at all. Here we have the biggest part of Ireland, the angry shout, the desires of the flesh, the hard lot of the young, the spirit that is of the earth, earthy, and none the worse for that same.

The translator has done well, though the whole vivacity of the Gaelic doesn't appear in the English idiom. For instance, the lass describing her hair:

> *ta m'urla sgainneach,*
> *Bachallach, buclach, cuplach, fainneach,*

what English could give, or imitate, the jaunty swinging sound of these adjectives?

Through the charm and liveliness of literature is a fine way of making friends; and the more we know of each other in this way, the better. I hope this delightful volume will have a fine sale.

A PROPHET IN THE THEATRE (1938)*

I never met Robert Loraine in the street or in the home; but his spirit, fast and furious, gentle and tragic, swept over me from the footlights in the theatre. I saw his bewilderment, his agony, his rage, and his madness in *The Father*; his terror, his selfishness, and his decay in *The Dance of Death*; and his enchanting swagger and heroic pathos in *Cyrano de Bergerac*. He came upon me first, like a soft and scented wind, in Barrie's *Barbara's Wedding*, and then, like a biting whirling wind in Strindberg's play. This, I said, is a man; a strange, gentle, tempestuous being, and an actor of the best that England can give as an offering for her soul. And now we have a book[1] telling us, finely and fairly, of the tremendous energy, the wild but sane enthusiasm, the great gifts possessed, and possessing, by this very remarkable man.

As long as I live, the acting (if it was acting; perhaps it was something more than acting) of Robert Loraine will forever live vivid in my mind. It is sad to think (as the book shows) that the theatre of England did not give this gifted man the opportunities he desired, and, more than that, the opportunities he needed.

What a strange young life he led! We are told that, in his infancy, he was filled with the idea that heaven was at the end of a long, long journey, and that he, with a little girl, held by the hand, tried to find where heaven was by following a funeral, an idea that is dark in the minds of many infants today; how his elders and his Aunt Bella talked to him about the Holy Ghost on Sundays 'when he sat between them on a hard bench in church for three or four hours at a time'; and that 'the family was deeply religious; a sweet, but firm woman was widowed,

---

* Book review published in the *Sunday Times*, Sept. 18, 1938.
[1] *Robert Loraine*, by Winifred Loraine (Collins, 1938).

lace-capped Aunt Bella'. I suppose they were 'deeply religious', though they seemed to carry child-baiting into their love of God. This idea of religion seems to explain, not his greatness but his occasional oddity.

After an attack of brain-fever, he was packed off to 'the best private school in Cheshire'. Here he expected to find endless excitement, including some snatch-and-grab raids into knowledge. Instead it provided 'endless copying out of text-books; arithmetic that had no relation to life; cheating; greasy potatoes and stale bread, as well as boys he was expected to fight, and then was punished for fighting'. I wonder what the better schools were like? So little Robert Loraine, prompted by his wild sanity, saved his life by running away to Liverpool; and, we are told, the head of 'the best private school in Cheshire did not notify the police, because his term's fee had not been paid'. Another example of deeply religious people.

Then follows an extraordinary account of the boy finding a job as an actor in a Sailors' Dive. He began his career in a cellar reeking of rum, bilge, kerosene, baccy, mixed with the smell of rotting vegetables, herrings, tar, and the body odours of unwashed humanity from every part of the globe. This terrible Dive was the making of the boy. It taught him to fight and so to live. The divinity that had remained hidden in church and school was revealed to this boy of thirteen in the Sailors' Dive.

Later came strenuous times in the Great War, where Loraine clung on to life, encaged in an aeroplane, high in the air, with a lung deeply channeled by a shrapnel bullet. But the great adventure of the man's life was the discovery of a play called *Man and Superman*. How hard it was to find a backer, even though Loraine, in his great faith, had sold all he possessed to secure this pearl of great price. Rich is the tale of a talk with a manager from 1-30 a.m. to 8-a.m., with the manager listening to every word of praise about the play, and ending up with a weary murmur of 'There may be something in it, Bob.' It makes one jubilant to read that Loraine made a fortune out of the play, the receipts 'breaking the takings of the Ziegfeld Follies for that season'. Hurrah! It's grand to watch idiotic managers being blown into the void.

When the war was over, and Loraine came back to life with a shattered knee, he found the remains of his temple down and a gaudy palace of joy in its place. 'Everyone wanted to dabble in shows; there were more plays than playhouses, and rentals had soared. Crazy speculation had taken the place of endeavour.' The artist was up against the ignorant moneybags, and, though they never defeated the artist, they eventually killed him.

The break with G. B. Shaw was an unfortunate event, and the subsequent alliance with Edgar Wallace, when Loraine joined up in the play called *The Man Who Changed His Name*, a much more unfortunate thing still. By passing from *Man And Superman* to such a play, Loraine became, indeed, a man who had changed his name: a name of glory for a name of nothing.

The book gives a remarkable account of the actor's association with Wallace. What a selfish, commonplace theatre was represented in the letter written to Loraine: 'Every laugh is a £100 in your pocket; every laugh killed takes about that amount off the play's value. . . . I'm so keen on the commercial side of the play that I didn't even bother to make your part supreme. . . . It was written so that it may go round the provinces for a couple of years and be for you a steady source of income.' What I have written, I have written.

His wife wanted him to play *Peer Gynt*, but he wouldn't. He would, had England been behind his wife, and England should have been there, with a banner of pride in her hand.

The book holds fine photographs, and some grand letters from G. B. Shaw. It is a most interesting book about a wonderful man: a man who brought dignity and power to the kip called a theatre.

The politicians may and do save England's face: Robert Loraine did a lot to save her soul.

A MINER'S DREAM OF HOME (1934)*

MR GARNETT in his introduction[1] tells us that D. H. Lawrence
pencilled a note on the MS., saying that he was but twenty-one
when he wrote the play, and that it was 'Most horribly green'.
It is green, certainly, but only in contrast to the withered things
that clutter the English stage and wait for a righteous judgment
and a general burning. It is not a great play, not even a fine play,
but it is a work which plainly shows the makings of a fine
dramatist in Lawrence. There is in the work the three-coloured
bud of force, humour, and dramatic feeling. There is, as Mr
Garnett points out in his introduction, a strong delineation of
character, and the ' "greenness" lies rather in the cocksureness
of the author'. But this 'cocksureness' is only the undisciplined
confidence of a young writer who knows too much and hasn't
learned enough. It is a confidence that every young dramatist
ought to have, must have, if he wants to put anything better than
popular successes on to the stage. This cocksureness of Lawrence
— childlike at times — is saturated with an intense and accurate
feeling in the vision of the life of the family he seeks to set upon
the stage. It isn't a play that the English managers would rush
out to meet, though many of them are ever in the market place
crying out for plays so that they may make hay while the sun
shines or the rain falls; but the moment they get a play with the
touch and go of life in it, they start to gibber like jays, close their
eyes, shake their heads, and say, how long, oh Lord, how long!
They are dead with a play, and dead without one.

Here is a play that was worth production when it was first

* Book review in *The New Statesman & Nation*, July 28, 1934.
[1] *A Collier's Friday Night*, play by D. H. Lawrence; with preface by
Edward Garnett (Secker, 1934).

written, and it is worth production now. Had Lawrence got the encouragement the play called for and deserved, England might have had a great dramatist. It's no use saying that the play was hid, and no one knew about it; the point is that even had everyone known about it the play would not have been produced, for the play is too good in essence to ensure a shower of gold into a manager's lap. Life has vanished, and art has vanished off the English stage. The pomp and circumstance of glorious life has been degraded down to the inglorious pomp and circumstance of a bed.

The play gives us, in the description of its scene even, a fine and lively idea of an English miner's home. It gives us a fine and sharp representation of a clash between a tired-out workman and his tired-out wife, and the clash between these two and their children. It gives us, too, an acute scene of a clash between woman and man, and woman and woman. Not as a cocktail-nourished dramatist gives them gives he them unto us, but as an earnest and young man, surprised and perplexed, sees them and feels them for the first time. The play is weak in dramatic action; it is not graceful, neither is there in it the sound of silken garments moving, but there is the sweat of life in it, and that is something. Some part of the play sinks to softness; a lot of it is hard and even brutal, and it ends on a note of puzzling, strange, and striking pathos. He shows us that the miner thinks more of the Miner's Arms than he thinks of the Miner's Dream of Home, which isn't a pleasant thing to the huge leaven of the sentimentally diseased among the great gang of theatre-goers.

There is a fine picture in the play when Lambert, the father, first enters. He is, the directions say, 'a man of middling stature, a miner, and black from the pit. . . . He wears a grey-and-black neckerchief, and, being coatless, his arms are bare to the elbows, where end the loose dirty sleeves of his flannel singlet.' He gets hold of the table, and pulls it nearer the fire, away from his daughter.

The Daughter: Why can't you leave the table where it was. We don't *want* it stuck on top of the fire.
Father: Ah dun, if you dunna.

Here, in a few chosen words, is sharply and closely depicted the irritated selfishness of the old man, and the corresponding irritated selfishness of the young daughter. It is very clever and very good.

There is humour at the edge and in the core of the play. Humour over the old man's damp breeches, when he ejaculates a naughty expression that sets his wife and his daughter's friend laughing, and flashes a flush of shame on to his daughter's cheeks; humour in the washing of his back by his wife who claps an ice-cold flannel on it and makes him yell resentment; humour in the visiting miner pounding 'The Maiden's Prayer' out of the piano; and humour over the baking of the bread when Ernest, deep in his puzzling and shrinking battle with the girls, forgets what he ought to do, and lets the loaves be burned to a cinder.

There is a gleam of poetry in the play when Ernest, after reading from a French book, says:

That's what they can do in France. It's so heavy and full and voluptuous: like oranges falling and rolling a little way along a dark-blue carpet: like twilight outside when the lamp's lighted.

Vivid flashes of anger and rage light up the quarrel between the old man and the young boy, and, later on, like sad summer lightning, the softer anger of the mother lightens the scene in which the woman's jealousy rebukes her son for allowing a girl to gather attentions from him that she wistfully and foolishly thinks to be still due to her.

It is maddening to think of the stillness that lay around the evident possibilities in Lawrence to create drama. A little more experience, a little more encouragement, and, in Lawrence, England might have had a great dramatist. It is no use saying that with more experience he wrote additional plays, plays deeper and greater than this effort of twenty-one. There never was a chance of him moving behind the curtain, and so getting into intimate touch with the hidden life of the theatre. The bugs and the bears of the theatre gave him the back of their hand. He came into the theatre, and the theatre received him not. Even today there isn't a theatre in England in which a writer like

Lawrence would be certain to get a chance.[1] Millions of money spent on football; millions of money spent on cricket; football grounds and cricket pitches everywhere, but ne'er a theatre to make a new-born dramatist sure of himself. And the community singers still sing Land of Hope and Glory. A great dramatist might have come from the ready acceptance of *A Collier's Friday Night*. Many and many a far worse play has been put on by the Abbey Theatre. There were the makings of a fine dramatist in D. H. Lawrence, but he is gone now, and the chance is gone forever with him.

[1] The play received considerable critical praise when it was performed by the Royal Court Theatre in Aug. 1965, but this was for only one Sunday evening presentation without decor. O'Casey's criticisms are valid, thirty years later, for no London management has given the play a commercial run.

CHARLES LEVER'S STORMY LIFE (1939)*

IT is strange and something fantastic to meet again, under the glimpses of the moon, the striding, curly-headed, tormented, rollicking figure of Charles Lever. Here he is running by us, quick as quicksilver, as a boy, as a student, as a doctor, and as a well-loved and much-criticised novelist, who died sadly and was buried with his books some fifty years ago.

This interesting book of his life, or a guess or two at his life (and no life-story can do much more), brings back an echo of an echo heard many years ago by those whose hair has gone quite grey now, when their fathers and mothers waxed enthusiastic over the adventures of Harry Lorrequer. Thackeray, we are told, when he travelled through Ireland, was gratified to see in thousands of humble homes the little pink-covered books that held firmly and lovingly together the story of *Harry Lorrequer*. And, indeed, in Ireland of that time all who could read (they weren't millions) had read or were reading the famous adventures of Harry Lorrequer, just as in England all who could read (they weren't millions either) had read, or were reading, the strange doings of the famous Mr Pickwick.

In my young nipper days Harry Lorrequer sat down in our little house, or, at least, in passing had looked in through the window. I had heard his name mentioned often, and had handled the paper-covered novel, having on its face the picture of a military parade in a barrack square, spiced with a senior officer glaring furiously at a junior who had come to join the assembly with a face blackened with burnt cork, while the soldiers of the regiment stood to attention trying to look as if

* Review of *Dr. Quicksilver* by Lionel Stevenson (Chapman & Hall, 1939), printed in *The Sunday Times*, Feb. 5, 1939.

nothing unusual were taking place. The things Lever had written were being read then, but they soon became an echo, growing fainter as the youngsters of fifty years ago grew up into men and women, finally fading away altogether till Charles Lever was completely forgotten. He had to give way to bigger men, though Charles Lever was a big man, a very big man in his own way, and did not deserve such a sharp oblivion.

Here in this book about *Dr. Quicksilver* he who was lost has been found again: Charles Lever once again gallops through the elegant and drab streets of Dublin; for a moment of time he drinks and laughs with the students of Trinity College; works as a doctor to deliver the wretched peasants of Clare and Galway from the misery and terror of cholera; then seeks a better chance to make a living in little Catholic Belgium; finally becoming one of the best-known novelists of his day, one of the first, maybe, to taint the vogue of romantic literature with the healthy salt of realism.

Lever was what in Ireland would be called 'one of the bright boys', one of those who, like the rest of those known as 'the Ascendancy', eked out life with a song, a laugh, a prank, and at all times pressed into life far more than it could comfortably or even safely hold. In Lever's day most activities, irresponsible or serious, were governed by the pistol. Rollicking and reckless men, hardy and foolhardy, in many cases cracking their wits to provide money for their curious and careless idea of what life should be; and at the beginning, or in the middle, or at the end of many of these boisterous activities there was often heard the sharp and ugly crack of a pistol shot. The best example of comic relief was the baiting of a friend, as the Elizabethans before them used to bait a bear. Today, more civilised as we are, instead of baiting a friend or a bear, everything that is possible is done to bait a whole community.

But Lever wasn't all merriment and make-believe. No one could have risked more or have done more for those who were stricken with cholera. We are told that at a military ball Lever was called to a sick child, and went riding to and from the ball just to snatch a dance, but always riding back till his patient was at ease.

Roving, ranting blade as he was, Lever went about with his eyes open, and, sad for himself, he couldn't keep his witty mouth shut. A silent mouth is sweet, says a Gaelic proverb, and, though Lever's tongue was sweet, many of the things he said had the sharp and sour savour of truth, and so he brought trouble on himself. The Orange clique of the *Evening Mail* went for him and the Green Dan O'Connell denounced him at a meeting in the Phoenix Park, denounced him so roundly that he was warned his life might be in danger if he ventured home before the crowds dispersed. Riding home, Lever and his children came to a crowded bridge, and the crowd refused to give a passage and began to boo and hoot. 'As the only hope of protecting his children, Lever stood up in his stirrups and shouted "Long live Daniel O'Connell!" The crowd lapsed into a doubtful silence, in the midst of which little Charlie, raising his miniature whip and bringing it down with a resounding smack, piped at the top of his voice, "Damn Daniel O'Connell!" The audacity appealed to the unpredictable Irish sense of humour, and, with a roar of laughter, the crowd made way for them to pass.'

It has often been said that Lever was not Irish, and mostly by the Irish themselves, or by some Irish among the Irish themselves. Because, it was said, he held the Irish up to ridicule; that he caricatured the Irish peasant and the Irish priest. And the gentlemen of Ireland, if I mistake not, said that he caricatured them, too. He did; he caricatured them all. But if we look at life as it was lived then in Ireland (and outside it, too), we'd see that life was nothing but a huge, sprawling, chaotic cartoon of life itself. He had, of course, the defects of the Irish (all races have got more or less of these), but he also had the high qualities of generosity, of savage devotion to work, as a doctor or as a novelist, and a personal courage well above even the courage that the Irish as a race have. And, besides, he had that important but torturing power of seeing through to the foolishness of many things, and the unworldly foolishness of setting his discoveries down for all to read. Yes, Lever was Irish right enough, whether his works are to be numbered among those of Irish literature I don't know enough to say. The dispute as to whether what is called Anglo-Irish literature is Irish or not is going on still. I myself think that all Irishmen are Irish — Craigavon as well as de Valera — and that what they write — if it be worthy — belongs to the soul of Ireland, if not to her body. And I have very little time for those — and never had — who talk of a 'hidden Ireland' that only themselves can see.[1]

As far as I know, the works of Lever exist today in the story of *Harry Lorrequer* in Everyman's Library, though possibly in other editions. This biography has brought a wish into my mind to read the best of Lever's stories over again before the day dawns and the shadows flee away.

[1] O'Casey is referring here, of course, to the extreme nationalist attitude propounded in books like Daniel Corkery's *The Hidden Ireland*.

GREAT MAN, GORKI! (1946)*

A strange soul, Maxim Gorki, and a very fine one too. A brilliant designer of the life he saw around him. A wanderer who sojourned in many strange places; yet one who always furnished a home wherever he went out of the thought and serenity of his own soul; a house not made with hands, eternal in the heavens. A man who, while he belonged to everybody, essentially belonged to himself. An example, if ever there was one, to show that an original mind, though always merged in the mass of men, however potent and clamorous that mass may be, never loses itself; but spreads itself out, leavening with brightness and valour the wider expanse in the slow and duller level of the common man.

While the great Tolstoy stayed, for the most part, within the hedged and set out monastery of his own district, finding within it the amazing panorama of the battles between Napoleon and Kutuzov, embedded in the sombre power and dazzling glitter of Russia's teeming life, Gorki ventured far and wide to find the favours and the facts of life, transmuting them into the true fantasy of story and of play. In foreign lands, up and down his own land, the gaunt, finely-chiselled head pushed forward, probing, so active in thought and observation that it seemed to be impatient of the slower body that kept it company.

Gorki and Tolstoy — how dissimilar and how alike they are. What a vivid picture Gorki draws of the two of them going along the low road on a hot day on the way to Livadia; the one on foot, the other on horseback; the one so eager to get to know God, the other so eager to get to know men; each of them close to Him as any man could be. Tolstoy afraid that his very gifts

* Article published in *Tribune*, May 3, 1946.

would keep him distant, for, thinking with Tertullian, he said, 'thought is evil'. Again, 'They make a fuss about my writing now; but, when I die, in a year or so, people will say "Tolstoy? Ah, that is the count who tried to make boots — is that the fellow you mean?"'

The aristocrat, Tolstoy, came quick into our knowledge; the proletarian, Gorki, came halting and slow; but sure; and today he is marching among our affections, almost shoulder to shoulder, step by step with the striding Tolstoy. How close, however different we may be, how close nature can bring us all together.

Ay, Gorki came slow into our ken. As a young man in the twenties, I heard a whisper of his name by someone, somewhere; as if a rare bird had visited the land, perched on a distant bough, whistled a curious note or two, heard but by a few, and then flown off again, to remain but a memory even with the few who had heard the bird sing suddenly. Years after, I picked up a secondhand book called *Three of Us*, for out of the memory of the whisper heard long before, the name of Gorki interested me. It was a sombre, realistic novel, but the pine forests were in it, the wretchedness of poverty, and all the dogged valour of life. In the book was a verse composed by one named Pashka, a young boy who had been taught to read and write by convicts, and this is what the verse sang:

> *People are moving along the street,*
> *They are all well-dressed and satisfied.*
> *But if you ask them for something to eat,*
> *They will just say to you — get away!*

Get away! That was the loudest cry, the shortest hymn, the world heard. It was sung by the policeman in his blue coat, by the soldier in his red one; by the lawyer in his sable gown, and by the cleric in his snowy linen surplice. Then I realised that the streets of St Petersburg and those of Moscow were, in all essentials, the very same as those of Dublin. Here, too, people passed who were well-dressed and satisfied, but if you asked them for something to eat, they would cry out — get away! Well, led by this man, we'll get away no longer.

Years later, the figure of Gorki loomed up again, dimly enough, in a play called *The Lower Depths*, performed indifferently by a company in an out-of-the-way shack in Floral Street, Covent Garden. So the little bird hopped back to our land again, staying a little longer this time to sing a low, plaintive, shrill and seductive song. Many saw its plumage clearly this time, and so did I, with its richly-black body and vividly crimson-capped head. Taking a step forward, Gorki became known as the man who wrote *The Lower Depths*; and almost all who knew this seemed to think that all he did began and ended there.

It was the dawn of knowledge of a great and unique man, and no false one either. Today his tall, lanky figure, topped by its handsome head, is very familiar to us. His name is heard oftener than that of Tolstoy; first, because he thought and moved more directly in the midst of the people's fight for deliverance; because, while Tolstoy sometimes ran from life, Gorki always ran forward to shake life by the hand; and because he was, by far, a greater dramatist than the towering Tolstoy; and drama is the nearest and quickest way in which a thinker can get to the people.

The critics, as usual, told Gorki he was no good. The blind fools could see nothing in him. They openly yawned the moment one of his plays began, and, when the curtain fell, hurried out to call him a cad. When the play *Enemies* was published, they cried out with turbulent voices, 'Gorki is finished'. As a lot of them are now, so most of them were then: they were horrified at anything novel, anything deeper than themselves, anything that tended to force them to sit straight in their chairs. So Gorki's heels were dogged by these fellows barking out their condemnations at every step he took. But Gorki, hurt no doubt, went on, taking his revenge by doing better than he did, and today these critics' names are never mentioned in our talk, while Gorki strides majestically about our streets.

One critic alone, Blok the poet, found time to praise him, saying, 'Gorki is bigger than he wants to be and than he always wanted to be, because his intuition is deeper than his intellect; inscrutably by the force of his talent, his blood, the nobility of his strivings, the affinity of his ideal and the scope of his spiritual suffering. If there exists that great boundless, spacious, melancholy and felicitous something, which we are accustomed to combine under the name of Russia, then we have to recognise Gorki as the man who expresses all this to a very high degree.' Right indeed, right you are, Alexander Blok.

Move up, there, Strindberg, Ibsen, Hauptmann, Chekhov, and the rest of you; ay, and those who came before you too: make room there for Gorki to come and sit down beside ye, for he is, indeed, worthy of a fair place at the highest table of honour.

PART THREE

PEOPLE AND PLACES

LONDON PASSES BY (1926)*

A STORY is told that an American, whipping up his valise in a heat, fixing with his other hand his spectacles more firmly on his nose, asked the Pope how long it would take him to see the whole of Rome. 'Stay a week,' said the Pope, 'and you'll see it all; stay five years and you'll see it less; live your life in Rome, and you'll see very little of the city.'

There are those who talk of the pigmies of Equatorial Africa, who have had a bed and breakfast in Cairo; and as one can talk with confidence and certainty of what one knows nothing about, so, having rambled through a few streets in Bloomsbury (as I have certainly done), I can speak graphically and authoritatively about the whole of London.

Not yet have I seen the hinderparts of the City, but I have looked in London's face, and a harried, restful, serious, curious, comical face it is! A pale, business-full, laugh-abandoned, pushing countenance, surrounded by a glittering, brilliant, dazzling medley of green, crimson, gold, blue, and purple illuminations, giving the appearance of the city as a whirling human form dancing with a mad intensity around a business totempole. . . . The wealth of its poverty and the poverty of its wealth. The bellow of its business; the eagerness to know all, leaving the strident students with a knowledge of nothing, where the flowers of the fields are huge pillars and Gothic buildings, and running brooks crimson, yellow, and blue buzzing buses; where the sun and the moon and the stars are darkened in a blaze of electricity.

And the crowds! How aimless, chaotic and feverish it all

* Published in *The Daily News* (London) on May 24, 1926, under the title 'London Passes By: Impressions of Five Weeks'.

looks. Streaming, churning, and eddying about in the torrent of traffic. And the helmeted, blue-coated Moses ever and again stretching out his hand and heaping up on each side of him the sea of traffic, that his people may safely pass over to the safety of the other side.

Piccadilly, Piccadilly, Piccadilly. The stranger's hope, and faith and charity. One is always safe and sound in Piccadilly. The gorgeously-illuminated crèche of the new-comer. Get to Piccadilly and you're safe; turn your back on Piccadilly and you're lost. Straying in Hammersmith, ask for a street a hop, step, and a lep away, and you excite no interest. Mention Piccadilly, and eyes are opened, ears are cocked, and voices say: 'Piccadilly, Piccadilly; ah, you want to get to Piccadilly, do you?' You say, 'Yes,' though you don't want to get to Piccadilly as much as you want to get out of Hammersmith.

Sauntering along the Embankment towards Westminster Bridge, silent as the river is silent, and a little sad. There you are, right opposite the Houses of Parliament, a dark mass in the dusk of the evening, with its pointed fretwork of lines zig-zagging across the sky. The lighted windows, like yellow eyes, blinking drowsily across the river, as if the building had awakened to take its part in the traffic of the evening. Inside are the specially-picked hands weaving and ripping, ripping and weaving again pattern after pattern, and border after border around the Ten Commandments, with Big Ben, standing stiff, like a confidential butler, ever and again booming out his approval of and pride in those who add a letter or a word to, and take away the word or the letter from, the British Constitution.

Five weeks in London and the only public building visited is the Tate Gallery! Oh, Sean, Sean, for shame! Passing by St Paul's with a wondering look at the church, wondering has it any influence on the people at all. With all its beauty of stone, gorgeousness of dyed glass, and wealth of sanctity, less than the glare, the gilded glamour, the roar and the gibbering in the Fancy Fair at Tottenham Court Road. Watching the foam of human life swirling around Westminster Abbey; thousands who have seen it hundreds of times, and have never seen it once, while the solemn silence of the Abbey seems to murmur, 'Am I nothing to you, all ye that pass by?' Sad, silent church, you are too great for the littleness of man; your message is too big to find room in his shrinking soul: Gloria in Excelsis Deo, excitingly beautiful — ah, here it is at last; here's the 'bus that goes to Piccadilly.

Hurrying past the long, elegant rank of the British Museum buildings, having, instead of the pensiveness of Westminster Abbey, a look of proud indifference, as if to say, 'Come in or stay out, whichever you like: you pay no money, but you take your choice,' and using its classic magnificence as a sign-post to show me the way to go home. The Tate Gallery seemed to be too huge a frame for a very small picture. What strange pictures the Turner landscapes seem to be! Trees that appear to have been planted in their full maturity by a gardener with a trowel; rivers and lakes whose water sparkles like the water in a basin. Pictures with lights that never was on sea or land. May God (and my London comrades) forgive me, for I didn't like the pre-Raphaelite school either. School, school. What a horrible word, school. Each example seems to say sweat fell to make this picture beautiful. One thought of the simplicity and elegant loveliness of a Japanese print. And Landseer, with his genteel dogs, and his genteel deer — Oh, God!

Sauntering into the room holding the French pictures given by Hugh Lane to Dublin, one felt the surge of hot blood, gazing upon these joys of colour and line raped from Dublin, proving the truth of Holy Scripture that 'from him that hath not shall be taken away even that which he hath'. How long shall these Anglo-Pharaohs harden their hearts, so that they will not let these pictures go, go back to Dublin?[1]

The noble public buildings, the dignified temples of God — where the Englishman comes to pray and goes away to scoff — the hurrying, hasty, business-racked people swarming the streets,

[1] In 1959 the British and Irish authorities came to an arrangement by which the Lane Collection was divided into two groups, one for exhibition in Dublin and the other in London; the groups were to be exchanged at five-yearly intervals.

rhythm-moved by the resolute drone of the scarlet, blue, green, and yellow buses, and the insinuating purr of the swift-gliding motor; the fat-bellied hotels pushing out a place for themselves everywhere; the quiet squares shrinking from the tumult and the shouting, offering a scant shelter to the harassed children of gentle-hearted solitude. Colour and gloom; luxury and misery; tumult and peace; loveliness and hideousness; strength and weakness; profit and loss — thy name is London!

The most ornamental and most amazing piece of fancy architecture in the whole of London, bar none, is the simply-beautiful, chastely conscious Memorial to Prince Albert, looking like a tippling piece of work that had staggered in, and was resting awhile in the quiet safety of Kensington. The beauty of the monument's gilded grandeur, the kingly columns, alluring allegories, magnificent mosaics, give a voice to the breezes murmuring through the trees gazing at the Memorial in sorrow and in anger, whispering unto all who come: 'Take off thy shoes from off thy feet, for the place whereon thou standest is holy ground.' And to think of that Epstein fellow creeping in to mar the peace of such good company! The brow of Egypt mocking the classic contours of Helen's beauty. Sneering at a work that has all the happy harmony of a well-decked Easter egg! Epstein should be driven out, driven out with a fool's bladder, or the Memorial should be carried to a place of safety: there's a ghastly mistake somewhere.

Anon, anon, we'll write some more, and tell of things that matter to the heart and head of London. Presently we'll say with that great man, unknown warrior in things spiritual, who shouted riotously in Hyde Park one Sunday afternoon, 'I thank Gawd for wot I am and w'ere I am t'day.' Amen, O Lord, Amen, Amen.

HYDE PARK ORATOR (1934)*

FROM the Glens of Antrim to a well-trodden part of Hyde Park is a long, long trail indeed, and, as pictured in the story told by Bonar Thompson, many halts had to be made before the pitch was reached. It is an interesting story, for it gives us interesting glimpses of the life of one, at least, of the strange men and stranger women who rant and rave there about politics and religion; and who settle Sunday after Sunday, once for all, the problems of life that have confused mankind from the first day he crept cautiously out of the primeval slime; or, according to another account, from the day on which he was banished from the Garden of Eden by a being holding a flaming sword in his hand which pointed to the left, to the right, before and behind Adam and Eve in a friendly effort to show them the best place to go, so that they both might settle down quietly for the night.

I have often listened to these speakers, and have sometimes wondered where they came from, how they lived, and where they would go when they had said or screamed their say, and the gates of the park were closing. Well, here in this book we are shown one place from which one speaker came, how he lived, and where he goes when he had said his say and the gates of the park are closing.

It is quite evident that Bonar Thompson has his knife in the bowels of what he calls the Labour Movement. After spending many years in its service, he would now, could the movement be personified, bind it to a tree, as Saint Sebastian was said to have been bound to a tree, and shoot it full of arrows till it died. And

* Preface to *Hyde Park Orator*, by Bonar Thompson (Jarrold's, London, 1934).

he hates what he calls the mob. But why does he confine the term of mob to the working-class? The mob can be very respectable and very well dressed, and can stamp its law and its customs in the books of the law, and in the pages of its constitution. The herd instinct is not confined to the workers: it spreads wider and goes deeper than this poor term permits. It is a human instinct. Besides, a mob can be a wonderful and a terrible thing. The mob that stormed the Bastille was a wonderful and a terrible thing. And the mob that poured into the armies of the first French Republic, first holding at bay, and then defeating, the massed and trained armies of the world, was a force and a power exciting amazement, and the centre of honour and glory.

The mob that poured into the armies that fought in the World War was a wonderful and a terrible thing, so terrible that it shattered a world to pieces. Now the mob that shattered a world to pieces must gather a world together again, and build it anew on a fresher and a cleaner plan. And the author admits himself that he submitted to a far meaner mob law when he put on an evening-dress suit to attend a gathering anxious to determine whether or no women were the intellectual equals of men. There is as much mob law on the Statute Book, and more, than there is, or ever will be, in a few stones shied at policemen or flung through a few plate-glass windows.

And the Labour Movement has passed by the passing phase of Trade Unionism. This method of attack was always useless, and is now out of date. In a speech given by General Knox, one of the political representatives of Bucks., the other day, the General seemed to be delighted that the membership of trades unions was declining. 'There has been a drop of a quarter of a million this year,' he said, and I'm sure, when he said this, there was a broad smile on his face. But a drop of a million would have sounded better from a Labour point of view. 'The trade unions,' he went on, 'say they represent the workers of the country, but this was not so, for there were only three and a quarter millions in the unions, while there were fifteen millions of workers in Britain at the present moment.' Well, so much the worse for General Knox, and so much the better for the Labour

Movement. The trade unions no longer represent the workers, and this fact is the beginning of hope for the Labour Movement. This is but one indication of the change in life which the brave and gallant officer cannot see is coming, and coming quick.

Before leaving this point of what is and what is not the Labour Movement, let me say that, in my opinion, the book written by Bonar Thompson, from the first to the last page, justifies the inner force and meaning of the Labour Movement. The first flight of his mother; the shame of his father, making him actively indifferent to his son; and the hard and precarious existence of the author afterwards, demands a change, and a drastic change, from the life that was and is to the life that is to come. Let me remind the author, too, that under a Communist State he and his pals, if they were able, but refused to work, would be compelled to join in the labour of all. This to him might be counted as tyranny, but to me it would be the meet and proper ordering of all things. That is why I think that when Asquith and Chamberlain each gave his friend a quid, and MacDonald gave him nothing, MacDonald was right, and Chamberlain and Asquith were wrong.

I'm afraid I have to say the same about what the author thinks of those who helped and of those who refused to help in the founding of *The Black Hat*.[1] As the end of the paper shows, those who helped were wrong, and those who refused to help were right. The paper wasn't so great as he evidently thinks; it wasn't really so terrifying as an army with banners. He tells us that the paper was 'original, unexpected, exceptional, provocative, pungent, trenchant, piquant, and never twice alike'. Well, well, if it were all these things, it must have stunned its readers, and, for the sake of the peace of humanity, it is good that it is gone.

And now a few words about the manner and the style of the book. I'm afraid I can't claim for it all the qualities that were in *The Black Hat*. The author's reminiscences of his young days, and of all that happened to him in Antrim, are, perhaps, the best things in the book; but the descriptions given are too fitful, as

[1] A periodical edited by Bonar Thompson and sold in Hyde Park.

indeed are all those given by the author of what happened to him in Ireland, and afterwards in England and in Hyde Park. Bonar Thompson hasn't observed things vividly. (I have been permitted to read only a portion of the manuscript, and am, of course, only dealing with the manuscript given to me.) He must learn to observe instinctively what is worth observing, then look long, and gather into his mind all that can and must be gathered in of the things he sees and of the things he hears. He must think a lot less of himself, and a lot more of others. By his own declaration, he finds it too easy to write. Had he found the gathering of thoughts together a hard thing to do, he would have written a far, far better biography of himself.

But he deserves a better abiding-place than a rickety platform in Hyde Park, and I hope this book may be his first step down from that high place to a safer, sounder, if less arrogant place on the paths and in the byways of life.

THERE GO THE IRISH (1944)*

IRELAND is a kaleidoscope of amazing contrasts. She is the oldest civilisation in Europe, though she is still in her teens. Her history begins in a mist, and has grown into a sun sending a gay green beam to the four quarters of the world. A country that believes everything, even the legend of Eden's garden, and yet she is always asking questions. She believes that all authority comes from God, bowing low in consecrated submission, and a second later, lifts her right hand to strike at an authority she dislikes, or thinks unjust. An irresponsible people, unable to concentrate on any one thing for a day (they say), yet a people who for a thousand years maintained the determination to drive out the English domination, succeeding at last, with the exception of one big bridgehead in Ulster, held for England by the Irish themselves, not for love of England, but because it seems to suit them to think so. A nation of Roman Catholics who abominate proselytism, but whose army and clans carried to the grave, with dirge of squealing pipe and beat of muffled drum, the body of the most proselytising English bishop ever usurping a See in Ireland, chiefs weeping over his grave, and hoping that they would have as fair a chance of heaven as the English bishop had. A people pathetically submissive to their clergy, who, whenever the clergy, through their lay adjutants, ban a book as bad, dangerous, and unwholesome, make every effort possible to get that book, read it, and see for themselves how bad a book it is. A people, who, in the First World War, cursed England, hoped and prayed she'd lose it, and then went out in droves to help her to win it. A people whose persistent prayer is for a long life, and

* Article published in *They Go, The Irish: A Miscellany of War-time Writing*, Nicholson & Watson, 1944.

245

death in Ireland, make things so that for the one who dies under an Irish sky, a thousand die under a foreign one, without feeling a bit the worse for it. A people who conceived the finest flag symbolic of a sensible and sensitive nationhood, the Plough and the Stars, long before the Hammer and Sickle was heard of, and yet today honours the meanest-looking and most colourless flag among the national flags of the nations. A nation with one of the loveliest collections of folk song and music the world over, yet sings, in season and out of season, a national anthem so miserable in its conception of ordered sounds that a sparrow would be half-ashamed to warble it if he thought another bird was listening. A people in whose Cathedral Church in Dublin, one can hear an imposing choir, endowed by a rich man, chanting Palestrina's divine creations, and a step away in the slums can hear the rag-and-bone collector lustily intoning, 'Rags an' bones an' bottles, sacred hearts for bones an' bottles'. A country, too, whose English army of Irishmen did the goose-step in Cork more than a hundred years ago; who tried ceremonially to raise the right hand long before Mussolini or Hitler were heard of, raising it, not to foster Fascism but, as Joseph Biggar, a Protestant Belfastman, told us, because it was the old way the old Gael gave a greeting to a comrade. But the habit was smothered in the laughter of the onlookers. The first, too, in anticipation of the future flag-days, to fix a paper disk in a lapel to signify that a subscription had been given to a good cause. A country that anticipated the Fascists themselves in the organisation known as the Molly Maguires, led by wee Joe Davlin and D. J. Nugent, replete with truncheon-armed stewards superintending all meetings at which they expected to meet with argued opposition, but whose power was eventually clipped into nothing by the Republican Brotherhood, the Gaelic League, and the Sinn Fein Movement.

Another curious thing about Ireland's manner of life is shown in that while always standing haughtily apart from England, she has always been by her side. Her dislike, her distrust, and even her hatred of England has invariably been exemplified in the Freudian way of a rush to help her in any difficulty she may happen to be in through, in most cases, some fault of her own. In the beginning, the Irish gave every help they could to the sons of the unfortunate monarch Harold, to drive the Norman Invaders out of England, hundreds of scores of them leaving their bones to lie forever in the Vale of Tamar. From the time King Henry the Second became Overlord of Ireland, there were always Irish soldiers to be found fighting under the banner of the King, or under the bannerets of his barons. Take the battle of Crécy, for instance, which is early enough in the struggle that began between the two nations. In this battle, fought in 1346, Edward the Third defeated the French badly. Looking at a plan of the battle in the *Everyman Encyclopaedia*, we find the King behind with the reserves, and in front, mind you, between three spearheads of British archers, under the Black Prince, the King's son, on the one hand the Welsh, and on the other the Irish. That they were at the battle of Agincourt, too, is certain, for in his *Henry V* Shakespeare gives us the picture of an Irish Captain, MacMorris, probably meant for MacMorrough, for the Mac proclaims a Gael, and none of your Norman gentry. Of MacMorris, the poet says, 'The Duke of Gloster, to whom the order of siege is given, is altogether directed by an Irishman, a very valiant gentleman, i'faith'; and with the Welsh, Scots, and English, the Irish, facing death as certain as death can be, waited for the dawn at Agincourt, starving, with 'lank-lean cheeks, and war-worn coats, presenting them unto the gazing moon so many horrid ghosts'. And when the dreaded dawn came, they rushed and roared into battle, helping in no mean way to make of Agincourt a fine familiar name, to be remembered over flowing cups for many a long day in England.

Even in the home-made wars of England, there the Irish were in the midst of them, pulling a white rose for York and a red one for Lancaster, and suffering more than the prick from a thorn in the doing of it. Indeed, if Shakespeare's authority stands good, it would seem that, without the Irish, there would have been hardly any fight at all, for in the second part of *Henry VI* he makes the Duke of York accept the command of the expedition into Ireland as a step towards getting the crown. Later on, when he returns, just after the King has escaped from the Irish Cade, leader of the men of Kent, Henry is assailed by a Messenger shouting,

> *The Duke of York is newly come from Ireland;*
> *And with a puissant and a mighty power,*
> *Of Gallowglasses and stout Kernes,*
> *Is marching hitherward in proud array.*

And these Irish-speaking gallowglasses and kernes were no easy thing to handle, for they were later editions of the Fenians, and earlier ones of the Connaught Rangers and Dublin Fusiliers. Standihurst tells us that 'The gallowglasses are grim of countenance, tall of stature, big of limme, lusty of body, wel and strongly timbered; they are armed with poleaxes. The Kernes are footsoldiers, armed with sword and target, and sometimes a piece, being commonly good marksmen.' And since the Earl of Ormond wore a red rose in his bonnet, and fought in all the battles up to Towton, it is probable he didn't run over from Ireland on his lone, but coaxed a few of the tall gallowglasses and rug-headed kernes to go along with him.

In the campaigns of the great Marlborough, there, under the rival banners, pierced by pike and musket ball, beset by the blustering cannon, were the Irish, Catholic Gaels defending the Protestant Succession for the Whigs against the Catholic Louis of France; and, it is said, Field-Marshal James O'Hara was regarded by Marlborough as one of his ablest generals. The Irish were thick on the other side, too, making sure for themselves that the right was on their side by facing both ways at once; and big deeds they did, for Thomas Davis, the Irish romantic versifier, tells us,

> *And when on Ramillies bloody field,*
> *The baffled French were forced to yield,*
> *The victor English backward reeled*
> *Before the charge of Clare's dragoons!*

And it is as certain as anything can be that among the English reeling back before the charge of the inflamed Irish dragoons,

were many who could claim the kinship of fellow-countrymen
with the charging and sabring horsemen.

I read somewhere, long ago, I think it was in the gossip
column of Viscount Castlerosse who has done so much for
Killarney's lakes and fells, em'rald isles and winding bays; that
place you know where the angels fold their wings, and jest, and
where at Muckross Abbey you must breathe a prayer, if there's
such a thing left dying in you. Well, this great man who was
interred recently amid the saying of a Requiem Mass, tolling of
bells, burning of incense and scattering of holy water and hyssop,
by Irish bishop, priest and deacon in return for what he had done
for heaven's reflex, this great man once in his gossip column said
that the Irish were thick as thieves in the regiments that fought
in the Peninsular War, facing with fury the veterans of Massena
and Soult. And, oddly enough, they were under a general as
Irish as a Sarsfield or a Shaw, a man who culled an army fit to
do battle anywhere from a mob, few of which knew the muzzle
from the butt-end of a musket; a man whom England never
understood, though Victoria burst into tears when he died, and
Tennyson put the shroud of a poor poem over him. Then
England stood up in Hyde Park a monster statue of Achilles to
show the world how well she comprenny vood her great general;
while in the centre of Ireland's capital city was set down and
built up the Pillar to her English Admiral, Nelson, who was one
with her, where every Irish citizen could see it, day and night,
awake or dreaming; sticking the obeliskean monument to their
Irish general away in a hollow in a park where it can be seen by
the citizens only on every other Sunday after Mass. Someone
recently writing about Wellington, said of him that he was a
man in whom sentiment never stirred, and pity found no dwell-
ing place. He had plenty of sentiment, right enough, but no
sentimentality, detesting Nelson's theatricality as a professed
hero, patriot, and rhapsode; all that sort of thing, as Shaw tells
us, meeting with the well-known Irish formula of *Don't be a
damned fool, sir*. And as for being destitute of pity, there is a
scene in Lever's novel in which he shows Wellington galloping
along with a hunting group. Suddenly he swerves aside, and

begins to ride in the wrong direction. An aide-de-camp stretches
out a whip, and says, Sir; the hounds are running over there;
but Wellington, answering never a word, goes on riding to
where his wounded are being cared for. Curious, too, to think
that as it was more than a hundred years ago, so it almost is
today. Lever describing an attack by the French which leaves
Wellington unruffled, but brings a look of worry to the face of
his Staff, tells us this:

Fourteenth, Fourteenth, cried a voice from behind, and at the same
moment a staff-officer, without his hat, and his horse bleeding from a
recent sabre-cut came up. You must move to the rear, Colonel
Merivale, the French have gained the heights!

In a moment we were in our saddles; but scarcely was the word
to 'fall in' given, when a loud cheer rent the very air; the musketry
seemed suddenly to cease, and the dark mass which continued to
struggle up the heights wavered, broke, and turned.

— What can that be? asked Colonel Merivale.

— I can tell you sir, I said proudly, while I felt my heart as though
it would bound from my bosom.

— And what is it, boy? Speak!

— There it goes again! That was an Irish hurrah — the Eighty-
eighth are at them!

— By Jove! here they come, said Hampden. God help the Frenchmen
now!

— Gallant Eighty-eighth! Gloriously done! shouted General
Picton, waving his hat.

— Aren't we Connaught robbers, now? shouted a rich brogue, as its
owner, breathless and bleeding, pressed forward in the charge.

> Oh! there's hope in the trumpet and glee in the fife,
> But never such music broke into a strife,
> As when at its bursting the war-clouds give way,
> And there's cold steel along with the Irish hurrah!

There it was, a loud and a frightening thing, making the
French troops hesitate, halt, and turn back, its sound shaking
the proud plumes in the cocked hats of Napoleon's haughty-
headed Staff; and its echo today in the deserts of North Africa,
Sicily, and in Italy is helping to make the Iron Cross hop about
in agitation on the boastful breadth of Hitler's bosom.

Ay, indeed; as it was a hundred years ago, so it almost is today. Connaught robbers are we to a lot of people still. The other day, I read this sort of thing about the book of an Irish author:

> *It is a singularly disgusting and repulsive piece of modern Irish writing. I cannot finish reading it. That Irish folk commonly use such words and express such ideas I know.*

And this is the feeling, not of one only, but of many. An up-to-date version of Pope Gregory's 'Non Angli, sed Angeli', which being interpreted, means, I think, not English, but Angels. Even were the Irish commonly low and repulsive, surely those who have been overlords in the country, controlling the lives of the people for a thousand years have some responsibility for this condition of heart and mind? Surely, they must have learned something of these things from their masters. And, indeed, it is so, for those people who see horns on Irish heads and wings on English shoulders should read the Bible and the plays of their Shakespeare to find what they think to be vulgar, low, and repulsive, well mirrored in both of these great books. And to go even farther, there isn't an Irish docker could beat St Peter, as a fisherman or apostle, in a flow of profanity when he wanted to express himself with due and proper force. No; this sort of thing won't do. It is as stupid as the Irish attitude — dead now for many years — of On our side is virtue and Erin; on theirs is the Saxon and guilt.

*   *   *

But the Irish didn't leave the battlefield when Wellington had finished with Napoleon. They were with England in the cold Crimea, where mine own uncle near lost an arm by a sabre-cut in the charge of Balaclava; in Egypt, fighting even while their people were being flung out of their poor hovels by the landlords, as the old song of 'The Irish Dragoon', testifies:

> *And the tears rolled down his sun-burned cheeks,*
> *As he gazed on the letter in his hand:*
> *Is it true? Too true;*
> *More throuble in my native land!*

All the time coercion acts were dropping all over Ireland like snowflakes in a hard winter, the Irish were doing good to those despitefully using them, and the names of the Fagans, Careys, Neills, Hayes, Buckleys, and Scullys were helping the English East Indian Company to hold fast on India that the Sepoys were trying in the Indian Mutiny to pry loose. Irish craftsmen strengthened the frame round this gorgeous jewel in England's crown. We learn from the *History of the Indian Mutiny* by G. W. Forrest, C.I.E., Ex-Director of Records, Indian Government, that at Lucknow Sir Henry Lawrence decided to withdraw the garrison of Muchee Bhawun to the main defence of the city. So the message, 'Spike your guns well, blow up the Fort, and retire at midnight,' was semaphored to the garrison there. Right enough, as the clock struck twelve, the column, headed by Lawrence's Company of the 32nd marched out, and reached the Residency safely, without losing a man. 'Then a fountain of fire leapt up to the sky, the earth rocked, a terrific report rent the air, and a coronal of black smoke hung over Muchee Bhawun.'

Wait till I tell you, though: One man who had been hopelessly drunk, and had hidden himself in a corner to be safe from prying eyes, couldn't be found when the muster-roll was called, and had to be left behind. So up, up he went in the centre of the blast, waking for a second in wonder, then deciding, when he came down again, to sleep on a little longer. When he woke next morning, he found himself the centre of a deserted mass of ruins, so he decided something must be done. And a few hours after, the soldiers within the guarded walls of Lucknow heard a shout of 'Ara, Jasus! open your gates, will yous!' And there was the bould Mulligan, sober now, not only with himself, but with two bullocks attached to a wagon, packed with precious ammunition that he had loaded up to bring home, which was needed badly by an anxious garrison.

And so it has gone on for hundreds of years, Ireland never failing, willy nilly, to be at England's side whenever England was beset by a foe; and so it goes on now, for to mention but three out of hundreds of heroes, Finnegan-Fogerty, Esmonde, and Finucane have been but for a few moments dead, and dying, they died for England.

The Times of the 9th June, 1922, says of a Munster regiment, 'In the Great War one battalion alone lost one hundred and eighty officers and over four thousand men.' One battalion alone of one Irish regiment, mind you. Just think of it: Eight hundred men gathered in Dublin to fight for Ireland, while four thousand, one hundred and eighty men out of one battalion of one Irish regiment alone perished that England might live; and England in the person of Herbert Henry Asquith roared out that Ireland stabbed England in the back! Silence all for a short prayer for the repose of his soul.

But it wasn't to England only that Ireland gave service. To every land, almost, Ireland has given of her best, and her best is always pretty good. True for you, Swift, when you wrote: 'I cannot too highly esteem those gentlemen of Ireland, who, with all the disadvantages of being exiles and strangers, have been able to distinguish themselves, in so many parts of Europe, by their valour and conduct above all other nations.' A French military historian estimates from the archives of that country that from 1650 to 1800, seven hundred and eight thousand Irishmen laid down their lives for France; and little as the more who died for England got, these who died for France got less. Poorly paid, wretchedly fed, the sure reward they got was certain death, for they were always planted in the most dangerous parts of the battlefields. The names of their commanders would form a litany too long to recite. Here are a few of them: One O'Donnell was governor of the Netherlands in 1762, another was a Marshal of Austria, and a third was governor of Carinthia, and a fourth was aide-de-camp to Emperor Franz Joseph of Austria. Field-Marshal de Lacy of Limerick was war minister and president of the war council of Vienna from 1766 to 1778; Field-Marshal Browne of Mayo was governor of Transylvania and Austrian general in Silesia against Frederick the Great — the 36th Bohemian Infantry bore his name down to 1918; Walsh of Carrickmines, Co. Dublin, was a general under Ferdinand the Third, and his eldest son, Marshal Oliver Walsh, commanded the

Austrian Army in Turkey, and was a Knight of the Polish White Eagle. There were Maguire of Fermanagh, Dalton of Tipperary, Nugent of Westmeath, O'Kelly of Galway, Wall of Waterford, and many others, all well-plumed generals in the service of the States of Europe. These fighters have stretched out to the present day, and, I daresay, will go on forever. Looks like there'll always be blossoms of blood on our sprigs of green.

Are we proud of these men? Not a bit; none but a few know anything about them, and their names are never mentioned at home.

* * *

The Irish are even a more scattered race than the Jews. They've gone to every land, sailed every sea, scanned every river, and climbed every mountain range. The lands of the Americas got to know them well soon after Columbus had come back from Hispaniola; indeed there is a legend in Galway and Chicago that an Irish pilot on the bridge of the Santa Maria showed Columbus the way to go. They dined on turkey and wild pigeon in the wigwams of Choctaw, Natchez, Muskogee, Chickasaw, and Cherokee. Near two hundred years ago, John Pope, an officer in the United States Army, sailing up the Mississippi to find out all he could about the river, writes in his diary: 'Just under Chickasaw Bluff — coloured red, blue, brown, grey, purple, yellow, and black — within six feet of the Shore, a first-rate Man of War might ride in Safety, unassailed by Winds. From the lower End of the Bluff, the river suddenly opens to the width of six Miles. Upon Examination, I find our crew consist of one Irishman, one Person born at Sea, one Anspacher, one Kentuckean, one Virginian, and one Welchman. March the 17th: The Irishman, in Honour of St Patrick, purloined all our Brandy, Sugar, and Eggs to make a Tub of Egg-Nog, of which he drank so copiously, that whilst at the helm, he insensibly run the Vessel into a strong Eddy, to get her out of which, employed all Hands in hard labour the Balance of the Day.'

The O'Carrolls founded Carrollton in Maryland; other Irish founded two towns in Massachusetts; the O'Sullivans built a Belfast in Maine; and many places in Virginia and Carolina owe their beginnings to Irish immigration. Professor Lecky, Conservative Member of Parliament, and a Historian, in his *History of England* states that 'disastrous circumstances (he jibs at saying British Governments) have driven great bodies of Irish to seek a home in America'. The same authority points out that the famous Pennsylvanian Line, the best regiments in Washington's army, were almost entirely Irish, and when Cornwallis surrendered to Washington at Yorktown, seventy-five per cent of the American Army were Irish; and New York owes its first parliament to an Irishman. Indeed, America was such a familiar object to the Irish, they had so close and constant connection with it — and have still — that the great continent was known to the Irish for centuries as An tOileán Úr — the New Island.

Just to show the curious diversity of Irish wandering, there is a little tavern down in Kerry called The South Pole Inn, a strange name for an Irish tavern, yet not strange, for it reminds all who come there in an Irish way that a Kerryman was the first to come to where poor Scott lay stretched under the glittering cold of the southern stars, shrouded in the silence of the snows of ages, a pioneer who had died with harness on his back, a dead comrade, a great man gone. Scott and his companions had fought to where but a few miles separated them from life; but a curtain of smiling, seductive snow fell slowly, dividing them from safety forever, so over a page of his diary Scott's icy hands wrote the words of *I can write no more*, meaning that a brave and gallant man could live no longer. So in a faraway Kerry cottage, there hangs on the simple wall, framed with quiet dignity, the last murmur of resigned resentment of a valorous man, whom the cold calculating spider of the sky was wrapping to death in its everlasting filmy fall of snowflakes.

* * *

All the things in the world weren't done by the fellows in the plumed hats, with glittering decorations jostling and envying each other on their breasts. The Irish workers have left a deeper mark than even these on the world. The English, even now (in spite of the portrait of poor Matt Haffigan, drawn by Bernard Shaw), think that we are the lazy ones of the universe. The fact is that the Irish worker has always toiled as hard as the Russian peasant. They have dug the coal from the English pits; they have loaded and unloaded her cargoes from her ships in every dock; they have reaped her corn and lifted her spuds from almost every field, and got small gains from it all. In one year twenty-two thousand farm labourers alone went to England to help in the harvest, and the Fen country, for instance, was well known, and spoken of as familiarly round the Mayo firesides as if it were in Ireland itself. In my young days, I often watched crowds of them, always in cargo boats, embarking for different places in England; in their corduroys, or heavy home-spun tweeds, each with a gay and gaudy scarf round his neck; off to earn enough rent that would keep a roof over their heads for the worst half of the year. Away into remote parts of Lincoln the priest often had to go, and it was no uncommon thing for a congregation of five hundred or more harvestmen to be hearing Mass in a barn lent for that occasion, and the descendants of some of them are still there, in Louth, Grantham, Crowle, and Luddington. They lost themselves in the hard work of the furnaces of South Staffordshire, some of the districts speaking more Gaelic than English, and weren't very well received. A. M. Sullivan, then a Member of Parliament, tells us 'Many were killed, many were murdered in the works at night of whom no word was ever heard, or trace ever found. If any of them went into a public house to have a drink, and an Englishman came in, they were struck dumb (and think what a fear must be that strikes an Irishman dumb); if he asked for our pipe, and didn't get it, he'd pull it out of our mouth. We daren't say anything, for there was neither law nor justice for the Irishman.'

They probably lowered the wages of the English workers, and so deserved a lot of what they got, though it was hunger that drove them to do it. Sullivan says again, 'Rain was pouring heavily as I stood on the furnace platforms to talk to the men. They wore but little clothing, and from this little, saturated and dripping, the heat of the furnace was driving a dense cloud of steam. In the snows and sleets of December, mid biting frosts and drenching rains, they are in this way exposed to the sudden and extreme changes of temperature — they are at the same moment being drenched and scorched, broiled and frozen; the strongest constitution sank under this fearful trial, and so the average length of life here is appallingly brief. At Oldbury it was even worse. Those at the copper works there commence the work fine, stalwart, young men, full of life, of powerful bone, and with sinews like iron — but they last only a few years. After a time, their teeth fall out, their noses bleed, they show every sign of arsenical poisoning, and in a few years become mere wrecks of humanity.' Of course they went to Mass on Sundays, and that was about all the clergy cared. The Irish have begun a good while ago to trust to God and a Trade Union.

In the United States of America and Canada the Irish navvies, the finest in the world, practically made the railways that connect the east of America with the west. They and the Scots did it all, or as much as all that matters. Here, too, they dig the mines, coal, iron, and copper, throwing out as a sideshow, J. L. Sullivan, the greatest fighter with his hands that this world will ever see. The seed of the Irish has fallen everywhere, on every kind of soil. Paul wrote an epistle to them that lived in Galatia; the Georgians of the Caucasus are their cousins; and the Crimea bears strong signs of the old Gael still.

We have knocked at every nation's door; looked in at every window; and sat down for a drink or two in the gardens of most of them — sometimes sword in hand that has helped the nation in whose garden they sat to either plenty or peace, or to both; oftener with bales of lovely black, white, or red cloth, silver and gold ware of cunning workmanship, dressed leather, fit for the finest horses, frieze to keep shepherd and farmer warm, fine linen to lie cool on the soft skin of fair ladies, oak for the roofs of Westminster Hall and Whitehall Palace, huge wolf hounds fit to tackle a bear, and splendid horses as grand as the twelve of a beautiful white colour, with purple reins, dressed with silver, led in for the Pope's train. In the opulent city of Florence the grandees, when a ship sailed in from Ireland, used to run races to the quay to be the first to get the noble stuffs that filled the belly of the vessel; all carried in Irish barques whose oars, Claudian the poet, says, churned the Irish Sea into a mass of foam. All this was in answer, I suppose, to St Patrick's prayer to God for

> *Gift of commerce from all parts,*
> *Gift of ever-widening marts,*
> *Gift in church of reverent hearts,*
> *Bless stout Dublin town.*

The four first things: commerce, fine markets, the grace of God, and stout in Dublin town.

* * *

What does it all come to? Well, to this anyhow: With all this behind them, close to right hand and left, the Irish race at home and abroad, won't shiver because they hear Mr Herbert Morrison say, 'My experiences in Northern Ireland will force me to modify my attitude to the Irish people.' Mr Morrison will be a long time dead before the Irish race hand in their guns. A Cabinet comrade should have flung into his ear the grand Wellingtonian phrase of 'Sir; don't be a damn fool!' Morrison's fiat proves the wisdom of Shaw when he wrote, more than thirty years ago, 'Englishmen are bullied today by the Protestant garrison in Ireland as no Bengalee now lets himself be bullied by an Englishman.' Bullied yesterday, bullied today, and probably bullied forever, if nothing happened. But even the hedgehog clique in Northern Ireland is cracking. Strangely enough, the Red Army has had something to do with it: their grand victories over the German Fascists have shown Ulster that there are other heroes besides William of Orange, just as they have shown those south of the Boyne that there are other warriors besides Brian the Brave Boru. Labour has intensified its resolution, and all intelligent men who are desirous of serving other interests as well as their own are helping to drive a wedge into the dug-in defences of a well-paid garrison. The North is realising that William is too long dead to be able to keep the auld house taegether when unemployment comes, and the South is beginning to be aware that the Pope isn't near enough to bring a hot meal on a plate to a hungry child. And now, Mr Morrison grandiloquently stands out in front, waves a hand like a polisman on point duty, and says, loudly, 'Yous can't do that there here.'

Leaving Mr Morrison roped in his orange and blue blanket, what does all that Ireland did in the past come to regarding Ireland herself today, as she tiptoes around outside the nations of the world, silent, suspicious, and suspect? A lot, but not enough, for the Ireland of today has been largely moulded by an English lord of misrule for the past thousand years; and this boyo is more responsible for her present-day neutrality than Ireland herself can ever be. It would be untrue and useless to set down anything else. Captain Stephen Gwynn, whose house was burned down by the I.R.A. because they didn't like what he wrote about them, can hardly be accused of partiality. In a recent review of a book he said, 'I can see clearly that neutrality was the only course for Ireland to take. Siding with Germany would have meant war; siding with England would have meant civil war, for Ireland was full of memories of things done by English officers to Irish prisoners which were like what Germans have been doing in this war.' We must take Ireland as she is, forgetting that she is technically neutral; remembering, rather, that as far as fighting goes, she has done as much, and, in many ways, more, than the next to stand in with the United Nations.

That is Eire political. Eire spiritual can be gauged by the threat of prosecution by Northern Ireland of parents whose children dared to stray into public parks (now railless because the old iron was commandeered for guns), and ventured to impose a smut on the whiteness of the Protestant sabbath by playing there; while Eire's minister, Sean McEntee refuses to allow a hot meal to be given to cold and hungry schoolchildren because the benefit might injure their souls. Well fed, the kids might start to read Anatole France, Voltaire, Chapman Cohen, or James Joyce, and then where would Eire or McEntee be! But in reserve, if this should happen, Eire has the Five Censors, led by Professor

Magennis, who, legend in Eire says, once climbed to the tip top of Sinai to roar up that he'd keep the minds of the Irish pure, wholesome, and innocent till God, who was tossing about above in a pillar of cloud, was ready to say: 'Relax, now, a little, me good man, for I think they're well on their way to virtue, Magennis, thanks.'

The present powers in Eire had a consecrated dream of a gigantic Catholic block coming out of the upheaval, in which Petainine France, Mussolinian Italy, Franconian Spain, and Salazarian Portugal would join hands in a ring of rosaries around Eire, and that the ring would widen till it formed a cordon sanctataire around the weary world. Somehow it didn't come off, for the world, apparently, isn't shaping the way the Vatican wanted it to go. So the Catholic Irish laity and the more progressive clergy have another chance to make 'the Vatican go the way of Dublin Castle, and the island of saints assume the headship of her own Church'.

But the present-day problem is that of what way are we to get on with England, now, and when the war is over?

Neither can ignore the other. Geography has caught us both by the neck and forced us to be neighbours. A thousand years of fighting is enough for anyone. To give Ireland her due, she has almost always been sensible. Security of tenure for the farmers was a reasonable demand. So was political and social liberties for the Catholics; so was the demand for Home Rule. Yet each had to be fought for tooth and nail. Then came the Treaty, born from a medley of blood and tears, a half-hearted thing, lopping off a vital part of Ireland's life. It is a malicious separation, and must be changed into a united Ireland. It is time now to end this damned strife so that we can see what is to be done to make both ends meet when this war ends. We'll need all our strength then to build up, and live again the life of decent people. England must remember (and so must we) that the Keltic fringe has been a bulwark of gay and lively steel around these islands. England must honour, and labour to preserve, the fine and furious characteristics of the Kelt in song, dance, story, and battle-rage. The Scot, the Cymru, the Gael, and the Manxman must be equal with the Englishman. Equal as individuals; equal as nationalities. Why do the more than hundred nations fight as one for the U.S.S.R.? Because they are co-equal, the one with the other, socially, politically, and nationally. Let England look back for a second from the great places, persons, and things, outside herself, to the great, half-forgotten things around her own borders. Unity in diversity — if this isn't to be, there can never be unity. If the Irish are to come visiting as friends to cancel the past, then we must come in the spirit of Tom Kettle's poem; poem of a man who died to save England's Commonwealth from the Germans.

> *Cancel the past! Why, yes!*
> *But when Cuchullin and Ferdeea fought,*
> *There lacked no pride of warrior courtesies,*
> *And so this fight must end.*
> *And when you make your banquet, and we come,*
> *Soldier with equal soldier must we sit,*
> *Closing a battle, not forgetting it.*
> *This mate and mother of valiant 'rebels' dead*
> *Must come with all her history on her head.*
> *No rudest man who died*
> *To tear your flag down in the bitter years,*
> *But shall have praise, and three times thrice again,*
> *When at that table men shall drink with men.*

CRABBED AGE AND YOUTH (1957)*

CRABBED age and youth cannot live together, says Shakespeare, and he was no fool. On the whole, this is very true, so what are we going to do with the old, even though they be not necessarily crabbed? What are we to do with them? In other words, how best can we get rid of them? To me the main question is, what are the old going to do for themselves? If they don't help themselves, assistance from the younger is of little use. But of this again.

Does creativity decline with age? No. Activity is bound to be less, but the creativity of an active mind goes on. In age many ills unknown to healthy youth slow down the aged; give him or her less time in which to work, for in times of [in]disposition, the aged have to rest and try to nurse themselves away from illness's worse pains, with the help of science; so the little time left with the old is lessened still more by age's infirmities. But even these [difficulties] can be conquered by the determined will. Beethoven wrote his greatest symphony when he was deaf; Prescott wrote his monumental works on the *Conquest of Mexico* when he was half-blind; and Renoir painted on when he had to tie a brush to a rheumatic hand.

What advice shall I give to the millions of men and women who are to retire in another five years? None, if they don't know what to do with themselves, I or no one else can tell them. Certainly, I say they shouldn't retire from life till life herself

* This article is based on the answers to five questions put to O'Casey by Thomas C. Desmond, chairman of the U.S. Senate Committee on Affairs of Cities; it was intended to be read at a public hearing of the New York State Joint Legislative Committee on Problems of the Ageing held on Dec. 18, 1957.

says go. To retire from a job doesn't mean the end; it means but another beginning; not such a long time, maybe, as before, but long enough to learn and practise a different, but useful and enjoyable, way of living. In a few more months, if I be spared that long, I shall be seventy-eight, and, if I be alive, I shall be still on the go. I have just finished a new play; I am working on a new book; I write many letters, and here, now, I am telling those who may be a little younger, or as old as myself, to go on too. Another thing — there must be still a tremendous amount of energy left within this crowd of millions about to retire, and, if the State be as wise as the State should be, then this energy should be organised and a chance given to this energy and intelligence to go on doing useful work, not only for those who have it, but for the whole community, so that they may not be wholly dependent upon the productivity of the young. To leave energy idle, is, to me, a woeful fault in the social system of a nation.

I can hear a murmur saying, 'Easy enough, when you're a writer, to go on with the job', and, maybe, the murmur is right. Here, though, are two examples of carrying on by old ones who hardly ever wrote a letter and probably never read a book in their lives. With our little flat goes a small garden which we have to take care of; a task which we, young and old, found beyond us. It was in a wild state when we took over, but our efforts at improvement, if it didn't make it worse, made it no better. Finally, we managed to get a man on pension, who knew something about the work. He was seventy-one, blind of one eye, with the good one not so keen as in his younger days. After a few months of quiet work, he brought tidiness and order out of its wildness, and when the summer came, it shone with a bright glow of colour from plants his cunning hand had set out for our enjoyment. Many an American has sat in that little garden, enjoying the blossoms and the finches, blackbirds, and thrushes hopping about in and out of them — all the work of the hands of my friend Harry, of the one eye and the bright heart. Another friend of mine, Charlie, an old lad of seventy-two, who went through the horrors of Mesopotamia during the First World War, living with his wife on the old-age pension, got hold of an old taxi that couldn't go, worked on it till it did, and now is very useful to us and other neighbours doing shopping and bringing the goods back, taking people to the station, and, in many other ways adding to the security of his own life and the comfort of the lives of others. Our son, Breon, knew two women in London, one ninety years old, the other but two years younger. The older one, when she sat in a chair for a while, found it difficult to rise, and the younger one had to come to help her out of it; but the glorious thing about these two very old women was that they were both busy learning Greek! They would never say die till death came. Remember, too, that Bernard Shaw didn't kill himself writing, but by manual labour, for he was on a ladder pruning a plum tree when he fell, broke his thigh, and never really recovered from the injury; but this warrior of ninety-four used his hands as well as his head during the last years of his life.

What is my daily regime in my later years? Work with hands and head, too, though the hands don't handle heavy things, and the head has to take an odd rest not needed in far younger days. When I was seventy and over, my favourite work was swinging a heavy axe, breaking up blocks of trees for the fires when winter made us need them, but this work became dangerous, and I had to give it up. I do the washing up, peel potatoes for a meal, at times get the breakfast in the morning, carry down the pail of rubbish to the ashcan, lay the table, and help my busy wife in any way I can. I take walks when the weather is not too bad, and find that even the same road changes its look during the different days and the differing seasons. I read a little, and am interested in painting and music, and science, too, reading *The New Scientist*, published in London every week, and *The Scientific American*, published in America every month; so I find that each day, not too long, but far too short to do all that my heart and mind so eagerly wish to do.

Do [I] have a 'formula' for long life? No. There is no formula that can make a life last a day longer. Life has lengthened over the years, but not through the force or inwit of any formula. It has become longer by the greater knowledge of health and by the great discoveries of medical and surgical science. Life owes a lot to the brave searchers in the world of science.

In my opinion the chief problems the old have to face are three: social, economic, and the young. From the viewpoint of corporal livelihood, they don't get enough to keep them safe and satisfied. They should receive enough in pension, that is in money, and in kind, to allow them to live within a very moderate independence. In kind, they should be provided with a fair-sized room, or even a one- or two-roomed cottage, if they be active enough to be able to care for themselves; and now, with the advance of the science of health, the far greater part of the ageing will retain their activity to a very late year; so this problem of provision is really for the Municipal authorities, the architect, and the engineer, with, of course, the advice of the social worker who has had an experience of the old in this respect.

The social problem is one more nearly concerning the old people themselves. Many of them find it hard to get along with their neighbours, and little envies, rivalries start up here and there when they live in communities, causing quarrels and un-pleasantness, though this, I think, will not be so prevalent in the present generation that is growing old as it was in the one preceding. But many of the old are inclined to be too querulous, and make themselves a nuisance and something of a burden to those who try to help them.

One fierce problem for the old is to keep their minds occupied so as to fix their attention on something outside of themselves; for the old have a tendency to think too much upon the conditions that age brings to them. They can't keep up with the young, and it is useless and distressing to try to do so, for the young can't be bothered with them — they have their own problems, and can't give too much time trying to lift the old out of theirs. The old must depend on themselves, using all the power left to them to do so. We old people try too much to get comfort and stimula-tion from sources outside of ourselves, from the younger ones, from television, from the wireless and from the cinema. These are good in their way, but they tire sooner or later. We who are old should try to get more entertainment out of ourselves than out of others who are busy with other things. Good reading from good books is one fine way to do it; but this needs practice, and is hardly possible for those who have not had some experience of good reading while they were young. These can enjoy lighter reading, and God knows there is enough of this to be found in all the libraries. Good music on the wireless, good painting — through looking at and enjoying the many art books to be had full of reproductions of the old and present masters of painting; but these again need practice, but once acquired, the enjoyment of mind and emotion in these arts will never allow one to feel that he or she is alone in the world, for they will link those who enjoy them with the mighty past and the busy present, with the everlasting communion of beauty and truth.

Then there are games for those who have never encouraged the habit of enjoyment in literature and art; cards, backgammon, draughts, and chess, each of which require but two players. Alone, there are a hundred ways of playing patience with cards. It is not difficult to get a simple idea of the game of chess, and many a delightful game can be played between two people who could never become masters of the game. The pity is that so many old people have always depended upon others for amusement when they were young, and never thought of creating within themselves the gift of providing their own interesting activities, the one thing that can really allow themselves to enjoy their own companionship.

The more important thing, to me, is the looking after of the old of tomorrow rather than the old of today, so that tomorrow's old people will be more adapted to take care of themselves, and serve themselves out of their own thought and emotion with pleasant and profitable entertainment when old age settles down upon them. We must begin with the young. Indeed, a beginning has been made, and today, in the schools, music, literature, art, and handicrafts are practised as they never were in my young days. The young of today who become old tomorrow will have a far better background, giving them a richer chance to enjoy themselves when youth has left them, going its own way in the eager activities of others.

One thing more — most important of all — the old must realise that they are old and not venture upon any activity that will distress them physically, making them an anxiety to the young; they must remember that their life is behind them, and that every evening is eternally drawing to a close. So they must look back with satisfaction, and be thankful that they have lasted so long. Of course, once in a while, we may regret our lost youth, but this must be quickly set aside, for we have had our day, and we must leave the world to the young, as Shaw and Tennyson so aptly tell us to do. We must not resent the young, their seeming thoughtlessness, for they are, as we were once, full of themselves; and must be if they are to become useful and sensible citizens of their nation. We must decrease, and they must increase, so we should be glad and rejoice in their energy and their eagerness. It is good to be alone in one's thoughts at times, to think of the end, to face it bravely, and go calmly and quietly when the time comes to go.

THE DAY THE WORKER BLOWS A BUGLE (1958)*

THE First of May! The Anniversary, the great day, when the workers parade themselves to take pride in what they have done, and what they are determined to do in the days to come. The day when the banners are unfolded, freshened up to take the air with colour and with gaiety; the day when the workers march in column of companies, trade following trade, each with its own symbol of what the trade does, all blending together in unity of achievement and harmony of endeavour; the day when the workers remember their strength, and renew their youth like the eagles; the day when the workers show that work, far from being a curse, is the activity that blesses all men; the day when all workers, those of the skilled hands and those of the clever minds, join together in parade and party to cheer as partners, and to cheer as one; the day when sounds of revelry by night tell of the joy, in song, in dance, and in story, of how blessed a thing it is to work together for the good of all.

These demonstrations, in the U.S.S.R. on the first day of the month, in other countries, not yet socialist, on the Sunday before or after the first day, show the importance and the power that Labour has achieved in many countries. Labour is now, thanks to the people of the Soviet Union's tremendous revolution, well on the road to a sensible and progressive socialism. The communist countries have reached the top, and face now towards the peak of communism; other lands are but half-way up, but climbing; others still are but planting their feet on the foothills of the higher ranges; but all face forward, and all look up to where they are determined to reach. It has become now but a question of time till the lowest in the climb join their comrades higher up,

* Article written for *New Times* (Moscow), May 1958.

268

for now they can clearly hear the cheering of the peoples who have reached the higher or the highest parts, and their longing eyes can see them weaving a coloured pattern of life bringing into being a safer, a more comfortable, and more colourful and joyous civilisation. All have now heard the battle-cry of Workers of all Lands, Unite! And all are echoing it, or singing it, as they climb upwards. Victory is certain now, and, even in the lowliest states, reactionary forces are kept on the defensive, presaging their final defeat.

To get where the workers are now was a bitter, long, testing, and a bloody climb; a long road first to the climb, then a rough and often perilous ascent. When did the climb begin? When and where was the first effort made to find the road on which the fight forward could be made to reach the place whereon to climb? God only knows. All we know — all I know, anyway — is that it began a very, very long time ago; thousands of years, thousands of years, if all were told. We do not know what stirrings went on in the hearts of the herdsmen who tended the flocks of their patriarchal masters; or of the discontent smouldering in the breasts of those who toiled in the building of the pyramids; who silently resented the crack of the foreman's whip around their shoulders, or the hatred for the scorn of those who flung away to die those who could no longer do the work demanded of them. We cannot tell how many mute-tongued rebels are now but deep dust in the plains of old Mesopotamia, or deeper still in the sands of the Egyptian deserts. We can surely guess that they were many, and, perhaps, spoke their resentment and their hatred in whispered words to their toiling comrades, or enshrined their feeling in a simple song, as so many workers did in the years that were to follow. We do not know when first the mills of man's mind first began to grind out thoughts of resentment, or think of ways by which to loosen the hold their masters held over them. All we can be sure of is that these thoughts must have been there, and that those who thought of them were braver than the many, and that they were few. But there they were, and a few seeds must have been sown before the life of [recorded] history began.

K

We know that there were artists among them by the way in which they decorated their primitive pots and pans, and the lively, and often beautiful, way in which they painted the walls of their caves. We know the story of Spartacus, the great gladiator, who hated the Roman grandees, those who used the toil of the slaves to produce their wealth, and those who used the stronger ones to provide their sport. This gallant Thracian slave organised his comrades into an army that defeated again and again the well-trained Roman Legions sent against him; but the time was not yet, the rest of the workers remained bewildered, for there had been no previous theory to guide them into co-ordinated thought, and Spartacus and his army was finally defeated, and the gallant leader slain. All fought and many died, becoming, perhaps, the first fine bugle-call for the workers of the world to hear and stand up for the freedom of all downtrodden men. No memorial yet marks the graves of these heroes who fell on the slopes of Vesuvius, but the time is coming when the name of the brave Spartacus will suddenly appear on the banner of Italy.

Afterwards the revolutionary ethical turmoil of Christianity, its tenets and teaching falling like the gentle dew from heaven upon the poor and the oppressed. However poor and miserable one might be, he and she now became, not only sons and daughters of men, but also daughters and sons of God. It was an hilarious thought! Do unto others as ye would that others should do unto you, promised a new life and a fine freedom from want and care. The life of the Christians set an example; goods were held in common, and, for a while a new earth seemed to be within the process of a great birth; a new dawn had come to all men, so all those who suffered, who were weary, all who laboured and were heavy-laden, flocked to the new idea. The workers had only to believe, and all would be well. It didn't turn out that way. It felt fine for a few years; many suffered death for their belief, and those who survived were strengthened in their hope that freedom was at their door. As soon as it was seen that Christianity could not be overthrown; as soon as it became powerful, the rich and powerful got busy. The then Emperor,

Constantine, blessed the new creed, and made it official, and struck it dead, as far as the poor, the needy, and the workers were concerned. They remained as poor, as needy, and as miserable as ever; the grandees, the rich, and their lick-spittle followers became the governors, not only of the Church, but of the State, too; and the lot of the workers became worse than ever; they could have heaven if they wished, but the rich and the privileged continued to inherit the earth. The workers lived in the earth's worst room; they still had a world to win. The poor workers! They had had the rich on their backs before; now they had the prelate and the priest there as well.

During the centuries following, we are only now beginning to forage out records of how the common people lived; they are few, but we know that life for them was both miserable and un-certain and short. They must have muttered together about their hard lot; maybe made rhymes in their own way, and chanted them softly as they toiled in the fields; but, by and large, the workers were poor dumb mouths; bearing all too patiently, depending on the talismanic benefits from Catholic sacrament and Catholic relic, fearful now not only of their earthly master, but of their heavenly one too. Obedience to their masters was what they had to keep in mind, in pain of punishment in this world and eternal penalties in the next. The workers most certainly rejoiced in the legend of bold Robin Hood, the outlaw who made the woods unsafe for the travelling rich, and who often raided them in their manors, exacting from them much money and goods for the better provision of those who needed those things more than they who had too much. The toiling people must have longed for a Robin Hood on every estate, close to the walls of every monastery, and among the clusters of filthy mud huts where the common people lived and died.

These people became children of God when they were born (so it was said), and were confirmed in this happy connection when they died, and became ashes, no longer of any use to those who had employed them; but throughout the long or short journey of life between birth and death, they toiled for eighteen hours a day, fed on the coarsest food, lived in a verminous mud

hut, slept on a pallet of straw, owning a rough bench at which
to eat, a stool or two, and a few pots to boil their porridge in. If
they were of the more fortunate few, having two cows and a
plough, a reaping-hook or scythe, when the possessor died, the
lord of the manor took the better cow, the better agricultural
tool, and the priest of the parish took what was left, leaving the
weeping widow with her mud hut, her pot and her pan, and her
pallet of dirty straw. It was taking a long time and many terrible
lessons to teach the common people that they had no aid to hope
for in anyone, or anything, but their own unity and organisation
to compel the privileged and powerful to recognise their right
to live decently, and to enjoy the fruits of their labour.

The workers were eternal, and development of thought went
on in their minds, and each attempt for freedom brought fuller
confidence, fuller knowledge, even in defeat. The peasants rose
in France, and showed their power for a time, shaking the
nobles with not a little fear. The peasants rose in Germany, and
the masters saw the fire and felt the blows of the risen workers;
and the peasants in England, galled into desperation by the poll-
tax, rose in revolt under Wat Tyler, swarmed from Kent and
Essex towards London, and took the city, but they were so
destitute of a preparatory plan that, with the king and government of nobles in their power, one dagger-blow ruined them and
turned a triumphant army into a fleeing rabble, followed by a
merciless slaughter of the peasants by the very nobles who a
moment before had promised them every reform they had
demanded.

The old slavery came back on them, but the echo of what
they had done lingered on, thought grew, and man, slowly and
unconsciously, went forward. The workers worked for their
masters, fought the wars for their masters, amassed new wealth
for them and went unrewarded; toiled till they could toil no
longer, and then died wherever they happened to be; but the
worker crept nearer and nearer his vindication.

A rifle-shot! from Bunker Hill, and colonialism, with all its
evils, suffered its first defeat; a rifle-shot that proclaimed the
birth of some of the world's grandest democrats — Jefferson,

Lincoln, Whitman, and Roosevelt; and the flag of the world's
first wide Republic was born; to be followed by the tremendous
French Revolution that shook Europe, put a cap of death on
absolute monarchy, and the Third Estate came to political life,
and the workers defeated the trained armies of Europe. Social
evolution was quickening its stir. The Industrial Revolution
came racing in on the scene, and the peasant now had a powerful
comrade in the proletarian. Organisation began, and the self-
educated miner, Keir Hardie, with his cloth cap, appeared among
the tall silk ones in the British House of Commons. The workers
were climbing the hill. The spearhead of revolution was being
fashioned by Trade Unions all over Europe, and political
Labour movements fashioned the workers' shield. Labour leaders
appeared out of corners into public places, and voiced a revolt
against the filthy and slavish conditions under which the workers
lived; while Lenin, bent over the works of Karl Marx, gathered
into his wide-ranging mind the visions of the poets, thinkers,
and scientists of the centuries, and forged them, with gigantic
skill, into an amazing plan of offensive and constructive action
to convert the upheaval of a revolution into a thriving and in-
vincible socialist republic. The workers were half-way up the
hill.

We honour those who fell in the many defeats suffered by the
struggling workers; honour them as much as we honour those
who rejoiced within the glory of victory, for those who fell went
down willingly for a cause they knew could never find defeat
final. Labour never suffered a defeat, for each defeat meant another
step on the way to the hill; and so we honour the numberless
unknown heroes equal to the greatest heroes known. The Red
Flag, respected now the world over, waves for them as it waves
for us; for the dead as well as the living. It was a long, long fight,
and those who carried it on in the earlier days of desperate odds
mingle with the dust of many places, Chicago, Detroit, Moscow,
Pekin, Dublin, Manchester, and many lesser places, laurelled
with no less of a glory. When Keir Hardie, the ex-miner,
became the first Labour leader to enter the English Parliament, I
was a young man of twenty years, and now, during my own life-

time, I have seen the workers become the great power of more than half of the world, with the other half beginning the climb of the hill; I have seen the workers, peasants and proletariat, widen their ranks to welcome home as workers, too, the poet, the artist, the scientist, the doctor, the teacher, and the thinker, who in their labour in their differing ways are all one, proving the truth of the old slogan of Each for All, and All for Each. There are many countries still within whose borders the workers still struggle; whose lives are unhappy and whose chances are few to enjoy a fuller and more harmonious life. But they are learning from those others who have done so much, and these undeveloped peoples are hearing now the Voice that said many years ago: 'The strongest bond of human sympathy, outside of the family relation, should be one uniting all working people of all nations, tongues, and kindreds.'

So, we the workers blow a bugle on May Day morning; blow long, blow loud for all to hear: a merry, merry sound. In the old days, the serfs used to dance on this day around the may-pole. The grandees danced in their castles or their manors, and the peasants danced beside the graveyard holding their dead; danced to depart for a moment from their hard life, and to colour their imagination with hope. So we dance now, not to forget our unhappy life, but in loud rejoicing that we have done so much, and that the worker now is a power, a great and eternal power in the world of life.

On this first day of May, under the birch tree or the oak; under the cedar of Lebanon or the palm; in the sandy places, the cold snows, or where the rich grapes grow, the worker blows a bugle; a moment for a dance and a song, a kiss from a girl, and a merry meal, for all of us who are 'too busy with the crowded hour to fear to live or fear to die'.

RESURGAM (1960)*

THE hunt for God goes merrily on without stop or standing. T'other day [July 17, 1960, in the *Observer*], there was a controversial wrangle in muted voices between Julian Huxley, the scientist, on the one hand, and the Rev. Dr E. L. Mascall, the Oxford theologian. Dr Mascall sets out on his controversial journey at an easy trot by admitting that 'most of his predecessors over the century failed almost entirely to see what were the real points at issue in the new and startling theory of Evolution'. This they have done, not over the present century only, but also over the many centuries which went before it; and they are still hard at it, telling all who have to listen to them the old, old story of the world's creation, the fall of man, and man's redemption, in school, from pulpit and lectern, reading the chapters of Genesis as if they were cross-me-heart gospels of truth and theological certainties. Even today there is a struggle going on between the prime minister of Guiana and the Roman Catholic clerics in that country over the schools, the Guiana Government making them secular because, the prime minister declares, 'the clerics are persistent in teaching the young theological tenets that have been [proved] utterly ridiculous to the mind of modern man; ideas now dust on a rubbish heap thrown out years ago by the discoveries of science'. And the missionaries — wherever they may get a chance — still carry on their back the old, workbasket of theological tricks to amaze and intimidate the heathen.

Dr Mascall tells us that man is unique, especially because of his power to reason out things which other animals cannot do; though he doesn't tell us how he knows that animals cannot

* This article is here published for the first time.

275

reason out things concerning themselves, which, after all, is all
that this unique thing called Man can do. The bee, for instance,
when it discovers a locality where nectar is abundant, seems to
be able to reason that it would be a good thing to tell the rest of
his winged tribe. He goes back, delivers a rhythmic dance, a sort
of a code, understood by the other bees so well that all who wish
can find their way to the honey-full locality without hesitation
or a single error of direction. There are those migratory birds
who regulate their passage from one place to another many,
many miles away, by the light and position of the stars; there is
the odd intelligence of the dog; of the blue-tits; the extraordinary acquirements of Kathy the porpoise in the giant
aquarium of Marineland, California, of whom, we are told, by
the scientists, that they are even now but scratching the ground
in the finding out of the nature and nervous abilities of this
amazing animal. We as yet know practically nothing about the
animal world, and only today, or, maybe, yesterday, are we beginning to try to discover new facts about them. This attribute
of uniqueness to Man, so stressed by Dr Mascall, is another
expression of that conceit which flourishes so fiercely in the
minds of the Christians; just another instance of the cry of
Anything you can do, I can do better. The fact is that there are
many things animals can do perfectly which Man cannot do
at all.

But Dr Mascall isn't done tossing up the bright bauble of his
uniqueness: he has yet another kind to offer us which he tells
us is much more than a mere biological uniqueness, that of an
intelligent species inhabiting the earth. This is that uniqueness
which the Christian theology asserts, namely, the uniqueness of
earthly beings with an eternal destiny and of the earthly species
in which God has become incarnate. When did this eternal
destiny begin? Just about two thousand years ago? But we are
told that before this, many souls were in paradise, in Abraham's
bosom, so that an eternal destiny began before what is called
The Incarnation. Then when did Man first assume the uniqueness of that 'something more'? Are our primitive ancestors, the
pithecanthepus, the neanderthal, and the other fossils of Man,

undergoing this 'something more' in Abraham's bosom; or have they been broken up and cast on to the spiritual scrapheap, like the useless and outworn robots of Rustum? Why does Dr Mascall separate the biological aspects of Man from the 'something more' that bounced somehow into his biological pattern unawares? Why does he seem to think that theology is too grand to bother about the earthly formation and physical limits of Man? Did not Thomas Aquinas build up his *Summa* on the then known physical and scientific knowledge, garlanded with the philosophy of Aristotle? So Dr Walter McDonald wrote when he was thinking of, and setting down, the then principle of Motion in relation to the findings of Christian theological thought and teaching. This was he who was Professor of Theology for forty years in Maynooth College, Kildare; and, surely, he must have known something to set him thinking in ways the Vatican condemned, though the present-day Pierre Teilhard Chardin, S.J., seems to have lapped himself in the mantle of McDonald when it [fell] from that Professor's shoulders the day he died; and, so far, escaping the odium and reprobation of the Vatican theologians, who, instead of bawling down any adventurous hypothetical ideas about the Universe, its origin and its evolution, must turn a deaf ear and blind eye to what is said and written by their own courageous thinkers, clerical and lay. All the meeting points on television, the talks of a Christian hour over the radio, the homely chats from the pulpits, are like a twice-told tale vexing the dull ear of a drowsy man. Pasquin in his or her fancy as it lies within the Catholic *Universe* can write gleefully: 'The newest scientific theory about the universe (not the Catholic one) is that every part of it acts, directly or indirectly, on every other part, but the degree of uncertainty about the behaviour of a given part increases with its distance from the observer, a condition which leaves room (says the article from which Pasquin is quoting) for endless surprises.' Now comes Pasquin's deep-minded comment (listen to it, you boyo and girlo scientists trying to find out facts about the Universe — it were well ye did). Here the comment goes: 'So, according to my own modest cosmographical research, does the trick of suddenly asking a given professor who or what started the whole thing rolling; apparently the last thing to occur to anyone in the trade. The reply may well be "What's your guess?" The answer, if it's the same as mine, immediately arousing surprise; genuine, pained, refined, tinged with pity, even annoyance and possibly endless. Exit professor trippingly, waving forepaws, baffled yet again.' A great mind, this Pasquin, employed by the great Catholic journal *The Universe*. How he or she makes game of the scientific boyos and girlos who watch the stars; watch them, and wonder. It is the flippant giggle of fear; a late reflection of the wisecracks of the chirruping Chesterton and the serene fiatical gaspels of the stout-drinking Hilaire Belloc. Odd to think some imagined these tremendous trifles would frighten away the scientific boyos and girlos from watching the stars; watching and wondering about the origin, nature, and evolution of the Universe; that these quivery quips could dull the probing mind of the scientist: paper arrows shot at a venture to defend the dying dogmatism of the church, of Christianity itself. The taradiddle which had developed into a magnetic and resounding drum-roll, has again diminished in a taradiddle beaten in slow motion, hesitant and dull, without a call in it.

We are, indeed, a wonderful way from the storms rushing round the publication of *Essays and Reviews*, the beginning of the biblical criticism which shook the literal meaning of the Bible and frightened the host of clericals blessed by a pure faith, good livings, and fat benefices; which shoved Stanley, a dean, Thirlwall, a bishop, and other men, clergy and lay, into a fiery pillory of abuse, repudiation, and outcries of fear from those who thought if this book wasn't banned and burned, in the Christian Church, fangs wouldn't be what they used to be, and wolves would ravage where once the good sheep grazed. So all things bright and beautiful led to a prosecution before lay judges, headed by the Lord Chancellor Westbury, and the bench of bishops, headed by Tait, Archbishop of Canterbury. The declaration was that it was no part of the duty of the Tribunal to pronounce any opinion upon the book, and that the Anglican

formularies nowhere declared against a humane cleric holding
the view that even the worst of the wicked would at length be
saved; so it was circulated, read, and carried about in procession
in the minds of many, many people, and the *virus veritas* spread
within many souls, so that the fangs were no longer what they
used to be. The Lord Chancellor like all mortals, came to the
end of life, and part of the epitaph over his clever and fair-
minded head, read

> *He abolished the eternity of punishment,*
> *Towards the close of his earthly career,*
> *In the Judicial Committee of the Privy Council,*
> *He dismissed Hell with costs,*
> *And took away from Orthodox members of the*
> *Church of England*
> *Their last hope of everlasting damnation.*

So having abolished the hell of superstition, used so often to put
the fear of God, spiritual pastors, and masters, into the hearts of
the common people, we have to bend to the job of doing away
with the real hells which still tarnish our earth; a task that has
been going on for centuries, but which has gone forward at an
amazing rate during the last forty years or so. The heretics
didn't escape scot-free; friends fled from them, efforts were
made to keep them away from a chance of making a living;
servants left them, frightened and furious, and excommunications fell on them like a sudden storm of hailstones; but the
people as a whole went their way regardless and gentle John
Keble was heard to moan about the indifference of the people to
clerical anathema. Excommunications now were less to them
than the firing of squibs on Guy Fawkes' Night. They had gone
a long way from King John kneeling before the haughty Pan-
dulf; gone a long way from the persecution of Colenso and
Ernest Renan, of the Abbé Loisy, of Monseigneur d'Hulst, and
the pathetic recantation of the scholar Lenormant; even from
the day of the Catholic scientist Mivart, contemporary of Dr
Walter McDonald; a long, long way from Tipperary, so far,
indeed, that when the Anglican Church is angry, she roars like

any sucking dove, and the Roman Catholic Church, even in Catholic countries, is beginning to call like a cuckoo. Pip, pip, hurray!

So here we come and there we go. Like little Jane Eyre asleep in the crib with her little friend, Helen Burns, the arm of Helen around Jane; the one asleep, the other dead: Helen to be buried, Jane to go through life for a little longer. The tale tells us that Helen's grave is in Brocklebridge churchyard. For fifteen years after Helen's death the grave was covered only by a grassy mound; but now a grey marble tablet marks the spot, inscribed with her name, and the word 'Resurgam'. The stone is probably tarnished now, the inscription hard to read; the author of *Jane Eyre* herself lies low, all dead as are the humble host in Gray's Country Churchyard, as is our own beloved boy, Niall, and since they went, not a sign has been seen of them, not a stir from where they lie buried or where their ashes are scattered over a garden of Remembrance. As far as we know — and discoveries of Science confirm all our doubts — there is nothing at the end of the road. Indeed, millions of people, always adding to their numbers, have abandoned the vanity of hope. We no longer bother about what the churches tell us, but only on what Science can find out for us. St Augustine and the present Catholic Archbishop of Dublin are indeed back-benchers in the world of thought. Few, I imagine, now read Milton's *Paradise Regained* or Dante's *Paradiso*, and fewer bother about the visions within them: they are, as far as thought and belief go, but faded pictures in a tattered album. The Scientific Eye On Research, the wonderful electronic-camera, today penetrates as far as sensible thought can reach, and shows us in vivid ways the early structure and present evolution of what we know as the human being, making, it seems, (though it doesn't set out to do this) the slogan of 'Resurgam' as pitifully faded as any slogan inscribed beneath the arms of a long-gone medieval family. It is, maybe, a sad conclusion, for with the idea of Hell banished from man's mind, it would be fine to think of ourselves, after lying low for long, to rise up bright and early upon a newer dawn of life. A dream, ladies and gentlemen, a dream.

Science has scattered many mists from the mind of man, she is busy scattering more, and no prayers or threats of the churches can prevent her. The Church cannot evade the searching eye of Science, not even were she to take the wings of the morning, and dwelt in the uttermost parts of the sea. This search of Science is in no way malicious, not even deliberate, only inevitable; for Science is now free from ecclesiastical control, free from menace, and can go forward, finding out the facts of the Universe, indifferent to whatever traditions or beliefs her discoveries may bring tumbling down upon our poor believing heads.

PART FOUR

STORIES

TOREADOR (1933)*

THE day had been very hot, but a delicious coolness had come into the evening air, as, work finished and over for the day, Stephen Benson sat and sipped his pint of beer in 'The Black Bull'. Stephen was a small, spare man, with a big moustache which flowed, rather than grew, over his upper lip, and trickled down both sides of his chin. He was bald to the back of his skull, where the hair still struggled to grow, getting a little thicker as it reached the neck. His arms were thin and sinewy, and his hands were as broad as the largest leaf on a chestnut tree. He stared dully out of the window of the tavern, gazing vacantly at every figure that passed by, and wondered how he could possibly brighten the next few days; for it was only halfway between the first of the week, and the uplift of payday.

'Huh,' he said, 'I'm fed up with life, finished and fed up with it all,' and he brushed off with his fingers the froth of the beer that lingered, like tawny drops of dew, on his shaggy moustache. 'Sitting on a lorry all day, and trying to get a dying horse to stick life out a little longer, and drag the lorry after him, isn't a life that would get a medal given to a man. Huh, that's it — I'm fed up with everything.'

He glanced over enviously at the barman washing the dirty glasses.

'He's pretty well placed,' thought Stephen, 'for he's never far from what can put a little sparkle into life.'

He noticed that the barman was now stretching his neck to look over the guard that covered half the window.

'Anything up?' he asked.

* This story, originally entitled 'The Bull of Bashan', was published in *Time and Tide*, Dec. 2, 1933.

'There's a lot of people running to the top of the street,' said the barman.

'Raise your little finger here,' said Stephen, 'and you'll get a crowd. All of them hunting after a thrill, and never getting one,' and he took a great gulp of the beer that remained in the glass.

'I got my chance ten years ago, and I let it pass.'

'Yes?' queried the barman, trying to look as if he were interested in all that Stephen was saying. 'Ten years ago?'

'Argenteena,' murmured Stephen, 'pressed to go out with a friend as a cowboy. Great life, exciting, galloping over the pampas, and trotting along the paths we cut through the cardoon thistles rounding up the bullocks and the bulls.'

'Dangerous pastime,' murmured the barman.

'No more danger in corralling bulls than there is in housing hens,' said Stephen, 'provided you've got the right kind of grit in you, for bulls is naturally afraid of man. Steers, not cattle, is what we call them in Argenteena, and, if your nerves are steady enough, fix even a pawing bull with your eyes, walk slowly and firmly up to him, he'll get frightened, and when you're near him, he'll wilt and almost go down on his knees to you.'

'I'd rather you'd do it, than me,' said the barman.

'Then,' went on Stephen, 'just slip a cord around his horns and lead him home. But once let the slightest sign of fear, even for a second, slink into your eyes, and he's down on top of you.'

'Curious the power that must be in the eyes of a man,' murmured the barman.

'No,' replied Stephen, 'the weakness is in the eyes of the bull. They're bigger than ours, and a bull sees a man ten or twenty times bigger than he really is, so that a man looks a kind of god to a bull; it's the way the animal's eyes is fashioned. I've often tried it on bulls when I was down in the country, and it never failed once.'

'Different countries, different customs,' said the barman.

'Aw,' said Stephen, as he filled his pipe, 'work, excitement, and animation are only midgets of things here. Everything out there's on a big scale. Butterflies, red, black, green, blue and orange, some striped and some speckled, millions of them, ten feet from tip to tip, and feelers on them as big as broom handles with knobs on.'

'I'd like a holiday, but I wouldn't care to live out there,' said the barman.

'Soon get used to it,' answered Stephen. 'It's the heat that does it. Tropical heat makes everything grow fast and furious. The bells of the blossoms out there are bigger than the funnels of Atlantic liners — a whole family could camp in one of them comfortable.'

'How do the bees manage?' asked the barman.

Stephen looked at him scornfully. 'There ain't no bees in Argenteena,' he said, and lay back on his seat to smoke thoughtfully.

Suddenly the swing door of the tavern opened and two corduroy-trousered men came in. Their faces lit up when they saw Stephen, and they made towards him at once. 'We've been looking for you, Steve, my boy,' said one of the men, 'and thought, at last, that we might find you here.'

'Ay,' said the second man, 'a quid waiting to be earned by you, Stephen, as easy as kiss hands.'

'The moment we saw what was happening, we set out in search of you,' said the first man.

Stephen wondered what was the cause of this anxiety to find him. He remembered that whenever he was wanted it was usually to tell him evil tidings, and his mind immediately became uneasy.

'Huh,' he muttered, 'let them want me, and let them wait — I'm having a quiet rest here after a hard day's work.'

The two men came over to him; each took hold of an arm, and tried to raise him from the seat; but Stephen sat firm.

'Drink up your beer and come along quick,' said one of them.

'Come along where, man?' asked Stephen.

'Think of the glorious hours of a night the pound'll give the three of us,' said the other man. 'The chance you've been waiting for years has come at last.'

'What chance, man?' asked Stephen.

'The same thing mightn't happen again for a century,' said the second man, 'so come along.'

'What thing, what thing, what thing?' shouted Stephen.

The first man looked wonderingly into Stephen's eyes as he murmured, 'Surely to God you're not afraid to chance it?'

Why does he ask me shall I be afraid? thought Stephen. There must be danger lurking around somewhere, or he wouldn't ask me that — so go careful, go careful, Stephen, my boy.

'Thousands'll watch you, and thousands'll cheer you while you're mesmerizing it,' said the second man.

'Till the steady stare of your eyes forces the animal to go down on its knees in front of you,' said the first man.

Stephen jerked himself free from the coaxing pressure of the two men's hands.

'What are you holdin' me for? — what mesmerizin', what animal?' he shouted.

The first man bent down, and looked admiringly up into Stephen's face.

'The bull,' he said; 'the bull that's broken loose, and is bellowing and running about wild in the street beyond.'

'A bull,' stammered Stephen, 'bellowing and running about wild in the street beyond?'

A crowd began to gather at the door of the tavern and make remarks.

'We've found him,' said the first man to the crowd, 'and he's coming along now in a second.'

'Get him to hurry up,' said a man in the crowd, 'for the bull's getting a bit restless, and may injure somebody if he isn't put under control.'

'The police,' said another man, 'are keeping the crowd back so that Stephen can have plenty of room to work.'

Stephen felt faint. He had been too open-mouthed, blathering round the whole district of how well and effectively he could handle a bull. Many a time, in the parlour of a house, or the parlour of a pub, he had shown how the thing was done. What mad moment put it into his head to meddle with bulls? And Argenteena? What the hell did he know about Argenteena or

care either? Find it hard to get it on the map, even though he had
been talking about the country a few seconds ago. And now he
was getting dragged out to get the better of a bull! He couldn't
back out of it either, without becoming the laughing-stock of all
who knew him and thousands who didn't. He felt his heart
beginning to beat faster. He'd go as far as it was safe to go slowly,
so that by the time he got there the bull might be under control.

'What sort of a bull is it?' he asked, as they were pushing him
towards the door.

'Oh,' replied one of the crowd, 'it won't really take a lot of
doing, Stephen, for it's only a young animal, and white.'

'A young animal, and white,' echoed Stephen, glaring vindic-
tively at him who spoke. 'Shows how you know sweet damn all
about it. Only a young animal, and white — it's the young bulls
are the most dangerous, especially when they're white, man.'

Stephen felt himself being pulled along the street like lightning.
Suddenly they all heard a deep, long bellow of a bull.

'Eh, don't rush me,' protested Stephen. 'None of you seem
to realize that I may be going to my death. There's nothing
easier for a young bull, when it's a white one, than to slip it
across a man.'

The two friends who had come to fetch Stephen walked by
his side, one on his left, the other on his right, carrying themselves with an air of importance and pride.

Damn easy for them to feel elated, thought Stephen, at
another poor man's expense. He could hear the busy, joyous
chatter of the crowd that followed.

'Stephen'll do it all right, he'll have the bull quietly tied up
with a rope in the twinkling of an eye,' said one.

'I've seen, myself,' said another, 'a bull, bigger than this
one, that was keeping a whole farm in under locked doors,
downed by Stephen with only just a shake of his finger and a
look from his eyes.' 'It was a lucky thing we thought of Stephen,'
said a woman. 'An' a luckier thing we found him,' said another.

'A gang of cannibals, that's what they are,' murmured
Stephen, 'a gang of cannibals.'

'Here we are,' said one of the men leading Stephen, with a

gay note of confidence in his voice: 'here we are, at last,' as they began to mix with and push through a large crowd which had gathered at the end of a street. 'Gangway there, make way, gangway, please.'

Stephen was shoved to the front, and somebody put a coil of rope in his hand. He looked round and saw, out of a mist, that he was in a long street, over each side of which towered huge, sombre-shaped stone warehouses, the walls broken at regular intervals by heavy wooden gates, all of which were now closed. Outside of one of the gates he noticed a low-decked lorry, from which the horse had been taken, standing idly there, the long, heavy shafts resting on the cobblestones of the street. Far away he saw a crowd of people gathered at the other end of the street, keeping close to the corners so that they might be able to dash off in different ways if the bull came too close. All the world like an arena, he thought; the warehouses, the dens; the heavy entrances, the gates that let the wild beasts in or out; the cobblestones the place where the battles were fought; and the crowds at each end, the audience that watched, laughed, cheered or turned their thumbs down. His eyes swam, his ears buzzed, his stomach felt queer, his legs felt like heavy columns of steel, and his heart thumped so madly that he almost saw his breast swelling out in front of him, sinking back and swelling out again. He felt a terrible desire to yell, to turn and fly, to yell and yell and turn and fly away to God knows where.

'You'd better make a start, me man,' said a heavy-headed policeman, to Stephen, 'if you're goin' to do it before the stars come out.'

'Let no one cough or laugh or cheer, to startle the animal,' said Stephen, as he moved forward.

He wished that the rope he held in his hand was a pair of rosary beads; but it wasn't, and it was getting as heavy as a hawser. He winked his eyes to shake off the gossamer mist which covered them and peered ahead. Then he saw the bull. A young, supple, yellowish-white fellow, with long curving horns tipped with black; powerful, muscular neck strong enough to toss a man over the warehouses; elegant, twitching flanks that a gleam from the setting sun turned to bronze. There he stood gazing fixedly at the crowd gathered at the far end of the street, slashing his back with his twitching tail — now on the right side, now on the left. As Stephen went on, his pace grew slower. The bull, with a stronger and more vicious switch of his tail, suddenly turned round, and looked at Stephen. Stephen stood still. He felt himself sinking down into a small, little man as the head of the bull grew bigger and bigger, till the eyes were like huge red November suns, and the horns spread over the sky like the branches of an oak tree. Then Stephen heard a sound, like thunder, and knew that the bull had bellowed. He let the rope fall from his hands, turned swiftly on his heels and fled. His legs that had been as heavy as lead moved like the wings of a swallow. He would rush headlong into the crowd at the end of the street, bury himself deep in the midst of the people, and put a crowd of soft bodies between himself and the charge of the bull. Then he heard the thuh thuh thuh thud, thuh thuh thuh thud of the bull's hooves on the cobbles as the animal came along after him. He glanced ahead and saw that the crowd had scattered, and were flying off in different directions. A wave of hatred surged through his soul as he raised his voice and shouted, 'Stand your ground, there, stand your ground.' But they heeded him not, and ran for their lives. Dirty cowards, the people, thought Stephen, as he rushed along; dirty cowards the whole of them — they wouldn't risk a pinprick to save a man's life. That's the thanks I get for showin' them an example of what a man ought to be.

Closer and closer came the sound of the thuh thuh thuh thud, thuh thuh thuh thud of the bull's hooves on the cobble-stones, and Stephen felt the hot, bitter breath from the bull's nostrils on the back of his neck.

His eye caught sight of the horseless lorry standing idly by one of the warehouse gates, a few yards away. He made for the lorry, swerving suddenly to the right as the bull swept past him. He heard the scratching of the bull's hooves on the cobbles as the animal checked his speed to turn and charge at him again. But as the bull was almost on top of him he dived under the lorry, sliding over the cobbles to the end farthest from the bull, tearing his trousers and tearing his knees as he did so. Thrusting its head under the lorry, the bull glared at him and bellowed. Stephen crawled out by the other side, but the bull trotted round, and he had to dive under the lorry again. He looked from beneath the lorry and saw that the crowd were gathering again in their old places to watch. First they had watched to see what he would do to the bull; but now they watched to see what the bull would do to him. The moment he got under the lorry the bull thrust his head under, too, and tried to reach him with his horns, so that Stephen had to scurry on his knees to the other side of the lorry. The bull trotted round, and again Stephen had to hurry on his knees to the other side of the lorry. Not one of the crowd stirred to help him. Stephen was getting exhausted; he wouldn't be able to keep up the dodging much longer. Crawling swiftly to the end of the lorry, Stephen shouted over to the crowd: 'For God's sake, dear Christian people, do something to drive him away before he rips me open, 'n leaves me in sthrips lying on the road.' He had hardly finished the sentence before the bull was round poking at him, and he was forced to crawl rapidly back to the other end of the lorry. Then he cocked his ears in amazement, for he heard the sound of laughter; the crowd were laughing and enjoying his terrible predicament. They even began to make ironical comments on the situation. Stephen heard them all as he was scurrying from side to side and from end to end of the lorry.

'He'll get away from you, Stephen, if you're not careful.'

'Don't interfere, now — Stephen has his own way of tamin' bulls.'

'He's doin' all this dodging just to tire the animal out.'

'Hope he won't be prosecuted for cruelty to animals.'

'He shouldn't tease the animal too much, for he's not in Argenteena now.'

With a lunge of his head, the bull thrust his horns between the spokes of one of the wheels, lifting an end of the lorry three or four feet from the ground, letting it down again with a thump which nearly cracked the skull of Stephen. He felt that he was done. But it was hard lines that he would have to slide into the unknown with his ears full of the hilarity of a cowardly, pleasure-seeking crowd. He'd make one last effort to get them to realize what a serious thing life was: lying on his belly, he put his hands to the sides of his mouth, making a rough megaphone of them, and shouted to the crowd: 'For the love of God, brothers, get the police to do something, or send for the fire brigade.' Then with his clothes torn and muddy, his hands and knees scratched, damp with sweat, he lay down flat and waited for the bull. He heard the rattling of the lorry as the bull savagely pulled it about, his horns caught in the spokes of a wheel. He heard the patter of feet and the murmur of many voices. He prayed that when the bull came, death might be swift and painless. Mother o' God, he felt the horns poking at his coat. A few seconds more, and the horns would be boring his vitals! He was roughly turned over on his back, and pulled and punched — the bull was going to worry him before he gave him the final prod. He heard laughter, and a loud voice telling him to get up an' be sensible. He opened his eyes, and saw a burly policeman bending over him.

'Where is he?' murmured Stephen. 'Is he gone; is he undher proper conthrol?'

'Here,' replied the policeman, 'get up ower that, man, an' don't be keepin' the crowd gathered to obsthruct the thraffic. If it's the bull you're thinkin' of, he's gone away long ago, roped liked a fly in a spider's web. We've had more than enough of your demonsthration of cow-punchin', so get up ower that an' go home — you an' your cocky walk an' your lassooin'.'

Stephen climbed painfully to his feet, dejected and crestfallen. With head bent down, he pushed his way through the crowd that murmured ironical praise as he passed.

'I'll be out of this disthrict,' muttered Stephen as he hurried away, 'before the week's out, for they're not Christians. They'd never get to the end of their jeerin' if I stopped among them — a nest of ignorant pagans, that's what they are.'

*   *   *

It was a sweltering hot evening, and Stephen was voluptuously drinking a foamy pint of beer as he sat in a pub at the other end of the town.

'I left the disthrict,' he was saying to the barman, 'because they weren't Christians. Savages with clothes on — that's what they were.'

'This must be the hottest evening yet this year,' murmured the sweating barman.

'Nothin' to the heat in Argenteena,' replied Stephen.

'Spent some of your time out there?' queried the barman.

'Best part of me life,' replied Stephen, 'cow-punchin'.'

'Dangerous job, that,' said the barman.

'Soon get used to it,' said Stephen carelessly. ''Course you have to keep your wits about you. I seen many a good man speared when he was off his guard.'

'Bulls are big out there, aren't they?' asked the barman.

'Big as bisons,' said Stephen. 'Everything's on a big scale out there. The bells of flowers out there are as big as the funnels of Atlantic liners — a whole family could camp in one of them comfortable.'

'How do the bees manage?' asked the barman.

Stephen emptied his pipe by tapping the bowl on the sole of his foot, and glanced scornfully at the barman.

'There ain't no bees in Argenteena,' he said.

DUM VIVIMUS VIVAMUS (1934)*

LORD CORNERSTONE sat rigidly in his enormous office, the
ceiling of which was invisible to the naked eye. He sat at a
marble desk that stretched across the room like the monument
of Stonehenge. Along the front of the desk engraven deeply
were the words, 'There is none that doeth good but only one,
and he is here.' To the left of the desk stood a telephone massive
as an obelisk. Embedded in the marble at the back was a gleaming silver sword, having under it the words, 'Nor shall my sword
sleep in my hand.' Over the table-top of the desk were battalions
of coloured switches, like regiments of toy soldiers, red, blue,
green, black, white, and yellow, which, when touched, sent the
official needed hurrying bareheaded to the call of the Great
Man. The walls of the office up to the stretched arm of a tall
man were lined with steel cabinets, divided into drawers locked
by many signs and complicated countersigns, containing, written
on steel plates, wisdom greater than the wisdom of the ages.
The building itself was the tallest for miles round, and the office
of the great man so high up in the building that only sky was
visible from the great tripledex soundproof glass windows,
though occasionally, before the steel shutters fell, a pale moon
looked in and wondered, or a gleam from the evening star fell
for a moment on the obelisk-like telephone of the Great Man.
The doors were of planed steel covered with the finest rubber
and, finally, jacketed with the brightest and smoothest silver
birch, so that no sound from the outside could ever creep in to
disturb the great thoughts of the Great Man, as he pondered out
solutions of the problems of the present and the past. A huge
clock on one of the walls told the time silently. The Great

* Short story published in *Time and Tide*, May 5, 1934.

Man wrote his leading articleens on a specially radioactive writing pad that carried the current thirty stories below to the chief editor's room, where word after word of the articleen as it was written by the Great Man appeared on a golden screen on a wall in letters of dancing flame.

A trimly built, cold-eyed, vibrating secretary sat typing like lightning at the far end of the room. Behind her, hidden by a partition, like a rood screen, made of Empire timber, was another great room in which seventy times seven under-secretaries were piling up records of a great mind and finding the work hard and never ending.

A pink light appeared on the Prime Secretary's desk whenever a message came over the phone, and a glance at the light brought the call through the headphone over her ears so that she could listen to the message and never lose a second over her work. When the call was finished she winked at a button on her left, and the pink light went out. Should the call be important enough, she winked at a button on her right, then the pink light vanished and a red light gleamed before the eyes of the Great Man.

Lord Cornerstone was dressed in a simple frock-coat over a nicely tailored black shirt. From the neck down he looked like an ordinary man, but the head, with its massive domelike forehead, nearly filled the room. He was thinking deeply. The Prime Secretary could see that he was thinking deeply, for a furrow deepened — and went on deepening in his mighty forehead till it looked like a cleft in a rock of ages. Suddenly he stretched out a hand and touched a tiny blue switch, took his hand away again and waited. The door opened softly, and a Young Man with a light tread and a light in his eyes entered swiftly and stood wordless and waiting beside the desk of the Great Man. Attention! softly shouted a tiny klaxon on the desk and the Young Man with the light tread and the light in his eyes became rigid. The Great Man wrote swiftly on a slip of paper and handed it to the Young Man. 'Go,' he said, 'aeroplane, get these and return for publication within twenty-four hours.' The Young Man read the words on the slip of paper. Karavanapore, India. 'Long journey, chief,' he said.

'Within twenty-four hours for publication,' murmured the Great Man.

'May drop into the sea, sir.'

'Within twenty-four hours,' said the Great Man.

'Duty to our readers, duty to our readers,' shouted the klaxon softly.

'May find it difficult to get them to sit,' murmured the Young Man timidly.

'Twenty-four hours,' said the Great Man.

'Dismiss,' shouted the klaxon softly, and the Young Man with the light in his eyes relaxed, saluted, and hurried from the office, the door softly opening before him, closing again as softly when he had passed out. He rushed like mad down the corridor and flung himself into the lift.

'Ground floor,' he said, and the lift shot down. The Young Man rushed out to a car that a touch of a button had brought to wait for him there, jumped in, and, with a lithe bound forward, the car swept to the aerodrome. The Young Man had dressed himself in leather overalls and crash helmet, which were ready in the car for him, as he sped along, so that all he had to do was to jump out and climb into a long slim aeroplane which a touch of another button had brought out, well oiled and engine running, to wait for him there.

'Karavanapore in eight hours,' he said to the pilot, as he jumped in and strapped himself into his seat in the cockpit.

'Karavanapore — long journey,' said the pilot.

'Duty to our readers, duty to our readers,' said the Young Man; 'Karavanapore, eight hours, go!'

The pilot connected the engine and seized the controls, the aeroplane taxied excitedly along the close-cut grass, rose and soared gracefully over the hedge seeking the sky. As they flew high up over a narrow road the pilot glanced down and saw what looked like a long straggling procession of tiny wooden figures marching along, half hidden by a cloud of dust. He heard a slight sound, and listening, he knew it was a song they sang as they marched along. He thought he heard and made out a few sentences as the aeroplane flew onwards:

Let cowards flinch and traitors sneer,
We'll keep the red flag flying here.

'Hunger marchers,' he murmured to the Young Man behind him.

'Karavanapore in eight hours,' responded his companion viciously; 'Karavanapore, man. We've work and not tinkering to do.'

The aeroplane soared horizontally up, up, till it cut through the clouds and swept out over the cliffs of Dover, seeking a straight line to make for the town of Karavanapore. The clouds through which they flew were bathed in the setting rays of the sun, and shone in crimson-gold masses dyed with the expert hand of God, deepening in their crevice to a deeper crimson cored with purple. 'Lovely cloud scene,' murmured the pilot, 'fit throne for Christ when he comes again in glory to judge both the quick and the dead.'

'Karavanapore, Karavanapore,' snarled the Young Man, 'we've no time to bother about Christ.'

On the aeroplane flew to the hurrying hum of the engines.

'Go lower till we see where we are,' said the Young Man to the pilot. The pilot pulled at levers, the aeroplane dipped and shot down towards the earth, ploughing through the lovely crimson-gold masses of the clouds. Both of them looked down and saw countless numbers of what looked like little black exes growing out of the green grass.

'Crossing the battlefields,' said the pilot. 'Millions and millions of dead lie buried beneath us.'

'We have no time to think of the dead now,' responded the Young Man; 'while we live let us live, and so on to Karavanapore.'

The aeroplane shot across the Rhine, and the sound of music and singing came to their ears. Staring down as the aeroplane flew on they saw thousands and thousands of battalions of little figures marching up hills and down dales, numbering off, forming fours, porting arms, wheeling to the right, and wheeling to the left in the hot amours of military manoeuvres.

'The Nazis on parade,' said the pilot, 'and looking for trouble again.'

'Curious how some men waste their time,' murmured the Young Man.

Hungary, the Balkans, and the Mediterranean Sea slid away from underneath them.

'What's she registering?' asked the Young Man.

'Five twenty-five,' said the pilot.

'Make it five hundred and fifty,' said the Young Man, 'for we're barely halfway there yet.'

'Crossing the desert of Sinai, now, I think,' said the pilot, as he accelerated.

The engines gave a deafening whining buzz as the aeroplane shot forward like a rocket. Suddenly they saw before them a solid bank of darkness, and the bank of darkness was sundered by continual flashes of red lightning that stretched from one end of the darkness to the other. And the heart of the pilot was afraid so that he lessened the speed of the aeroplane and the machine shivered from its nose to its tail. Thunder rumbled loud in the midst of the darkness and the lightning formed letters of fire, and the pilot would fain have covered his eyes as he spelled out the terrible name of Jehovah.

'What shall we do, what shall we do?' he asked, and his voice shook with the great fear that was on him.

'Down and under it,' shouted the Young Man.

Down and down went the aeroplane, but nowhere could they find a way to get over the bank of darkness.

Down to the centre again came the aeroplane, and faced towards the bank of darkness and the terrible name of fire that flamed thereon.

'Go on, go on, straight through it!' shouted the Young Man.

The pilot hesitated.

'Go on, go on, man,' shouted the Young Man, 'a nation waits on its knees for the results of what we have to do today!'

The pilot clenched his teeth, bent his head, pulled a lever right and a lever left, the aeroplane plunged into the darkness which parted before it, like the parting of the Red Sea before Israel, the roar of the aeroplane rose above the rumbling of the thunder in the midst of the darkness, and the lightning sprinkled sparks over the machine and the two men, but on and on they flew till suddenly the aeroplane burst from the darkness into the fresh air full of the scent of cinnamon just as the sun sank down below the horizon and the stars came out in the sky.

'A mile now from Karavanapore,' murmured the pilot, as he wiped the sweat pouring down his brow.

They dropped quickly down, watching from the darkened sky thousands of black and white figures picked out in the rays of powerful searchlights, running wildly about from place to place filling the air with shouts and screams. They saw them scattering, joining in groups, then scattering again. They saw men in turbans, gowns, and loincloths, struggling with each other, screaming fiercely as they struggled, while lithe men in khaki shorts and sleeveless tunics lammed the various groups with long bamboo batons.

'Moslems and Hindoos having a set-to over a cow, and the police knocking sparks out of them,' murmured the pilot, as the aeroplane landed gracefully before the entrance of a long and high white building with pillars in front, back, and side, and a dome over all. On the roof of the building was a group of tall, fine-looking young men looking at the row. Before the machine stopped the Young Man had climbed out and had rushed into the building. A few seconds later, the pilot saw him come out on to the roof and shoo those who were there back into the building. After a few moments, the Young Man came galloping out again, and climbed back into the cockpit.

'Got all I wanted,' he said, as he climbed back; 'six fine shots at them all, in four different positions. Full speed now for home.'

The pilot pulled a lever left, a lever right, and grasped the controls tensely. The aeroplane taxied swiftly along knocking several groups of disputants out of her way, rose lightly from the ground, and, with engine roaring, soared swiftly towards the sky as the stars began to grow big.

*   *   *

Lord Cornerstone sat at his stone desk, monumental as Stonehenge, and spread the morning paper in front of him with the picture page under his eyes. The furrow had gone from his huge forehead, and there were smiling clefts in the corners of his mouth. The great thing had been done. Within twenty-four hours. Here were the pictures of the Australian Football Team in front of them — four of them, each in a different position. And, underneath the notice:

'These photos have travelled four thousand miles in twenty-four hours. Their publication was made possible by a triumph of organization, aeroplane, wireless, and telegraphic transmission. Once more the *Morning Mercury* has provided the most up-to-the-minute service of photos of national interest.'

THE DOG (1943)*

JOHNNY stood behind Archie sitting near a rousing fire, for it was a cold night and a sharp feeling of frost invaded every corner, eagerly watching Archie attending to the sack. He watched Archie putting a patch over a hole in the sack with a packing-needle and some thin strong twine. When the patch was on and firmly fixed, Archie ran wide loose stitches in and out round the mouth of the sack, using a thicker cord, so that when the ends were pulled the mouth of the sack closed. A dog's muzzle, roughly made of thicker twine, lay on the table beside him.

Archie's dog, a black-and-tan terrier, had darted out one fine morning and had placed, with a sudden vicious bite, a number of tiny evil-looking holes in a little child's white-fleshed leg. The frightened child had screamed, bringing out Mrs Cassidy with a run, to haul the dog away by its scut of a tail and shut it safe inside; then out again to bear the screaming child to its mother, insisting that the child must be taken to the hospital immediately to have the wound cauterised, while the raging mother shouted to a curious world that she didn't know why, under God's heaven, she didn't know why people who hadn't one penny to rap against another wanted to keep wild and threacherous animals lying slyly asleep in hidin', ready to leap out at any moment an' leave the red mark of its venom in the fresh whiteness of a little girl's leg.

Her mouth fixed in a firm line, Johnny's mother had said what's done is done and what must be done must be done now without waiting, so as to be sure that the evil of the wound would

* Chapter of autobiography published in *Million: New Left Writing*, [No. 1], William MacLellan, Glasgow, 1943.

stay where it is and strike no deeper, by having a sure hand cauterise it, so that after a day or two of pain, the wound would be harmless.

The child's mother had wept and barged her way to the doctor, her weeping hurried along with the warning that if she didn't let the doctor see it the child would lose its leg, the whole street and all the passers-by hearing of the day's evil and her child's hurt, Mrs Cassidy tight-lipped and striding beside her.

'For God's sake, Mrs Cassidy,' the woman had whispered outside the surgery door. 'You go in with the kid yourself, for it's fallin' flat in a faint I'd be, if even one o' me eyes caught a glimpse of what the docthor'll have to do.'

And Johnny's mother had gone in, plump and plain, crooning encouraging sentences to the frightened little one in her arms; helping the surgeon by holding the child to be probed and cauterised, calm and callous over the child's cries, or so its mother said afterwards; carrying the child back in her own arms and putting her to bed, as if she owned it, as the mother observed; then running off and coming back again with sheets of transfers, fair and finely coloured, of birds and butterflies, of England's rulers from the time of Edward the Confessor, to the first years of our own liege lady, Queen Victoria; and then ordering the child's mother, if you please, as if she were the be-all and end-all of the whole world's healing, to let the child rest; in no way to remind her of the accident, not to mention it in the child's presence, so that with the healing of the leg all shock might fade away; and finishing with the remark that she would now return to her own place, that the dog would be dead within a day, and the child well within a week.

'Where's the howler now?' asked Archie.

'Under the bed in t'other room. He ran off when he seen you sewing the sack.'

'Sometimes,' murmured the mother, 'dogs seem to have a second sense.'

'It won't be long now till he's none,' said Archie shortly.

'Will I go in and pull him out?' asked Johnny, eager to begin the exciting task.

'Oh, let th' poor animal be at peace till the last minute,' said the mother quickly.

'A minute or two won't matther one way or another,' said Archie, knotting the last stitch to make the whole thing firm. 'There, now,' he said, holding up the sack for all to see, 'strong enough to hold a tiger, an' he in a temper.' He tugged at the sack, putting a corner under his foot, and tugging again with all his might. Then he tied two great bricks together with bits of rope and dropped 'em in the sack.

'Slip out now,' he said to his mother, 'an' see if the sky is dark enough, an' the street is still an' no life movin'.'

Mrs Cassidy went to the door, opened it, and stepped out on to the path, looked up at the sky, down the street, then came back again into the lighted room.

'It's cold an' quiet an' still outside,' she said, 'with nothin' to be seen save the shiverin' stars thrying to shelther an' shine in the blackness of the night sky.'

'Then we'd better get ready to go,' said Archie. 'Coax him from undher the bed with an oul' bone or something.' Mrs Cassidy went into the other room, and knelt down beside the time-worn bed.

'Boxer, here; Boxer, Boxer, good doggie, come on out an' see the lovely thing I've got for you.' She pushed her head under the bed. 'Boxer, poor Boxer, come on here.' But Boxer didn't stir.

'Isn't he coming, where is he, can't you see him?' wailed out Archie. 'He's in the farthest corner, pressed up against the wall, lookin' as if he guessed full well what was in store for him.' 'He'll soon be where he won't have to guess any more,' said Archie viciously, catching hold of the bed and switching it from the wall, and pouncing on Boxer, who tried to press away from the clutching hands, his ears hanging limp on his head, his little eyes gleaming, the stump of a tail wagging timidly, and a soft whimper shaking itself from his mouth.

Johnny held Boxer while Archie fixed the muzzle over his snout, binding the end-strings tightly round his neck so that he couldn't edge the muzzle off him. The terrier tried several times to snap with the muzzled mouth, but the snap and snarl ended only in a long low whimper. Then, while Mrs Cassidy and Johnny held the mouth of the sack wide open, Archie gathered the dog tightly in his arms, bunched the legs together, and thrust him firmly down, down into the depths of the sack, pulling the running cord that was threaded through the mouth, and tying it into a black knot, so that Boxer was safely housed and hindered and hearsed for the last short journey to the dark that would never grow light again.

Making a loop in the thick cord, Archie thrust a broom-handle through the loop, saying to his mother, 'See now, for the last time, if the coast's clear.'

She thrust her head and shoulders as far out into the night as she could, and then drew in again.

'It's all clear,' she said. 'Only a cold an' nipping night air to put speed into both your feet.'

Gripping the broom-handle, one at each end, Archie and Johnnie lifted it to their shoulders, so that the sack swung between them, and set off up the street, looking like they were carrying corn out of Egypt. Through the cold and frosty night they went, Archie leading, with Johnny steadying the swinging sack. They kept well to the middle of the street, lest a door of one of the houses should suddenly open, and someone come out and grow too curious. They went on their toes, as much as was endurable, like drunken ballet-dancers, like Indian braves, in single file, avoiding any little pool of light, hugging the darkness, and loving the darkness, fearful that some might think their deed evil.

Archie pulled up with a jerk, and said, 'Hush.' He swung over to the farther side of the street, and crouched down in the deeper darkness of a sheltering door. A little way up, Johnny heard a slow heavy haunting tread, heavy-footed, and through a pool of gaslight glitter, he soon saw a heavy form, thick and strong, firm and footy, passing through the pool, and Johnny knew that a policeman was passing by, passing by, here's a policeman passing by, my fair ladies.

They waited quite a time till the form had vanished and the

sound of the mighty tread had ceased before they slung the sack
up between them again. Coming near the top of the street, they
heard the sound of singing in the corner house.

'Prendergasts are havin' a party,' said Archie. 'That's Mouse
Prendergast singin' now — I'd know his voice among a
million. An' he's still singing the only song anyone ever heard
him singin'.'

They listened for a few moments to the squeaky voice of
Mouse trickling faintly out through the brightly-lighted
window:

> *'O'er thy grave I weep goodbye,*
> *Hear, oh hear my lonely cry,*
> *Oh, without thee, what am I?*
> *Sweet Belle Mahone.'*

Then the full swell of the chorus came pouring out through the
lighted window as everyone joined in:

> *'Sweet Belle Mahone! Sweet Belle Mahone!*
> *Wait for me at Heaven's gate,*
> *Sweet Belle Mahone!'*

'Oh, let's get on,' said Johnny, 'for the frost's going through
me bad boots, and me hands are numb with the cold.'

They turned, right, round the corner at the head of the street
into the waste field running alongside the high grey walls of
Mountjoy Prison, standing like a great grey wolf in the midst of
the Irish fold. They paused to look at the high stone walls,
made higher by three or four tiers of bricks, each barely resting
on the other's edge, held from falling by a thin splash of mortar,
so that if any convict, tired of his stay there, tried to escape by
climbing over the loosely joined bricks on the top of the wall, they
would come tumbling down like a cascade, rousing the sleepy
warder in the watchtower, causing him to leap to attention,
pointing his gun and let bang at the place the noise came from.

Johnny gazed at the hardy high walls, blacker than the blackest
night, and the watchtowers, seeming to tip the stars, where
warders stood stretching their eyes through the darkness, with
guns already loaded, watching and waiting to see that nothing

crept from a lonely cell out of the light into God's marvellous
darkness to creep and creep to the wall, and climb and climb
on and up to the top, taking down brick after brick, softly and
slowly, and laying them, softly and slowly, on top of others as
far away as an arm could stretch, clearing a gap, a space, then
to lift a leg, cautiously, the right leg, straddlewise over the wall
through the gap, waiting, still and stony, like the wall itself,
listening and listening while the other leg, the left one, was being
brought over as softly and shyly as a butterfly's wings brushing a
petal, over the wall, through the gap, cautiously and slowly, and
slyly, to crouch, stony and still, listening and waiting, without
stir or breath, for the flash and the bang from the rifle of a
warder in one of the towers, firing at an escaping prisoner,
escaping prisoner, escaping, making the alarum bells go ring
ring a ringling, waking the other warders out of a dense deep
sleep, and sending them, half naked, with batons and bayonets,
charging out through the passages into the square, bent for the
place on the wall where the convict was escaping, half-way out,
hovering on the wall with his hands gripping the ledge, his body
stretched down as far as it could string in a stretch to lessen the
last quick sliddering drop down, scattering the frightened frogs
and madly coiling eels squirming in the muddy moat below.

Suddenly, in the midst of the shining stars and the sparkling
frost, from somewhere behind the dark grey walls facing them, a
voice rang out in a challenging chant, Number One, an' all's
well, to be echoed by another answering strongly, Number Two,
an' all's well, to be echoed by a third till they faded away into the
quietness of the frost and the stars again.

'Number nix,' said Archie, 'an' all's well'; and on he led
Johnny, both of them stumbling over the mounds of rubbish
thickly studded with weeds, towards the canal, the sound of
water pouring over the lock gates coming nearer and nearer to
them as they hurried forward.

Archie caught his foot in a tangle of weed, and lurched forward, pulling Johnny down so that his face for a moment was
pressed against the living thing in the sack, and he felt the paws
clawing violently against his cheek, and a muffled growl and a

snarl came curling into his ear, forcing his heart into a quickening beat.

'The damned brute has snapped his muzzle,' said Archie. 'Up you get, quick, an' let's get it over, before the world hears him howling, an' a warder, thinking something's up, let's fly at a venture, and sends a bullet into one of our backsides!'

They hurried over the rest of the way in fear that anyone should hear the snarling coming out of the darkness, and at last reached what Archie said was the bank of the canal; and Johnny, peering ahead, saw a cold, dark, shiny mass moving slowly along ending in a gurgle and a loud splashing as the slow shiny mass pressed over the sluice-gates and tumbled down into the lock below.

Archie took the broom-handle from the mouth of the sack. 'Now,' he said to Johnny, 'you take the top an' I'll take the bottom, give three fine firm swings, and at the third go, let fly!'

Each took his grip of the sack and swung it back in a wide swing. The thing inside let out a long sickening howling moan. 'One,' said Archie, 'two, three — go!'

The sack shot away high over the soft moving shiny mass in a curving line, the howling moan rising higher and higher, to be suddenly stilled by a loud splash that stabbed through the sound of the tumbling waters falling through the sluice-gates down into the lock below.

Archie shouldered the broom-handle and turned to go. Johnny thought he saw him give a little shiver.

'*Mors omnibus communis*,' said Archie, bravely.

'Ay,' said Johnny proudly, rubbing his frost-frayed hands vigorously together, 'it takes us, doesn't it!'

INDEX

INDEX

311

T. Gallagher
295 Riverside Drive.
Detroit 48 2145.
Michigan.

Elizabeth (Parkinson)
c/o Grrington Vigella,
24 great Pulteney St,
London W1.
01 - 437 - 0466 extn 106.